EDINBURGH TEXTBOOKS IN EMPIRICAL LINGUISTICS

Series Editors: Tony McEnery and Andrew Wilson

Corpus Linguistics

Tony McEnery and Andrew Wilson

EDINBURGH UNIVERSITY PRESS

EDINBURGH UNIVERSITY PRESS

© Tony McEnery and Andrew Wilson, 1996

Edinburgh University Press
22 George Square, Edinburgh EH8 9LF

Typeset in 11/13pt Bembo by
Koinonia, Manchester
and printed and bound in Great Britain

A CIP record for this book is available from the British Library

ISBN 0 7486 0808 7 (cased)
ISBN 0 7486 0482 0 (paperback)

Contents

Acknowledgements

We are grateful to the following for permission to reproduce illustrations from published work: Gunter Narr Verlag and Dieter Mindt for the dendrogram in Figure 3.3; *ICAME Journal* (Editor: Stig Johansson) and Junsaku Nakamura for the plots in Figures 3.4 and 3.5.

We are equally grateful to the following for providing us with samples of their corpora: Patricia Kelly, Editorial Secretary of the CURIA project at the Royal Irish Academy, for the old/early middle Irish text and TEI header in Figures 2.2 and 2.3. Atro Voutilainen of the University of Helsinki for the example of Helsinki English Constraint Grammar tagging and parsing used as Figure 2.11.

For reading, commenting and correcting, we are grateful to Ilka Mindt, Chris Tribble, Josef Schmied, Michael Oakes, Eva Hertel and all students on courses 253 and 266 at Lancaster University.

Above all we would like to thank Ed Finegan (also of our editorial advisory board), who not only read the work in draft but also contributed much more in getting this book and the series off the ground. We are grateful also to our other board members – Dieter Mindt, Bengt Altenberg, Jan Aarts, Pam Peters and Knut Hofland.

On a personal level, Tony McEnery would like to thank Paul Baker and Jason King for their marvellous support in times of stress. Andrew Wilson would like to thank Ilka Mindt for her constant support as a friend throughout this project, and Julia Watson for inspiration in times of crisis.

Last, but by no means least, we must thank our two successive editors at Edinburgh University Press – Jonathan Price and Jackie Jones – without whom none of this would have been possible.

Abbreviations

ACH	Association for Computers and the Humanities
ACL	Association for Computational Linguistics
AI	artificial intelligence
ALLC	Association for Literary and Linguistic Computing
APBH	American Printing House for the Blind
ARCHER	A Representative Corpus of Historical English Registers
BNC	British National Corpus
CALL	computer-aided language learning
CEC	Commission of the European Communities
d.f.	degrees of freedom
DTD	document type description
EAGLES	Expert Advisory Groups on Language Engineering Standards
EBHT	example-based machine translation
ESL	English as a second language
EU	European Union
FSD	feature system declaration
FSM	finite-state machine
ICAME	International Computer Archive of Modern English
ICE	International Corpus of English
IPA	International Phonetic Alphabet
ITU	International Telecommunications Union
LOB	Lancaster–Oslo/Bergen Corpus
MDS	multidimensional scaling
MT	machine translation
NITCS	Northern Ireland Transcribed Corpus of Speech
NLP	natural language processing
OCP	Oxford Concordance Program
POW	Polytechnic of Wales Corpus
SEC	Lancaster/IBM Spoken English Corpus

SEU	Survey of English Usage
SGML	Standard Generalised Markup Lanuage
TEI	Text Encoding Initiative
TLG	*Thesaurus Linguae Graecae*
WSD	writing system declaration
ZEN	Zurich Corpus of English Newspapers

Early corpus linguistics and the Chomskyan revolution

Corpus linguistics is perhaps best described for the moment in simple terms as the study of language based on examples of 'real life' language use. It has a long and interesting history. Yet the term corpus linguistics is a relatively modern term. This chapter examines how this modern phenomenon, corpus linguistics, has come to be an increasingly prevalent methodology in linguistics, in spite of the unpopularity of the approach in the 1960s and 1970s.

A staggering number of myths surround corpus linguistics. When we consider that it is nothing but a methodology, it is surprising to observe the heated debates it has caused. The history of corpus linguistics exists almost as a body of academic folklore. Nearly any linguist will be able to cite parts of this body of anecdotal knowledge, for example, 'More people live in New York than Dayton Ohio', 'Corpus linguists study real language, other linguists just sit at their coffee table and think of wild and impossible sentences', 'A corpus can't describe a natural language entirely' and 'Natural language is infinite.' All of these statements express twisted, partial views of linguistic methodology. Some contain mis-truths and exaggeration. Some put forward dislocated facts as irrefutable evidence. All are only part of a rich and fascinating topic – the history of corpus linguistics. This chapter will seek to dispel myths, and collect together often fragmented pieces of evidence to reconstruct a coherent view of corpus linguistics. The aim is for an understanding of the topic framed in an overall view of linguistic methodology and theory.

In this chapter we examine the history and methodology of the corpus-based approach to the study of language, and show how corpus linguistics has evolved over time. The 1950s were an important period for the development of corpus linguistics. As a consequence much of the chapter will be devoted to examining the reasons put forward against a corpus-based approach to linguistics in that decade. We will also concern ourselves with how modern corpus linguistics has sought to overcome these objections.

1. IS CORPUS LINGUISTICS A BRANCH OF LINGUISTICS?

The answer to this question is both yes and no. Corpus linguistics is not a branch of linguistics in the same sense as syntax, semantics, sociolinguistics, and so on. All of these disciplines concentrate on describing/explaining some aspect of language use. Corpus linguistics in contrast is a methodology rather than an aspect of language requiring explanation or description. A corpus-based approach can be taken to many aspects of linguistic inquiry. Syntax, semantics and pragmatics are just three examples of areas of linguistic enquiry that have used a corpus-based approach (see Chapter 4, sections 4, 5 and 6 respectively). Corpus linguistics is a methodology that may be used in almost any area of linguistics, but it does not truly delimit an area of linguistics itself.

Corpus linguistics does, however, allow us to differentiate between approaches taken to the study of language, and in that respect it does define an area of linguistics, or at least a series of areas of linguistics. Hence we have corpus-based syntax as opposed to non-corpus-based syntax, corpus-based semantics as opposed to non-corpus-based semantics, and so on. So while corpus linguistics is not an area of linguistic enquiry in itself, it does at least allow us to discriminate between methodological approaches taken to the same area of enquiry by different groups, individuals or studies.

2. EARLY CORPUS LINGUISTICS

'Early corpus linguistics' is a term we will use here to describe linguistics before the advent of Chomsky. Field linguists, for example, Boas (1940), and later linguists of the structuralist tradition all used a basic methodology that we can undoubtedly call corpus-based. That is not to suggest that we will find the term 'corpus linguistics' used in texts and studies from this era. We will not. The term 'early corpus linguistics' is being coined here to categorise all of this work. In some ways it describes all linguistics before Chomsky and links it to the modern methodology of corpus linguistics to which it has affinity. To illustrate this point and to demonstrate the wide use of corpora in linguistics before the 1950s, below is a brief overview of interesting corpus-based studies predating that time.

2.1. Language acquisition

Linguistics proceeded by corpus-based description[1] in the nineteenth as well as the early twentieth century. The studies of child language in the diary studies period of language acquisition research (roughly 1876–1926) were based on carefully composed parental diaries recording the child's locutions. These primitive corpora, on which later speculations were based by the researchers of the period such as Preyer (1889) and Stern (1924), are still used as sources of normative data in language acquisition research today, for example, Ingram (1978). Corpus collection continued and diversified beyond the diary studies period. Indeed it is of interest to note that language acquisition studies can be split into longitudinal and large sample studies on the basis of the sampling technique used to collect the corpus of utterances representing the language of the child or children under study.

Large sample studies covered the period roughly from 1927 to 1957. The corpora for analysis were gathered from a large number of children with the express aim of establishing norms for development in language acquisition, (see, for example, McCarthy 1954).

Longitudinal studies have been dominant from 1957 to the present. They are again based on the collection of utterances, but this time around three children are used as a source of data over time. Brown (1973) and Bloom (1970) are both examples of longitudinal studies.

2.2. Spelling conventions

Käding (1897) used a large corpus of German – some 11 million words – to collate frequency distributions of letters and sequences of letters in German. The corpus, by size alone, is impressive for its time, and compares favourably in terms of size with some modern corpora.

2.3. Language pedagogy

Fries and Traver (1940) and Bongers (1947) are examples of linguists who used the corpus in research on foreign language pedagogy. Indeed, as noted by Kennedy (1992) the corpus and second language pedagogy had a strong link in the early half of the twentieth century, with vocabulary lists for foreign learners often being derived from corpora. The word counts derived from such studies as Thorndike (1921) and Palmer (1933) were important in defining the goals of the vocabulary control movement in second language pedagogy.

2.4. Comparative linguistics

Comparative linguistics also shows evidence of a corpus-based inclination. A good example here is Eaton's (1940) study comparing the frequency of word meanings in Dutch, French, German and Italian. The work is very sophisticated even by today's standards. Only in the early 1990s are corpora again being created which could even begin to be used to derive such information, for example, McEnery & Oakes (1996).

2.5. Syntax and semantics

The semantic frequency lists used by Eaton were also used by other researchers interested in monolingual description. Lorge (1949) is an example of this. Syntax was also examined. Fries (1952) is an early example of a descriptive grammar of English based on a corpus.[2] This work pre-dates the corpus-based grammars of the late 1980s, for example, *A Comprehensive Grammar of the English Language* (Quirk *et al.*, 1985), by thirty years and more.

This type of work was not merely limited to English. Gougenheim *et al.* (1956) used a corpus of transcribed spoken French from 275 informants to describe high frequency lexical choices and grammatical choices.

It is fairly clear to see from these examples that the basic corpus methodology was widespread in linguistics for a long period of time. Yet the fact remains that we can pinpoint a discontinuity in the development of corpus linguistics fairly accurately in the late 1950s. After this period the corpus as a source of data underwent a period of almost total unpopularity and neglect. Indeed it is no exaggeration to suggest that as a methodology it was widely perceived as being intellectually discredited for a time. This event can be placed so accurately because its source lies almost exclusively with one man and his criticisms of the corpus as a source of information. That man was Noam Chomsky.

3. WHAT CHOMSKY SAID

Chomsky (1957, 1965), in a series of influential publications, changed the direction of linguistics away from empiricism[3] and towards rationalism[4] in a remarkably short period of time.

But what is this empirical–rationalist distinction referred to here? Is it peculiar to linguistics? Well to deal with the second point first, the answer is no. This fundamental division exists, in principle at least, within any discipline faced with the basic decision of whether to rely on naturally occurring observations or to rely on artificially induced observations. Let's make this distinction sharper. A rationalist theory is a theory based on artificial behavioural data, and conscious introspective judgements.[5] This may be a native speaker of a language reflecting on that language and making theoretical claims based on those reflections.

Rationalist theories are based on the development of a theory of mind in the case of linguistics, and have as a fundamental goal cognitive plausibility. The aim is to develop a theory of language that not only emulates the external effects of human language processing, but actively seeks to make the claim that it represents how the processing is actually undertaken.[6]

On the other hand, an empiricist approach to language is dominated by the observation of naturally occurring data, typically through the medium of the corpus. In this case, we may decide to determine whether sentence x is a valid sentence of language y by looking in a corpus of the language in question, and gathering evidence for the grammaticality, or otherwise, of the sentence.

In essence our empirical–rational divide is one predicated upon the nature of the data used to inform theory. There are advantages and disadvantages to both approaches, which will be discussed later in this chapter. But for the moment we shall use this characterisation of empiricism and rationalism within our discussion without exploring the concepts further.

Chomsky changed the object of linguistic enquiry from abstract descriptions of language to theories which reflected a psychological reality, cognitively plausible models of language. In doing so he apparently invalidated the corpus as a source of evidence in linguistic enquiry. Chomsky suggested that the corpus could never be a useful tool for the linguist, as the linguist must seek to model language competence rather than performance. Chomsky's distinction between competence and performance has now been somewhat superseded by the concepts of I and E Language (see Chomsky 1988), but for the purposes of this discussion we will consider Chomsky's original concepts.

Competence is best described as our tacit, internalised knowledge of a language. Performance, on the other hand, is external evidence of language competence, and is usage on particular occasions when, crucially, factors other than our linguistic competence may affect its form. Chomsky argued that it was competence rather than performance that the linguist was trying to model. It is competence which both explains and characterises a speaker's knowledge of the language. As the linguist is attempting to explain and characterise our knowledge of language, it is this that he or she should be trying to model rather than performance. Performance, it was argued, is a poor mirror of competence. As already stated, performance may be influenced by factors other than our competence. For instance, factors as diverse as short-term memory limitations and whether or not we have been drinking can alter how we speak on any particular occasion. This brings us to the nub of Chomsky's initial criticism. A corpus is by its very nature a collection of externalised utterances; it is performance data, and as such it must of necessity be a poor guide to modelling linguistic competence.

But what if we chose to waive this fact and suggest that it is good enough anyway? Is it possible that this is a mere quibble with the nature of the data? Chomsky (1957) suggested not. How, for example, can a theory of syntax develop from the observation of utterances which only partly account for the true model of language – one's linguistic competence? This externalised language not only encodes our competence but also, as noted, an indeterminate number of related features on any particular occasion of language use. How do we determine from any given utterance what are the linguistically relevant performance phenomena? This is a crucial question, for without an answer to this, we are not sure whether, for any set of observations we make based upon a corpus, that what we are discovering is directly relevant to linguistics. We may easily be commenting on the effects of drink on speech production without knowing it!

To paint an extreme example, consider a large body of transcribed speech based on conversations with aphasics. If we are not told they are aphasics, we could easily end up modelling features of aphasia as grammatical competence unless we are made aware of the nature of the corpus. Chomsky believed that ultimately it was not possible to tease apart linguistic competence from related features in performance data. Chomsky saw the main task of the linguist to be the definition of a model of linguistic competence, so it is hardly a great

surprise to discover that he saw the corpus as a bad starting point for achieving this goal. Consequently Chomsky urged a move away from empiricism
towards rationalism. Rather than try to account for language observationally,
one should try to account for language introspectively.

This then was one of Chomsky's criticisms. To appreciate fully the next
criticism, we must consider some of the basic assumptions underlying early
corpus linguistics. All of the work seems to be underpinned by two fundamental, yet flawed, assumptions: first, that the sentences of a natural language
are finite, and second, as a corollary of the first point, that the sentences of a
natural language can be collected and enumerated. Both points are based on a
simple belief. Language is finite. Like blades of grass on a lawn, the sentences
of language are great in number, but if one has sufficient patience one may
collect and count them all. They are finite. There are just so many blades of
grass, and there are just so many sentences. Language is an enumerable set
which can be gathered and counted.

Why may we assume that this view was tacitly held by these linguists?
Primarily for this reason: the corpus was seen as the sole source of evidence in
the formation of linguistic theory. It therefore follows that *complete* observation must be possible via a corpus. To use Leech's (1991: 8) observation, 'This
was when linguists ... regarded the corpus as the sole explicandum of linguistics.' Can it be that corpora could ever be so comprehensive as to enumerate
language − be the sole explicandum of linguistic research?

To be fair to the early corpus linguists, not all of them made such bullish
statements. Harris (1951) is possibly the most bullish exponent of this point of
view, yet other researchers such as Hockett (1948: 269) did make weaker
claims for the corpus, suggesting that the purpose of linguist working in the
structuralist tradition 'is not simply to account for all utterances which
comprise his corpus' but rather 'to account for utterances which are not in his
corpus at a given time'.[7] This view, however, was a decidedly minority one,
and the ability of the corpus to act as the sole explicandum of linguistics was
largely an unchallenged assumption leading up to Chomsky's criticisms of
corpus-based research.

If the above view holds, many exciting possibilities open up. To be able to
use solely empirical methods to describe language would be feasible. It would,
in short, be possible to make language description a matter of objective fact
and not a matter of subjective speculation. It is possible to see why such an
approach to language may be attractive. To set linguistics up alongside other
empirical sciences such as physics may indeed seem a laudable goal. But is it a
valid one? Is it possible to eschew introspection totally? When we consider
Chomsky's criticisms we must conclude, unfortunately, that this is not possible.
Note that Chomsky shifted the grounds of debate away from phonemics,
which the structuralists of this era had as their main goal of study, towards
syntax. This, in effect, amplified his criticisms.

The number of sentences in a natural language is not merely arbitrarily large. It is no use sitting around speculating about the number of sentences in a natural language. The number is uncountable – the number of sentences in a natural language is potentially infinite. The curious reader may try a simple test at this point. Go to any page in this book and choose any sentence which is not a direct quotation. Now go to your local public lending library and start to search for that exact sentence in another book in the library. Unless it is a very formulaic sentence (such as those sentences appearing as part of a legal disclaimer at the beginning of the book) it is deeply unlikely that you will find it repeated in its exact form in any book, in any library, anywhere. The reasons for this become apparent when we consider the sheer number of choices, lexical and syntactic, which are made in the production of a sentence, and when we observe that some of the rules of language are recursive. Recursive rules may be called repeatedly; indeed they may even call themselves The following phrase structure rules include a recursion:

Index	
Symbol	*Meaning*
S	Sentence
NP	Noun Phrase
VP	Verb Phrase
AT	Definite Article
N	Noun
PP	Prepositional Phrase
Prep	Preposition
V	Verb
JP	Adjectival Phrase
J	Adjective

Rules
S → NP VP
NP → AT N
NP → AT N PP
PP → Prep NP
VP → V JP
JP → J

In this set of rules the second NP rule and the sole PP rule refer to one another. In principle, there could be an infinite number of prepositional phrases enclosing an infinite number of noun phrases within a sentence, according to these simple rules. There is a certain circularity in the phrase structure of English here. These rules alone, by continued application, may give infinitely many sentences. We may even begin the infinite sentence:

The dog of the man (one recursion) was old

S   → NP VP
NP   → AT N PP
PP   → Prep NP
NP   → AT N
VP   → V JP
JP   → J

The dog of the man from the house (two recursions) was old

S   → NP VP
NP   → AT N PP
PP   → Prep NP
NP   → AT N PP
PP   → Prep NP
NP   → AT N
VP   → V JP
JP   → J

The dog of the man from the house by the pond (three recursions) was old

S   → NP VP
NP   → AT N PP
PP   → Prep NP
NP   → AT N PP
PP   → Prep NP
NP   → AT N PP
PP   → Prep NP
NP   → AT N
VP   → V JP
JP   → J

The dog of ... (infinitely many recursions) was old

S   → NP VP
NP   → AT N PP (infinitely many recursions start here)
PP   → Prep NP
.
.
NP   → AT N
VP   → V JP
JP   → J

Observing the recursive nature of phrase structure rules shows clearly how the sentences of natural language are not finite. A corpus could *never* be the sole explicandum of natural language. Our knowledge of, say, grammar is enshrined in our syntactic competence. This may be composed of a *finite* set of rules which give rise to an *infinite* number of sentences. Performance data, such as a corpus, would not describe this competence. Corpora, by their very nature, are incomplete. Language is non-enumerable, and hence no finite corpus can adequately represent language. Corpora are 'skewed'. Some sentences are in the corpus because they are frequent constructions, some by sheer chance. To quote Chomsky (1959: 159) on the matter:

> Any natural corpus will be skewed. Some sentences won't occur because they are obvious, others because they are false, still others because they are impolite. The corpus, if natural, will be so wildly skewed that the description [based upon it] would be no more than a mere list.

This is a perfectly accurate observation by Chomsky. Corpora are partial, in two senses of the word. First, they are partial in the sense that they are incomplete. They will contain some, but not all of the valid sentences of a natural language. Second, they are partial in the sense that they are skewed, with frequency of a feature in the language being a significant determiner of inclusion. As Chomsky himself stated so amusingly, the sentence *I live in New York* is fundamentally more likely than *I live in Dayton Ohio* purely by virtue of the fact that there are more people likely to say the former than the latter. This partiality was seen by Chomsky as a major failing of early corpus linguistics.

One final practical criticism remains to be made. Even if language was a finite construct, would the corpus methodology still be the best? Why bother waiting for the sentences of a language to enumerate themselves, when by the process of introspection we can delve into our own minds and examine our own linguistic competence? The corpus had cast the linguist in a somewhat passive, and often frustrating mode. Fillmore (1992: 35) comments most amusingly on this. He satirises the corpus linguist thus:

> He has all of the primary facts that he needs, in the form of a corpus of approximately one zillion running words, and he sees his job as that of deriving secondary facts from his primary facts. At the moment he is busy determining the relative frequencies of the eleven parts of speech as the first word of a sentence versus the second word of a sentence.

Not a very attractive idea for many linguists! Fillmore's depiction of the corpus linguist is an admittedly extreme and comic one. But it underlines an important point. Why look through a corpus of a zillion words for facts which may be readily available via introspection? As we shall see shortly, for accurate frequency-based information this may be our only option. But we must concede that at times intuition can save us time in searching a corpus.

So the manifesto laid out by Chomsky saw the *linguist*, or **native speaker** of a language, as the sole explicandum of linguistics. The conscious observations of a linguist who has native competence in a language are just as valid as sentences recorded furtively from somebody who did not know they were swelling some corpus. Indeed, it is not a simple question of empowerment. Without recourse to introspective judgements, how can ungrammatical utterances be distinguished from ones that simply haven't occurred yet? If our finite corpus does not contain the sentence:

*He shines Tony books.

how do we conclude that it is ungrammatical? Indeed, there may be persuasive evidence in the corpus to suggest that it is grammatical. We may see the sentences:

He gives Tony books.
He lends Tony books.
He owes Tony books.

There is nothing to suggest that the complementation of *shines* is any different from that of *gives*, *lends* and *owes*, if we have never seen *shine* before. It is only by asking a native or expert speaker of a language for their opinion of the grammaticality of a sentence that we can hope to differentiate unseen but grammatical constructions from those which are simply ungrammatical and unseen. This may seem a minor point, but as language is non-finite and a corpus is finite, the problem is all too real.

Let us sum up the arguments against the use of corpora so far. First, the corpus encourages us to model the wrong thing – we try to model performance rather than competence. Chomsky argued that the goals of linguistics are not the enumeration and description of performance phenomena, but rather they are introspection and explanation of linguistic competence. Second, even if we accept enumeration and description as a goal for linguistics, it seems an unattainable one, as natural languages are not finite. As a consequence, the enumeration of sentences can never possibly yield an adequate description of language. How can a partial corpus be the sole explicandum of an infinite language? Finally, we must not eschew introspection entirely. If we do, detecting ungrammatical structures and ambiguous structures becomes difficult, and indeed may be impossible.

The power and compulsion of these arguments ensured the almost total rejection of corpus-based (empirical) methodologies in linguistics and the establishment of a new orthodoxy. Introspection (rationalist) based approaches rose in the ascendant.

I will not present any justifications of Chomsky's theories here. The purpose of this section is to summarise Chomsky's criticisms of early corpus linguistics, not to review what path Chomsky's theories followed. For readers interested in this, Horrocks (1987) presents an engaging overview, while Matthews (1981) presents an expressly critical review.[8]

3.1. What others said

There was another problem which faced early corpus linguists which was somewhat more pragmatic than those presented by Chomsky, but which loses nothing for that. There was a basic problem of data processing. Abercrombie (1965) summed up the corpus-based approach as being composed of 'pseudo-techniques'. Can you imagine searching through an 11-million-word corpus, such as that of Käding (1897), using nothing more than your eyes? The whole undertaking becomes prohibitively time consuming. It also becomes very expensive and error prone. A risible variety of workforces were used by early corpus linguists, from Käding's (*ibid.*) 5,000 Prussian analysts through to West's (1953) horde of analysts from the Indian subcontinent. All of these analysts cost money, and all were possible sources of error in analysis. Processing 11 million words using humans alone is to put it simply, slow, expensive and prone to error.

Abercrombie (*ibid.*) made a very real criticism. There were plenty of things which may have seemed like a good idea, but were well-nigh impossible in practice in the 1950s and before. Most of the techniques described in this book would be nearly impossible to perform on corpora of an average size today if we were still relying on humans alone for the analysis. Whatever Chomsky's criticisms, Abercrombie's was undoubtedly correct. Early corpus linguistics required data processing abilities that were simply not readily available at the time. Without that data processing ability, their work was necessarily made more expensive, more time consuming, less accurate and therefore, ultimately, less feasible.

The impact of the criticisms levelled at early corpus linguistics in the 1950s was immediate and profound. It seems to the casual reader that almost overnight linguistics changed, and the corpus became an abandoned, discredited tool. But, as the next section shows, that was certainly not the case.

4. WHY IS THIS BOOK BEING WRITTEN?

Having read this book so far, you may well be asking yourself this question. This is not a book about what happened in linguistics before Chomsky's criticisms. This book concerns itself with corpus linguistics as practised today. Yet having read the above criticisms, you may well be wondering why on earth anybody ever bothered to look at a corpus again.

Well, several points must be made here. First, and perhaps most importantly, these criticisms did not stop *all* corpus-based work. In the field of phonetics, naturally observed data remained the dominant source of evidence with introspective judgements never making the impact they did on other areas of linguistic enquiry. In the field of language acquisition also, the observation of naturally occurring evidence remained dominant. In this particular example we should not be overly surprised. Introspective judgements are not available to the linguist/psychologist studying child language acquisition. If you doubt this try asking the next eighteen-month-old child you meet whether the word *moo-cow* is a noun or a verb! On a more serious note, introspective judgements can only become available to us when our metalinguistic awareness has developed. There is no evidence that the child in the one-word stage of language has metalinguistic awareness. In brief, its language use is not something the child thinks of talking about. Chomsky himself (1964) cautioned that his rejection of performance data as a source of evidence was inappropriate for language acquisition studies.[9]

On a general note, work based on the corpus methodology was undertaken in the 1960s and 1970s, but, as we will examine more closely in the next section, as a somewhat minority methodology. The next question we must ask ourselves then is this: why did some researchers bother to continue to use a corpus-based approach to linguistics? The answer is that in the rush for rationalism sparked by Chomsky drawbacks became apparent which were, in their own way, just as profound as the drawbacks he had so clearly pointed out in the position of the early corpus linguists. At this point we must recall the earlier description of the nature of the data Chomsky wanted to observe. The great advantage of the rationalist approach is that by the use of introspection we can gather the data we want, when we want, and also gather data which relates directly to the system under study, the mind. Chomsky had rightly stated that a theory based on the observation of natural data could not make as strong a claim on either of these points. But there are advantages to the observation of natural data, and it may also be that the case against natural data was somewhat overstated.

Naturally occurring data has the principal benefit of being observable and verifiable by all who care to examine it. When a speaker makes an introspective judgement, how can we be sure of it? When they utter a sentence we can at least observe and record that sentence. But what can we do when they express an opinion on a thought process? That remains unobservable, and we have only one, private, point of view as evidence: theirs. With the recorded sentence we can garner a public point of view – the data is observable by all and can be commented on by all. This problem of public vs. private point of view is one which bedevils not only linguistics, but other disciplines where the divide exists between natural and artificial observation, such as psychology, as discussed by Baddeley (1976: 3–15). The corpus has the benefit of rendering public the point of view used to support a theory. Corpus-based observations are intrinsically more verifiable than introspectively based judgements.

There is another aspect to this argument. The artificial data is just that – artificial. Sampson (1992: 428) made this point very forcefully in some ways, when he observed that the type of sentence typically analysed by the introspective linguist is far away from the type of evidence we tend to see typically occurring in the corpus. It almost seems that the wildest skew lies not in corpus evidence, but in introspectively informed judgements. It is a truism that this can almost not be helped. By artificially manipulating the informant, we artificially manipulate the data itself. This leads to the classic response from the informant to the researcher seeking an introspective judgement on a sentence: 'Yes I could say that – but I never would.' Chomsky's criticism that we would never find certain sentences or constructions in a corpus overlooked an important point. If we do not find them, this is an interesting and important comment on their *frequency*.

Frequency brings in another point. There are certain types of language data which can only be gathered accurately from a corpus. Human beings have only the vaguest notion of the frequency of a construct or word. Natural observation of data seems the only reliable source of evidence for such features as frequency. Of course, Chomsky may counter this point by suggesting that the gathering of such quantitative information is actually pointless. Remember his views on the relative likelihood of people living in Dayton, Ohio or New York! A response to this criticism will be presented shortly. For the moment let us satisfy ourselves with the observation that corpora are sources of quantitative information beyond compare. At this moment it is useful to consider the earlier point made by Chomsky: to paraphrase, why look in a corpus for what lies in your head? Here we can see one example of data which is not susceptible to recovery via introspection, that is, frequency-based data. We must also consider that the process of introspection may not be at all systematic and in fairness look at the extremes reached by the non-corpus linguist. If the corpus linguist can often seem the slave of the available data, so the non-corpus linguist can be seen to be at the whim of his or her imagination. Fillmore (1992: 35) provides satire once again in describing the almost mystic persuits of the non-corpus linguist:

> He sits in a deep soft armchair, with his eyes closed and his hands clasped behind his head. Once in a while he opens his eyes, sits up abruptly shouting, 'Wow, what a neat fact!', grabs his pencil, and writes something down ... having come still no closer to knowing what language is really like.

So it seems that the type of evidence provided by the corpus does have advantages after all. Not only does it seem that the corpus appears a rather more reliable source of frequency-based data, it is also the case that it provides the basis of a much more systematic approach to the analysis of language, a point argued eloquently by Leech (1992). Leech argues that the corpus is a more powerful methodology from the point of view of the scientific method, as it is open to objective verification of results.[10] This cannot be said of thought processes on the other hand, the stock-in-trade of introspection.

Setting these important points aside for the moment, let us consider again the supposed disadvantages of using a corpus. Is it also possible that some of the disadvantages of the approach had been overexaggerated? Central to the attack on corpus-based approaches was the idea that natural data of this variety was a poor mirror of our competence, as the production of language was influenced by factors other than our competence. Chomsky (1965), in a rather off-handed way, categorised '95 per cent' of utterances as ungrammatical, hence performance data was a bad representative of competence knowledge. Yet this picture has turned out to be somewhat over-simplified. Labov (1969) showed that 'the great majority of utterances in all contexts are grammatical'. Along one dimension at least, we can suggest that corpus-based enquiry may not be as invalid as originally supposed. The corpus is not necessarily a mish-mash of ungrammatical sentences. It would appear that there is reason to hope that the corpus may generally contain sentences which are grammatical. Note we are not saying here that all of the sentences in a corpus are grammatically acceptable. They are not necessarily so, a theme that will be returned to in Chapter 4. But it does at least seem that good grounds exist to allow us to believe that the problem of ungrammatical sentences in corpus may not be so common as was initially assumed.

This brings us back to a point made earlier. We showed that corpora are excellent sources of quantitative data, but noted that Chomsky may well respond that quantitative data is of no use to linguists. Well here again we can suggest that his point, though well made, is actually not supported by reality. Setting aside the fact that quantitative approaches to linguistic description have yielded important results in linguistics, such as in Svartvik's (1966) study of passivisation, the quantitative data extracted from corpora can be of great practical use to linguists developing tools for analysis. To take the example of part-of-speech analysis, all of the successful modern approaches to automated part-of-speech analysis rely on quantitative data derived from a corpus. We will not labour this point here as it is properly the province of Chapter 5. But one observation must be made. Without the corpus, or some other natural source of evidence yielding comparable quantitative data, such powerful analytical tools would not be available to any linguist or computational linguists today. 'The proof of the pudding is in the eating' is an old English saying, and it certainly allows us to dismiss Chomsky's suggestion that quantitative data is of no use or importance.

So some of the criticisms of corpus linguistics made by Chomsky were in part valid, and, as will see shortly, have helped to foster a more realistic attitude towards corpora today. But these criticisms were also partially invalid, and avoided a genuine assessment of the strengths of corpora as opposed to their weaknesses. This observation begins to suggest why some people continued to work with corpora, yet fails to suggest why they did so in the face of the other important criticism of early corpus linguistics reviewed here, that of Abercrombie (1965). So let us turn finally to this criticism. The pseudo-technique objection made by Abercrombie was, at the time, somewhat accurate. We could argue that it need not necessarily have been so, as we shall see. But for the moment, we will take its accuracy for granted. A crucial point, however, is that today, a remark such as Abercrombie's is no longer accurate, and that lack of accuracy is solely attributable to one source – the digital computer.

As will be discussed in the next chapter, the term *corpus* is now almost synonymous with the term **machine-readable** corpus. This is no accident. The computer has allowed techniques previously thought of as being distinctly in the realm of the pseudo-technique to be used. The computer has allowed this because of its ability to *search for, retrieve, sort* and *calculate* data (after Leech 1991). Before examining what each of these abilities allows the machine to do, let us recall how simple computers are, conceptually at least. The modern digital computer only takes data, carries out a process on that data and, as a result of the processing it undertakes, provides us with some information. The range of processes it can carry out, the data it can work with and the information it can yield can be bewildering. We must not be beguiled by this diversity, however. In reality, nothing more than the processing of data to provide information occurs even on the most advanced super-computer.

So to refine Leech's point a little, it is truer to say that the interest in the computer for the corpus linguist comes from the ability of the computer to carry out the processes of searching for, sorting, retrieving and calculating linguistic data, whether that be textual (most common) or digitised speech (increasingly common). These processes are those which, when required of humans, ensured some corpus retrieval techniques could only be described as pseudo-techniques. Although these processes were possible using a willing army of human analysts they were wildly unattractive. Willing armies of analysts cost money, work slowly and make mistakes. The computer, over the last fifty years, has become cheaper, faster and is capable of total accuracy in text processing. The type of analysis that Käding waited years for can now be achieved in a few moments on a desktop computer. The computer alone has rendered the pseudo-technique criticism invalid.

Considering the importance of the marriage of machine and corpus, it seems worthwhile to consider in slightly more detail what these processes that allow the machine to aid the linguist are. The computer[11] has the ability to search for a particular word, sequence of words or even perhaps part of speech in a text. So if we are interested, say, in the usage of the word *however* in a text, we can simply ask the machine to **search for** this word in the text. Its ability to **retrieve** all examples of this word, usually in context, is a further aid to the linguist. The machine can find the relevant text and display it to the user. It may also **calculate** the number of occurrences of the word so that information on the frequency of the word may be gathered. We may then be interested in **sorting** the data in some way – for example, alphabetically on words appearing to the right or left. We may even sort the list by searching for words occurring in the immediate context of the word. We may take our initial list of examples of *however* presented in context (usually referred to as a **concordance**), and extract from that another list, say of all examples of *however* followed closely by the word *we*. These processes are often included in a *concordance program*. The concordance program is the tool most often used in corpus linguistics to examine corpora. After using a concordance program it is all too easy to become blasé about the ability to manipulate corpora of millions of words. In reality we should temper that cavalier attitude with the realisation that without the computer, corpus linguistics would be terrifically impractical, and would hover Grail-like beyond reasonable reach. Whatever philosophical advantages we may eventually see in a corpus, it is the computer which allows us to exploit corpora on a large scale with speed and accuracy, and we must never forget that. Technology has rendered the pseudo-technique argument obsolete.

Maybe now it is possible to state why this book is being written. A theoretical and technical shift over the past half-century has led to some of the criticisms of the corpus-based approach being *tempered*. Note that the term 'tempered' is used rather than discarded. Only in the case of the pseudo-technique can we safely say that the argument against the corpus is refuted.

Chomsky's criticisms are not wholly invalidated, nor indeed could they be. Chomsky revealed some powerful verities, and these shape the approach taken to the corpus today. Chomsky stated that natural language was non-finite. This book will not argue with that finding. Chomsky argued that externalised speech was affected by factors other than our linguistic competence. This book will not argue with that finding. Some other criticisms of Chomsky's may be reduced in degree, but with the possible exception of his denigration of quantitative data, this text would not seek to dispute the fundamental point being made. The argument being made here is that in abandoning the corpus-based approach, linguistics, if we can speak idiomatically, threw the baby out with the bath water. The problems Chomsky rightly highlighted were believed to be fundamental to the corpus itself, rather than being fundamental to the approach taken to the corpus by the post-Bloomfieldian linguists. In other words, if you think language is finite, then your interpretation of the findings in a corpus may reflect that − if we can change the interpretation of the findings in a corpus to match the verities Chomsky revealed, then the natural data provided by the corpus can be a rich and powerful tool for the linguist. We must understand what we are doing when we are looking in a corpus and building one.

The mention of natural data brings in the other general point. Why move from one extreme of only natural data to another of only artificial data? Both have known weaknesses. Why not use a combination of both, and rely on the strengths of each to the exclusion of their weaknesses? A corpus and an introspection-based approach to linguistics are not mutually exclusive. In a very real sense they can be gainfully viewed as being complementary.

The reasons for the revival of corpus linguistics should now be quite obvious. It is, in some ways, an attempt to redress the balance in linguistics between the use of artificial data and the use of naturally occurring data. As we have stated already, and will see again in later chapters, artificial data can have a place in modern corpus linguistics. Yet it should always be used with naturally occurring data which can act as a control, a yardstick if you will. Corpus linguistics is, and should be, a synthesis of introspective and observational techniques, relying on a mix of artificial and natural observation.

Before concluding this chapter and moving on to review the constitution of the modern corpus, however, we will present a brief overview of important work in corpus linguistics that occurred during the interregnum of the 1960s and 1970s.

5. THROUGH THE INTERREGNUM TO THE REVIVAL OF THE EARLY EIGHTIES

We have examined why corpus linguistics underwent a period of unpopularity, and how the modern methodology of corpus linguistics has regained theoretical ground to reach a position of generally accepted respectability in modern linguistics. Some of the myths and fables we discussed at the beginning of this chapter have been swept away in this process. But not all. A common belief is that corpus-based linguistics was abandoned entirely in the

1950s, and then adopted once more almost as suddenly in the early 1980s. This is simply untrue, and does a disservice to those linguists who continued to pioneer corpus-based work during this interregnum. We must not think in terms of corpus linguistics being set aside in the early 1960s, and suddenly revived after some intrepid explorer-style linguists rediscovered it, like some ancient pyramid overgrown by a jungle, and rescued it from obscurity. The history of corpus-based studies over these two decades is actually a very interesting one.

As stated, some linguists did not abandon the corpus-based methodology at all. Quirk (1960) planned and executed the construction of his ambitious Survey of English Usage (SEU) which he began in 1961. In the same year Francis[12] and Kucera began work on the now famous Brown corpus, a work which was to take almost two decades to complete. These researchers were in a minority, but they were not universally regarded as peculiar and others followed their lead. For example, in 1975, fourteen years after work began on the Brown corpus, Jan Svartvik started to build on the work of the SEU and the Brown corpus to construct the London-Lund corpus.

Note that during this period the computer slowly started to become the mainstay of corpus linguistics. Svartvik computerised the SEU, and as a consequence produced what some, including Leech (1991: 9) still believe to be 'to this day an unmatched resource for studying spoken English'. Francis and Kucera set out with the explicit aim of producing a computer readable corpus. So perhaps at least part of the answer to 'Why didn't all linguists abandon the corpus?' is the fact that some of them had seen how computerising the corpus invalidated one main criticism of the approach – the pseudo-technique.

The availability of the computerised corpus and the wider availability of institutional and private computing facilities do seem to have provided a spur to the revival of corpus linguistics. The growth of corpus linguistics between 1965 and 1991 illustrated in Table 1.1 (from Johansson, 1991: 312) was fuelled almost exclusively by a handful of machine-readable corpora, such as the Lancaster-Oslo/Bergen (LOB) corpus, the London-Lund corpus and the Brown corpus.

6. CONCLUSION

So a more accurate pattern of the development of corpus linguistics is now apparent. During the 1950s a series of criticisms were made of the corpus-based approach to language study. Some were right, some were half-right, and some have proved themselves, with the passage of time, to be wrong or irrelevant. The first important point is that these criticisms were not necessarily fatal ones, though they were widely perceived as such at the time. The second important point is that some linguists carried on using the corpus as a

Date	Studies
To 1965	10
1966–1970	20
1971–1975	30
1976–1980	80
1981–1985	160
1986–1991	320

Table 1.1 The revival of corpus linguistics

technique and tried to establish a balance between the use of the corpus and the use of intuition.

Although the methodology went through a period of relative neglect for two decades, it was far from abandoned. Indeed, during this time essential advances in the use of corpora were made. Most importantly of all, the linking of the corpus to the computer was completed during this era. Following these advances, corpus studies boomed from 1980 onwards, as corpora, techniques and new arguments in favour of the use of corpora became more apparent. The following chapter deals in more depth with what constitutes the modern corpus exactly and what beliefs lie behind its use. But for the moment we can say that the availability of computer-based corpus material, the acceptance that a corpus could never be the sole explicandum of language and a growing awareness of the usefulness of quantitative data provided major impetuses to the re-adoption of the corpus-based language study as a methodology in linguistics. Most important of all, it was realised that the corpus and the linguist's intuition were complementary, not antagonistic. Fillmore (1992: 35) seems to sum it up so well when discussing corpus and non-corpus linguists, so we shall allow him to have the last word in this chapter:

> I don't think there can be any corpora, however large, that contain information about all of the areas of English lexicon and grammar that I want to explore ... [but] every corpus I have had the chance to examine, however small, has taught me facts I couldn't imagine finding out any other way. My conclusion is that the two types of linguists need one another.

7. STUDY QUESTIONS

1.   Take a sentence, at random, from this chapter. Ensure that it is not a quotation from another book. How likely are you to find that exact sentence repeated anywhere in the English language? Having decided this, if you have access to a large corpus, look for the sentence in that corpus to aid your observation. If not, find a book in which you think the sentence is likely to be repeated and use the index, if appropriate, to help you search for the sentence. What does this experiment show us about the nature of natural languages?

2. Start an infinite sentence. How easy is it to do this? Why can you do it? What does your ability to do it say about human languages?

3. If you used a corpus in answering question (1), try this exercise to see how important the use of computers are in corpus linguistics: try to produce a list of sentences in which the word *sorting* is used in this chapter. If you attempt this exercise, how long did it take you?

4. Using your intuition, try to estimate what the ten most frequent words are in this chapter, giving for each an estimated number of occurrences. How sure are you of the results you produce?

8. FURTHER READING

Leech (1991, 1992) has written two important articles on the origins of corpus linguistics. Both cover the history of corpus linguistics in some detail, though the 1992 article is of particular interest in that it considers corpus linguistics as a paradigm contrasting with the generative framework of language study. Francis 1979 is of historical interest – an early work from the renaissance of corpus linguistics. Hockett 1948 is of particular importance – it shows that some 'early corpus linguists' did have more progressive views of the role of corpus data in the investigation of language than one might imagine.

NOTES

1. Though the corpora used were merely large collections of transcribed interactions. Important notions such as representativeness (see Chapter 2) were not used in the construction of these 'corpora'.
2. Fries based his grammar on a corpus of transcribed telephone conversation. This is interesting as the modern corpus grammars are based almost exclusively on written data. Fries, in some respects, has yet to be surpassed.
3. See the Glossary for a definition of this term.
4. See the Glossary for a definition of this term.
5. It is of interest to note that Chafe (1992: 87) has suggested that naturally occurring, almost subconscious, introspective judgements may be another source of evidence we could draw upon. It is difficult to conceive of a systematic method for recovering such observations, however, so for the purposes of this discussion we shall dismiss this source of natural data and refer the curious reader to Chafe (*ibid.*).
6. We shall return to and refine the notion of cognitive plausibility in Chapter 5, section 2.
7. Sebba (1991) gives an interesting account of early corpus linguistics.
8. Or to use Chomsky's definition, from his 'Lectures on Government and Binding', a 'pathological' set of criticisms.
9. Note that in historical linguistics, corpora of sorts remained in use too – here again it is impossible to question native speakers.
10. One is irresistibly drawn to remembering Galton's words, 'until the phenomena of any branch of knowledge have been submitted to measurement and number, it cannot assume the dignity of a science'.
11. In the following discussion, it is assumed that the computer is running an appropriate program to achieve the various tasks required by a corpus linguist.
12. Francis (1979) describes the early days of the Brown corpus.

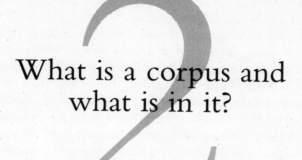

What is a corpus and what is in it?

1. CORPORA VS. MACHINE-READABLE TEXTS

Empirical research may be carried out using any written or spoken text. Indeed, such individual texts form the basis of many kinds of literary and linguistic analysis, for example the stylistic analysis of a poem or novel or a conversation analysis of a television talk show. But the notion of a **corpus** as the basis for a form of empirical linguistics differs in several fundamental ways from the examination of particular texts. In principle, any collection of more than one text can be called a corpus: the term 'corpus' is simply the Latin for 'body', hence a corpus may be defined as any body of text. It need imply nothing more. But the term 'corpus' when used in the context of modern linguistics tends most frequently to have more specific connotations than this simple definition provides for. These may be considered under four main headings:

sampling and representativeness

finite size

machine-readable form

a standard reference.

1.1. Sampling and representativeness

In linguistics, we are often more interested in a whole variety of a language, rather than in an individual text or author. In such cases we have two options for our data collection: first, we could analyse every single utterance in that variety; or second, we could construct a smaller sample of the variety. The first option is impracticable except in a very few cases, for example, with a dead language which has few extant texts. More often, the total text population is huge, and with a living language such as English or German the number of utterances is constantly increasing and theoretically infinite. To analyse every utterance in such a language would be an unending and impossible task. It is therefore necessary to choose the second option and build a sample of the language variety in which we are interested.

As we discussed in Chapter 1, it was Chomksy's criticism of early corpora that they would always be skewed: in other words, some utterances would be excluded because they are rare, other much more common utterances might be excluded simply by chance, and chance might also act so that some rare utterances were actually included in the corpus. Although modern computer technology means that nowadays much larger corpora can be collected than those Chomsky was thinking about when he made these criticisms, his criticism about the potential skewedness of a corpus is an important and valid one which must be taken seriously. However, this need not mean abandoning the corpus analysis enterprise. Rather, consideration of Chomsky's criticism should be directed towards the establishment of ways in which a much less biased and more generally repesentative corpus may be constructed.

In building a corpus of a language variety, we are interested in a sample which is maximally representative of the variety under examination, that is, which provides us with as accurate a picture as possible of the tendencies of that variety, including their proportions. We would not, for example, want to use only the novels of Charles Dickens or Charlotte Brontë as a basis for analysing the written English language of the mid-nineteenth century. We would not even want to base our sample purely on text selected from the genre of the novel. What we would be looking for are samples of a broad range of different authors and genres which, when taken together, may be considered to 'average out' and provide a reasonably accurate picture of the entire language population in which we are interested. We shall return in more detail to this issue of corpus representativeness and sampling in Chapter 6.

1.2. Finite size

As well as sampling, the term 'corpus' also tends to imply a body of text of a finite size, for example 1,000,000 words. This is not, however, universally so. At Birmingham University, for example, John Sinclair's COBUILD team have been engaged in the construction and analysis of a collection of texts known as a **monitor corpus**. A monitor corpus, which Sinclair's team often prefer to call simply a 'collection of texts' rather than a 'corpus', is an open-ended entity. Texts are constantly being added to it, so that it gets bigger and bigger as more samples are added. Monitor corpora are primarily of importance in lexicographic work, which is the main interest of the COBUILD group. They enable lexicographers to trawl a stream of new texts looking for the occurrence of new words or for changing meanings of old words. Their main advantages are: (a) the age of the texts, which is not static and means that very new texts can be included, unlike the synchronic 'snapshot' provided by finite corpora; and (b) their scope, in that a larger and much broader sample of the language can be covered. Their main disadvantage is that because they are constantly changing in size and are less rigorously sampled than finite corpora they are not such a reliable source of quantitative (as opposed to qualitative) data about a language. With the exception of the monitor corpus observed, though, it should be noted that it is more often the case that a corpus has a finite number of words contained in it. At the beginning of a corpus-building project, the research plan will set out in detail how the language variety is to be sampled, and how many samples of how many words are to be collected so that a pre-defined grand total is arrived at. With the Lancaster-Oslo/Bergen (LOB) corpus and the Brown corpus the grand total was 1,000,000 running words of text; with the British National Corpus (BNC) it was 100,000,000 running words. Unlike the monitor corpus, therefore, when such a corpus reaches the grand total of words, collection stops and the corpus is not thereafter increased in size. (One exception to this is the London-Lund corpus, which was augmented in the mid-1970s by Sidney Greenbaum to cover a wider variety of genres.)

1.3. Machine-readable form

It should also be noted that nowadays the term 'corpus' almost always implies the additional feature 'machine-readable'. For many years, the term 'corpus' could be used only in reference to printed text. But now things have changed, so that this is perhaps the exception rather than the rule. One example of a corpus which *is* available in printed form is *A Corpus of English Conversation* (Svartvik and Quirk 1980). This corpus represents the 'original' London-Lund corpus (i.e. minus the additional examples of more formal speech added by Sidney Greenbaum in the 1970s). Although these texts are also available in machine-readable form within the London-Lund corpus, this work is notable as it is one of the very few corpora available in book format. There is also a limited amount of other corpus data (excluding context-free frequency lists, and so on, prepared *from* corpora) which is available in other media. A complete key-word-in-context concordance of the LOB corpus is available on microfiche, and, with spoken corpora, copies of the actual recordings are sometimes available for, amongst other things, instrumental phonetic analysis: this is the case with the Lancaster/IBM Spoken English Corpus, but not with the London-Lund corpus. Corpora which are machine-readable possess several advantages over the original written or spoken format. The first and most important advantage of machine-readable corpora, as noted in Chapter 1, is that they may be searched and manipulated in ways which are simply not possible with the other formats. For instance, a corpus in book format, unless pre-indexed, would need to be read cover to cover in order to extract all instances of the word *boot*: with a machine-readable corpus, this task may be accomplished in at most a few minutes using concordancing software, or even, slightly more slowly, simply using the search facility in a word processor. The second advantage of machine-readable corpora is that they can be swiftly and easily enriched with additional information. We shall turn to this issue of **annotation** later in this chapter.

1.4. A standard reference

Although it is not an essential part of the definition of a corpus, there is also often a tacit understanding that a corpus constitutes a standard reference for the language variety which it represents. This presupposes its wide availability to other researchers, which is indeed the case with many corpora such as the Brown corpus of written American English, the LOB corpus of written British English, and the London-Lund corpus of spoken British English. The advantage of a widely available corpus is that it provides a yardstick by which successive studies may be measured. New results on related topics may, for example, be directly compared with published results (so long as the methodology is made clear) without the need for re-computation. A standard corpus also means that a continuous base of data is being used and thus variation between studies may be less likely to be attributed to differences in the data being used, and more to the adequacy of the assumptions and methodologies contained in the study.

So a corpus in modern linguistics, in contrast to being simply any body of text, might more accurately be described as a finite-sized body of machine-readable text, sampled in order to be maximally representative of the language variety under consideration. However, the reader should be aware of the possibilities for deviation in certain instances from this 'prototypical' definition.

2. TEXT ENCODING AND ANNOTATION

Corpora may exist in two forms: **unannotated** (i.e. in their existing raw states of plain text) or **annotated** (i.e. enhanced with various types of linguistic information). Unannotated corpora have been, and are, of considerable use in language study, but the utility of the corpus is considerably increased by the provision of annotation. The important point to grasp about an annotated corpus is that it is no longer simply a body of text in which the linguistic information is implicitly present. For example, the part-of-speech information 'third person singular present tense verb' is always present implicitly in the form *loves*, but it is only retrieved in normal reading by recourse to our pre-existing knowledge of the grammar of English. By contrast, a corpus, when annotated, may be considered to be a repository of linguistic information, because the information which was implicit in the plain text has been made explicit through concrete annotation. Thus our example of *loves* might in an annotated corpus read 'loves_VVZ', with the code VVZ indicating that it is a third person singular present tense (Z) form of a lexical verb (VV). Such annotation makes it quicker and easier to retrieve and analyse information about the language contained in the corpus. We shall discuss part-of-speech and other forms of linguistic annotation further in section 2.2.3.

Leech (1993) identifies seven maxims which should apply in the annotation of text corpora. These may be paraphrased as follows:

1. It should be possible to remove the annotation from an annotated corpus and revert to the raw corpus. Thus if the raw corpus contains the sentence *Claire collects shoes* (BNC)[1] and this is annotated for part of speech as 'Claire_NP1 collects_VVZ shoes_NN2', then it should be possible to remove the annotation and revert to the original *Claire collects shoes*. The ease of recoverability in this case (simply by stripping everything between an underscore character and a space or punctuation mark) may be contrasted with the prosodic annotation in the London-Lund corpus, which is interspersed within words – for example 'g/oing' indicates a rising pitch on the first syllable of *going* – and means that the original words cannot so easily be reconstructed.

2. It should be possible to extract the annotations by themselves from the text for storage elsewhere, for example in the form of a relational database or in an interlinear format where the annotation occurs on a separate line below the relevant line of running text. This is the flip side of (1). Taking points (1) and (2) together, in other words, the annotated corpus should allow the maximum flexibility for manipulation by the user.

3. The annotation scheme should be based on guidelines which are available to the end user. For instance, most corpora have a manual available with full details of the annotation scheme and the guidelines issued to the annotators. This enables the user to understand fully what each instance of annotation represents without resorting to guesswork and to understand in cases where more than one interpretation of the text is possible why a particular annotation decision was made at that point.

4. It should be made clear how and by whom the annotation was carried out. For instance, a corpus may be annotated manually, sometimes just by a single person and sometimes by a number of different people; alternatively, the annotation may be carried out completely automatically by a computer program, whose output may or may not then be corrected by human beings. Again, this information is often contained in a printed manual or a documentation file issued with the corpus.

5. The end user should be made aware that the corpus annotation is not infallible, but simply a potentially useful tool. Although, as prescribed by point (6), annotators normally try to aim for as consensus based an annotation scheme as possible, any act of corpus annotation is by definition also an act of interpretation, either of the structure of the text or of its content.

6. Annotation schemes should be based as far as possible on widely agreed and theory-neutral principles. Thus, for instance, as we shall see below in section

2.2.3(b), parsed corpora often adopt a basic context-free phrase structure grammar rather than an implementation of a narrower specific grammatical theory (e.g. Chomsky's Principles and Parameters framework).

7. No annotation scheme has the a priori right to be considered as a standard. Standards, where they exist, emerge through practical consensus, as we shall see in the next section.

Although it is desirable that corpus annotators should adhere to these principles, which aim to maximise the usability and interchangeability of annotated corpora, there is scope for considerable variation in what distinctions are made within the annotations which are applied. One particular conflict which Leech (1993) draws attention to is between the utility of annotations to the end user and the ease of annotation for the annotator. For instance, the end user of a corpus annotated with semantic field information might want distinctions to be made between the different senses of the preposition *on*; but such distinctions might be so fine that it is impossible for automatic annotation software to make them with an acceptable degree of accuracy, and there may be no time or money for the annotation to be checked by a human analyst. In such cases, therefore, the pragmatic necessities imposed upon the producer of large quantities of annotated text must override the desiderata of the potential end user, and *on* might be assigned to a blanket category of grammatical words or prepositions. In practice, most annotation schemes are a compromise between the two poles of this dichotomy, and aim at the maximum potential utility, tempered by the practicalities of annotating the text.

2.1. Formats of annotation

There is currently no widely agreed standard way of representing information in texts. In the past, many different approaches have been adopted. But some approaches have been more lasting than others, and work is now progressing towards the establishment of truly international standards. One long-standing annotation practice has been that known as COCOA **references**. COCOA was a very early computer program used for extracting indexes of words in context from machine-readable texts. Its conventions were carried forward into several other programs, notably to its immediate successor, the widely-used Oxford Concordance Program (OCP). The conventions have also been applied to the encoding of corpora themselves, such as the Longman-Lancaster corpus and the Helsinki corpus, to indicate textual information (see below). Very simply, a COCOA reference consists of a balanced set of angled brackets (< >) containing two entities: a code standing for a particular variable name, and a string or set of strings, which are the instantiations of that variable. For example, the code letter 'A' could be used to stand for the variable 'author' and the string or set of strings would stand for the author's name. Thus COCOA references indicating the author of a passage or text would look like the following:

<A CHARLES DICKENS>
<A WOLFGANG VON GOETHE>
<A HOMER>

But COCOA references only represent an informal trend for encoding specific types of textual information, for example, authors, dates, and titles. Current moves are aiming towards more formalised international standards for the encoding of any type of information that one would conceivably want to encode in machine-readable texts. The flagship of this current trend towards standards is the **Text Encoding Initiative** (TEI).

The TEI is a project sponsored by the three main scholarly associations concerned with humanities computing – the Association for Computational Linguistics (ACL), the Association for Literary and Linguistic Computing (ALLC), and the Association for Computers and the Humanities (ACH). The aim of the TEI is to provide standardised implementations for machine-readable text interchange. For this, the TEI employs an already existing form of document markup known as SGML (Standard Generalised Markup Language). SGML was adopted because it is simple, clear, formally rigorous, and already recognised as an international standard. The TEI's own original contribution is a detailed set of guidelines as to how this standard is to be used in text encoding (Sperberg-McQueen and Burnard 1994).

In the TEI, each individual text (or 'document') is conceived of as consisting of two parts – a **header** and the **text** itself. The header contains information about the text such as: the author, title, date, and so on; information about the source from which it was encoded, for example the particular edition/publisher used in creating the machine-readable text; and information about the encoding practices adopted, including any feature system declarations. The actual TEI annotation of the header and the text is based around two basic devices: **tags** and **entity references**. Texts are assumed to be made up of **elements**. An element can be any unit of text – word, sentence, paragraph, chapter, and so on. Elements are marked in the TEI using SGML tags. SGML tags – which should be distinguished from the code strings that are often known as 'tags' in linguistic annotation (e.g. NN1 = singular common noun) – are indicated by balanced pairs of angled brackets (i.e. < and >). A **start tag** at the beginning of an element is represented by a pair of angled brackets containing annotation strings, thus: < ... >; an **end tag** at the end of an element contains a slash character preceding the annotation strings, thus: </ ... >. To give an example, a simple and frequently used TEI tag is that which indicates the extent of a paragraph. This would be represented as follows:

The actual textual material goes here.

In contrast to tags, entity references are delimited by the characters & and ;.

An entity reference is essentially a shorthand way of encoding detailed information within a text. The shorthand form which is contained in the text refers outwards to a **feature system declaration** (FSD) in the document header which contains all the relevant information in full TEI tag-based markup. For example, one shorthand code which is used in annotating words for parts of speech is 'vvd', in which the first *v* signifies that the word is a verb, the second *v* signifies that it is a lexical verb, and the *d* signifies that it is a past tense form. In the following example, this code is used in the form of an entity reference:

polished&vvd;

The entity reference here (*&vvd;*) might refer to a feature system declaration such as the following, which presents the information represented by the shorthand code 'vvd' fully in terms of its component features:

```
<fs id=vvd type=word-form>
      <f name=verb-class><sym value=verb>
      <f name=base><sym value=lexical>
      <f name=verb-form><sym value=past>
</fs>
```

This is essentially the same as looking up the identical shorthand code (*vvd*), which has been attached to a word in a corpus, in a table of codes and explanations of those codes. In a pre-TEI corpus such as the Lancaster/IBM Spoken English Corpus, the same word plus annotation might look something like this:

polished_vvd

with the tag attached to the word using an underscore character, and the user would then be able to look up the meaning of the code in a table listing all the codes used in annotating the corpus:

vvd   past tense form of lexical verb (e.g. ...)

The overall entity of a text is in the TEI based around the notion of a **document type description** (DTD). This is a formal representation which tells the user or a computer program what elements the text contains, how these elements are combined, and also contains a set of entity declarations, for example representations of non-standard characters. The TEI has already defined standard DTDs for basic text types such as poems, letters, drama, and so on. The DTD for drama, for example, includes tags for elements which delineate the different parts of dramatic texts such as stage directions, cast list, and so on. A DTD can be used by a special computer program known as an SGML **parser** in order to check whether the document is truly TEI-conformant.

Several major electronic text projects now employ fully TEI-conformant markup schemes. These projects include the 100,000,000-word British National

Corpus; the International Corpus of English, a collection of 1,000,000-word corpora from many countries where English is used as a first or second language; and the CURIA project, an initiative sponsored by the Royal Irish Academy which aims to provide a range of machine-readable texts in the various languages which have been used in Ireland during its history – Irish, Hiberno-Latin, and Hiberno-English. It should be noted, however, that the TEI's guidelines refer only to the final user-ready text and need not affect the annotation practices adopted during the preliminary processing of the text: at Lancaster University, for example, initial part-of-speech is carried out using the same practice which has in use for over a decade (i.e. attaching a tag to the end of a word using the underscore character) and this is only converted to TEI-conformant format at a later stage in the processing.

The TEI only provides quite broad guidelines for the encoding of texts. There exists, therefore, considerable scope for variation, even within the broad remit of being TEI-conformant. Hence, further standards are necessary if groups of researchers and resource users wish to specify in more detail the content and form of annotations. The European Union (EU), for example, has set up an advisory body known as EAGLES (Expert Advisory Groups on Language Engineering Standards), whose remit is to examine existing practices of encoding and annotation for the official languages of the European Union, and to arrive at specifications for European standards which are to be employed in future EU funded work. EAGLES consists of a number of working groups which deal with the various types of resource, including lexicons, computational linguistic formalisms, and, most importantly for our present purpose, text corpora. The text corpora working group is particularly concerned with defining standard schemes for annotation which may be applied to all the EU languages: for example, it has produced a base set of features for the annotation of parts of speech (e.g. singular common noun, comparative adverb, and so on) which will form the standard scheme for all the languages, but will be sufficiently flexible to allow for the variations between languages in how they signal different types of morphosyntactic information. Thus the EAGLES initiative, as compared with the TEI, aims more directly at specifying the *content* of text annotations rather than their *form*. However, a representation working group will also examine the form of annotations, including the issue of whether EAGLES will recommend full TEI conformance or whether it will employ a less rigorously constrained application of SGML markup. But little more can be said on this issue at present, since the EAGLES working groups have not, at the time of writing, made their final reports, and follow-up consultations will continue after the submission of these reports.

2.2. Types of annotation

2.2.1. Textual and extra-textual information

Having considered the ways in which additional information may be encoded in machine-readable texts, we now move on to consider the types of information which are typically found in corpora.

The most basic type of additional information is that which actually tells us what text or texts we are looking at. Sometimes the name of the computer file which contains the text will give us a clue to this: for example, *loba.tag* might tell us that we are looking at the part-of-speech tagged version (tag) of section A of the LOB corpus (loba). But filenames only provide us with a tiny amount of information and cannot cope with telling us about files which contain more than one text, hence this information is often encoded explicitly within the file, using one of the text encoding styles discussed above.

This basic information about the nature of the text can often be much more detailed than simply giving a title and author. Sometimes it will tell us more about the contents of the file: for example, it may give the age of the author, the sex of the author, the date the text was published or written, the variety of the language (e.g. US English, New Zealand English, British English), a broad subject domain (e.g. science, religion, detective fiction), and so on. These information fields provide the document with a whole document 'header' which can be used by retrieval programs to search and sort on particular variables. For example, we might be interested only in looking at those texts in a corpus which were written by women: in that case, we could ask a computer program to retrieve only those texts where the 'author's gender' variable (call it X) is equal to 'FEMALE'.

These kinds of information are given in COCOA format in both the Longman-Lancaster corpus and the Helsinki corpus. Figure 2.1 shows an example of a COCOA document header from the Helsinki corpus. Similar sorts of information may also be encoded in TEI conformant markup. Figure 2.2 shows an extract from such a document header taken from a Middle/Early Modern Irish text encoded by the CURIA project.

On the left-hand side of the page in Figure 2.1 is the COCOA-format header as it appears in the corpus; on the right-hand side of the page we have glossed each code for you (e.g. we have said that code 'N' represents the feature 'name of text'). Where an 'X' occurs as the instantiation of a particular code (e.g. <M X>), this means that the information for that code either was not relevant to this text or was not available.

As will be gathered from the names of the TEI tags in Figure 2.2, the header to this document provides a wealth of detail about the origins of the text, and how and when it was encoded. The CURIA project also marks a variety of other information within its texts using the TEI form of markup, and these may give a further idea of the vast range of information which we may find

```
<B CEPRIV1>                     Short descriptive code
<Q E1 XX CORP EBEAUM>           Text identifier
<N LET TO HUSBAND>              Name of text
<A BEAUMONT ELIZABETH>          Author's name
<C E1>                          Sub-period
<O 1500-1570>                   Date of original
<M X>                           Date of manuscript
<K X>                           Contemporaneity of original and manuscript
<D ENGLISH>                     Dialect
<V PROSE>                       Verse or prose
<T LET PRIV>                    Text type
<G X>                           Relationship to foreign original
<F X>                           Language of foreign original
<W WRITTEN>                     Relationship to spoken language
<X FEMALE>                      Sex of author
<Y X>                           Age of author
<H HIGH>                        Author's social status
<U X>                           Audience description
<E INT UP>                      Participant relationship
<J INTERACTIVE>                 Interactive/non-interactive
<I INFORMAL>                    Formal/informal
<Z X>                           Prototypical text category
<S SAMPLE X>                    Sample
```

Figure 2.1 COCOA document header from Helsinki corpus

explictly annotated in corpora. For example, CURIA indicates those words in the texts which are in a language other than the main language of the document, and says which language they belong to. A variety of what might be termed 'encyclopaedic knowledge' is also encoded in the CURIA texts: for instance, all words which are personal or place names are annotated as such. Figure 2.3 shows a short TEI-encoded extract from a Middle/Early Modern Irish text from CURIA.

Note in Figure 2.3 the various kinds of information encoded using SGML tags delimited by < ... > and </ ... >:

encloses a place name

encloses a person's forename

encloses words in another language; lang="Lat" indicates in this example that that language is Latin

encloses a correction to the manuscript of the text; sic=" ... " indicates the original reading in the manuscript

<l> indicates a new line in the printed edition

<page n="56"> indicates a new page (p. 56) in the printed edition

<milestone unit="folium" n=59vb> indicates a new unit in the original manuscript

```
<TEI.2><TEIHEADER><FILEDESC><TITLESTMT><TITLE>Lives of the Saints from the
Book of Lismore: an electronic edition</TITLE>
<AUTHOR>Anonymous</AUTHOR><RESPSTMT><RESP>compiled by</RESP><NAME>Elva
Johnston</NAME></RESPSTMT></TITLESTMT><EDITIONSTMT><EDITION N="1">First
draft, revised and corrected.<DATE>1993-04-
30</DATE></EDITION><RESPSTMT><RESP>Proof corrections by</RESP> <NAME>Dr
Nicole Mueller </NAME></RESPSTMT></EDITIONSTMT> <EXTENT>98,436 words</EXTENT>
<PUBLICATIONSTMT><PUBLISHER>CURIA, the Thesaurus Linguarum Hiberniae: a joint
programme of the Royal Irish Academy and University College Cork,</PUBLISHER>
<ADDRESS><ADDRLINE>19 Dawson Street,</ADDRLINE> <ADDRLINE>Dublin
2,</ADDRLINE> <ADDRLINE>Ireland,</ADDRLINE></ADDRESS> <DATE>1993.</DATE>
<DISTRIBUTOR>CURIA online at University College Cork, Ireland.</DISTRIBUTOR>
<IDNO TYPE="curia">11</IDNO> <AVAILABILITY><P>Available with prior consent of the
CURIA programme for purposes of academic research and teaching
only.</P></AVAILABILITY></PUBLICATIONSTMT> <SERIESSTMT><P></P></SERIESSTMT>
<NOTESSTMT><NOTE></NOTE></NOTESSTMT> <SOURCEDESC> <BIBLFULL><TITLESTMT>
<TITLE>Lives of Saints from the Book of Lismore.</TITLE> <EDITOR>Whitley
Stokes</EDITOR> </TITLESTMT> <EDITIONSTMT><EDITION>First
edition</EDITION></EDITIONSTMT> <EXTENT>cxx + 411 pp</EXTENT>
<PUBLICATIONSTMT><DATE>Created 1890.</DATE> <PUBLISHER>Clarendon
Press</PUBLISHER> <PUBPLACE>Oxford</PUBPLACE> <DATE>1893</DATE>
<IDNO></IDNO><ADDRESS></ADDRESS><AUTHORITY></AUTHORITY> </PUBLICATIONSTMT>
<NOTESSTMT><NOTE>Chatsworth, Book of Lismore (at Chatsworth since 1930),
folios 41ra1-84ra9 (facsimile foliation); published in facsimile: R. A. S.
Macalister (ed), The Book of Mac Carthaigh Riabhach otherwise the Book of
Lismore, Facsimiles in Collotype of Irish Manuscripts V (Dublin Stationery
Office 1950). There are two MS copies: (1) Dublin, Royal Irish Academy, MS 23
K 5 (477), made by Eugene O'Curry, c. 1839 and (2) Dublin, Royal Irish
Academy, MS 23 H 6 (474), made by Joseph O'Longan in 1868. Stokes's edition
was made from the original, lodged for him in the British
Museum.</NOTE></NOTESSTMT></BIBLFULL></SOURCEDESC></FILEDESC>
<ENCODINGDESC><PROJECTDESC><P>CURIA: Thesaurus Linguarum
Hiberniae</P></PROJECTDESC> <SAMPLINGDECL><P>All editorial introduction,
translation, notes and indexes have been omitted. Editorial corrigenda (pp.
404-411) are integrated into the electronic edition. In general, only the
text of the Book of Lismore had been retained, since variants are cited from
other MSS in a non-systematic way and most are non-significant. Only
significant variants are retained and these are tagged as variants. Missing
text supplied by the editor is tagged.</P></SAMPLINGDECL>
<EDITORIALDECL><CORRECTION><P>Text has been thoroughly checked and proofread.
Corrections are tagged.</P></CORRECTION>
```

Figure 2.2 Partial extract from TEI (P2) document header (CURIA project)

encloses an expansion of an abbreviation in the
   original manuscript

<q> </q> encloses a question

<persongrp role="genus"> </persongrp> encloses a phrase referring
   to a group of people. In this case that group is a genus.

```
<q>Ni ricthe a leas te<expan>cht</expan> damsa libh anbhar t&iacute;r,
&aacute;r ita <lb>gein ocuibh i m- broinn mhna, &ampersir; is d&oacute;
dor<expan>a</expan>dadh o Dia b<expan>ur</expan>dadh o Dia b<expan>ur</expan> tir-si: is iarnachul
<lb>bheithi, is d&oacute; fhoighentai &ampersir; foighen<expan>us</expan> in
cenel-sa <persongrp role="genus">ua Figennte</persongrp>. IS e bus
<lb><forename>Pat<expan>raic</expan></forename> duibh. <foreign
lang="Lat">Et</foreign> bidh m&oacute;r a cata in gein <corr
sic="gignighter">gignith<expan>er</expan></corr> lib. Mogenar bias 'na<page
n="56"> <lb>aircill. <foreign lang="Lat">Et</foreign> ann inis tall tiar a m-
beluibh in mara, in fil <milestone unit="folium" n=59vb>aitreabh
<lb>innte?</q> ar <forename>P<expan>&aacute;traic</expan></forename>, .i.
<placename>Inis Cathaigh</placename>.</p>
```

Figure 2.3 Extract from a TEI-encoded (P2) Middle/Early Modern Irish text from the CURIA project

Note also the use of *&aacute*; and similar *entity references* indicating accented characters. See further section 2.2.2.

2.2.2 Orthography

Moving on from general, largely external, attributes of the text, we now consider the annotation of specific features within the text itself.

It might be thought that converting a written or spoken text into machine-readable form is a relatively simple typing or optical scanning task. But even with a basic running machine-readable text, issues of encoding are vital, although their extent may not at first be apparent to English-speakers.

In languages other than English, there arise the issues of accents and, even more seriously, of non-Roman alphabets such as Greek, Russian, Japanese, Chinese and Arabic. IBM-compatible personal computers, along with certain other machines, are capable of handling accented characters by using the extended 8-bit character set. Many mainframe computers, however, especially in English-speaking countries, do not make use of an 8-bit character set. For maximal interchangeability, therefore, accented characters need to be encoded in other ways. Native speakers of languages with accented characters tend to adopt particular strategies for handling their alphabets when using computers or typewriters which lack these characters. French speakers on the one hand typically omit the accent entirely, so that, for example, the name *Hélène* would be written *Helene*. German speakers on the other hand either introduce the additional letter *e* for the umlaut (which is historically what the umlaut represented), so that *Frühling* would be written *Fruehling*, or alternatively they place a double quote mark immediately before the relevant letter, for example Fr"uhling; at the same time, they simply ignore the variant *scharfes s* (ß) and replace it with the ordinary *ss*. However, although these strategies for text encoding are the natural practice of native speakers, they pose problems in the encoding of electronic text for other purposes. With the French strategy, one loses information which is present in the original text, and with the German

strategies this problem is compounded with the addition of extraneous orthographic information. In encoding texts, we want to aim as much as possible at
a complete representation of the text as it exists in its natural state. In response
to this need, the TEI has recently put forward suggestions for the encoding of
such special characters. Although the TEI provides for the use of several standard character sets (e.g. the extended character set including the basic
accented characters), which must be defined in a **writing system declaration** or **WSD**, it is strongly recommended that only the ISO-646 subset (which
is more or less the basic English alphabet) is used, with special characters being
annotated in other ways. The guidelines suggest that the characters are
encoded as TEI entities, using the delimiting characters of & and ;. Thus, for
example, *ü* would be encoded in the TEI as *&uumlaut;*. This can make the text
somewhat hard for the human user to read (see, for example, Figure 2.3
above),[2] but has the huge advantage that all the information in the original
text is encoded.

As to the problem of non-Roman alphabets, a number of solutions have
been adopted by text encoders. One of the most common approaches, now
quite frequently used for machine-readable Greek texts such as the Fribergs'
morphologically analysed Greek New Testament, is to represent the letters of
the non-Roman alphabet by an artificial alphabet made up of only the basic
ISO-646 ('English') characters which are available to nearly all computers. In
the Friberg Greek text, for instance, ISO-646 letters which have direct correspondences to Greek letters are used to represent those letters so that, for
example, A = alpha; ISO-646 letters which do not exist in Greek (e.g. W) are
used to represent those Greek characters which do not have direct equivalents
in the computer character set (e.g. W is used for omega, as it closely resembles
a lower-case omega). An alternative approach to this, which has been adopted
by some projects, is actually to use the non-Roman character set itself. The TEI
guidelines, as noted above, do allow for the use of a number of different character sets, but such an approach makes text exchange and analysis less easy:
special graphics capabilities are required to display the characters on screen
and the encoding may pose problems for some of the commonly available text
analysis programs (e.g. concordancers) which are geared solely towards
Roman alphabets.

In encoding a corpus, a decision must also be made at an early stage as to
whether to represent the language as unaffected by external aspects of typography and so on, or to represent as fully as possible the text in all its aspects.
Representing the text in the latter way means that one needs to account for
various aspects of its original form – these include the formal layout (e.g.
where line breaks and page breaks occur), where special fonts are used for
emphasis, where non-textual material such as figures occurs, and so on. Again,
in the past these aspects have been handled in various ways – for example, the
LOB corpus used asterisks to represent changes of typography. However, the

TEI has now also suggested standard ways of representing these phenomena, based upon their concept of start and end tags.

The transcription of spoken data presents special problems for text encoding. In speech there is no explicit punctuation: any attempt at breaking down spoken language into sentences and phrases is an act of interpretation on the part of the corpus builder. One basic decision which needs to be made with spoken data is whether to attempt to transcribe it in the form of orthographic sentences or whether to use intonation units instead, which are often, though not always, coterminous with sentences. There also follows from the intonation unit/sentence decision the issue of whether to attempt to further punctuate spoken language, or leave it at the sentence level without punctuation. The London-Lund corpus, which exists solely in a prosodically transcribed form (see 2.2.3(g) below), was transcribed using intonation units alone, with no punctuation whatsoever. In contrast, the Lancaster/IBM Spoken English Corpus used intonation units for its prosodic version, but orthographic transcriptions of the speech were also produced; where possible, these transcriptions were made using the actual scripts used by speakers (given that most of the corpus is made up of radio broadcasts) or from transcriptions made by the speakers themselves.

Spoken language also entails further encoding issues. One major issue in spoken discourse involving several speakers is overlapping speech, that is, where more than one speaker is speaking simultaneously. This could be ignored and treated as an interruption, that is, giving each speaker a different turn, but this distorts what is actually occurring in the discourse. A common way of approaching turn taking and overlaps in written transcriptions is to use 'staves', such as the following:

```
D did you go to the doctor     hmmm
P               I went to the clinic
N                                    did they weigh you
```

Here we have a conversation between three people – D, P and N. The movement of the speech with time is from left to right. We can see clearly here who is speaking at any one time and where speech overlaps: for example, P starts speaking as D is saying the word *go* and their speech then overlaps. In this method, when one reaches the end of a line of the page, a new three-person stave is begun, so one 'line' of text is actually made up of three parallel lines, one representing each speaker at each point in the discourse. But staves are almost impossible to manipulate computationally, so other techniques need to be adopted in machine-readable text encoding. Typically, these involve enclosing the overlapping speech in some kind of marker to indicate where the overlap occurs: the London-Lund corpus used balanced pairs of asterisks (★★ ... ★★) for this, whereas the TEI uses its normal tag-based markup to indicate the extent of overlapping sections (see above).

In transcribing speech one also needs to make a decision whether to attempt to indicate phenomena such as false starts, hesitations, associated 'body language' (such as the direction of eye contact between speakers), and non-linguistic material such as laughs, coughs, and so on. Corpora vary considerably in the extent to which these features are included, but, where included, they are also typically included as comments, within some form of delimiting brackets.

2.2.3 Linguistic annotations

We now move on to consider the annotation of specifically linguistic features in corpora. But, before reading on, a detail of terminology should be observed at this point. Certain kinds of linguistic annotation, which involve the attachment of special codes to words in order to indicate particular features, are frequently known as 'tagging' rather than 'annotation', and the codes which are assigned are known as 'tags'. These terms will be encountered in much of the primary literature on corpus annotation, and will also be used in the sections which follow.

2.2.3(a) Part-of-speech annotation The most basic type of linguistic corpus annotation is part-of-speech tagging (sometimes also known as grammatical tagging or morphosyntactic annotation). The aim of part-of-speech tagging is to assign to each lexical unit in the text a code indicating its part of speech (e.g. singular common noun, comparative adjective, past participle). Part-of-speech information is a fundamental basis for increasing the specificity of data retrieval from corpora and also forms an essential foundation for further forms of analysis such as syntactic parsing and semantic field annotation. For instance, part-of-speech annotation forms a basic first step in the disambiguation of homographs. It cannot distinguish between the verbal senses of *boot* meaning 'to kick' and 'to start up a computer', but it can distinguish *boot* as a verb from *boot* as a noun, and hence separate away the verb senses from the noun senses. This means that in examining the way in which *boot* as 'footwear' is used in a corpus, we might need to dredge through only 50 examples of *boot* as a noun instead of 100 examples of the ambiguous string *boot*. Figures 2.4 to 2.7 show examples of various part-of-speech tagging schemes.

In Figure 2.4 the first two columns on the left are references to the text (P05) and the line numbers in the text. In the text itself, part-of-speech codes are attached to words using the underscore character. The following codes are used:

.	punctuation tag, full stop
BED	past tense form of *to be*
HVD	past tense form of *to have*
IN	preposition
JJ	adjective

```
P05  32   ^ Joanna_NP stubbed_VBD out_RP her_PP$ cigarette_NN with_IN
P05  32   unnecessary_JJ fierceness_NN ._.
P05  33   ^ her_PP$ lovely_JJ eyes_NNS were_BED defiant_JJ above_IN cheeks_NNS
P05  33   whose_WP$ colour_NN had_HVD deepened_VBN
P05  34   at_IN Noreen's_NP$ remark_NN ._.
```

Figure 2.4 Example of part-of-speech tagging from LOB corpus (C1 tagset)

```
^ For_IF the_AT members_NN2 of_IO this_DD1 university_NN1 this_DD1
charter_NN1 enshrines_VVZ a_AT1 victorious_JJ principle_NN1 ;_; and_CC
the_AT fruits_NN2 of_IO that_DD1 victory_NN1 can_VM immediately_RR
be_VBI seen_VVN in_II the_AT international_JJ community_NNJ of_IO
scholars_NN2 that_CST has_VHZ graduated_VVN here_RL today_RT ._.
```

Figure 2.5 Example of part-of-speech tagging from Spoken English Corpus (C7 tagset)

```
Perdita&NN1-NP0;,&PUN; covering&VVG; the&AT0; bottom&NN1; of&PRF;
the&AT0; lorries&NN2; with&PRP; straw&NN1; to&TO0; protect&VVI;
the&AT0; ponies&NN2;'&POS; feet&NN2;,&PUN; suddenly&AV0;
heard&VVD-VVN; Alejandro&NN1-NP0; shouting&VVG; that&CJT; she&PNP;
better&AV0; dig&VVB; out&AVP; a&AT0; pair&NN0; of&PRF; clean&AJ0;
breeches&NN2; and&CJC; polish&VVB; her&DPS; boots&NN2;,&PUN; as&CJS;
she&PNP;'d&VM0; be&VBI; playing&VVG; in&PRP; the&AT0; match&NN1;
that&DT0; afternoon&NN1;.&PUN;

&bquo;&PUQ;I&PNP;'ll&VM0; polish&VVI; your&DPS;
boots&NN2;,&PUN;&equo;&PUQ; he&PNP; offered&VVD;.&PUN;
```

Figure 2.6 Examples of part-of-speech tagging from the British National Corpus (C5 tagset in TEI-conformant layout)

NN	singular common noun
NNS	plural common noun
NP	singular proper noun
NP$	genitive proper noun
PP$	possessive pronoun
RP	adverbial particle
VBD	past tense form of lexical verb
VBN	past participle of lexical verb
WP$	genitive *wh*-pronoun
^	start of sentence marker

The example in Figure 2.5 uses a later development of the tagset used in Figure 2.4. Again, the tags are attached to words using the underscore character. Note the change to a more divisible tag scheme as discussed in the text: compare HVD (past tense of *to have*) with VHZ (present tense of *to have*). These are the codes used:

	punctuation tag, full stop
AT	article neutral for number

AT1	singular article
CC	coordinating conjunction
CST	*that* conjunction
DD1	singular determiner
IF	*for*
IO	*of*
NN1	singular common noun
NN2	plural common noun
NNJ	singular group noun
RL	locative adverb
RR	general adverb
RT	temporal adverb
VBI	infinitive form of *to be*
VHZ	third person present from of *to have*
VM	modal verb
VVN	past particple of lexical verb
VVZ	third person present form of lexical verb
^	start of sentence marker

The example in Figure 2.6 shows a further development from the tagsets shown in Figures 2.4 and 2.5. All the tags here contain three characters (for example JJ has been replaced by AJ0). Two more important things to note about this example are (a) that the use of the underscore character to attach tags to words has been replaced by the use of TEI entity references delimited by & and ;, and (b) that some words (such as *heard*) have *two* tags assigned to them. The latter are known as 'portmanteau tags' and have been assigned to help the end user in cases where there is a strong chance that the computer might otherwise have selected the wrong part of speech from the choices available to it (unlike the corpora in Figures 2.4 and 2.5, this corpus has not been corrected by hand).

The codes used are:

AT0	article neutral for number
AVP	adverbial particle
CJC	coordinating conjunction
CJS	subordinating conjunction
CJT	*that* conjunction
DPS	possessive determiner
NP0	proper noun
PRF	*of*
PRP	preposition
VVB	base form of lexical verb

The example in Figure 2.7 shows the part-of-speech tagging of a language other than English – in this case Spanish. The conventions are similar to those in Figures 2.4 and 2.5 above. The codes used are:

```
De_PREP conformidad_NCFS con_PREP la_ARTDFS Recomendación_NCFS
Q.13_CODE,_, debe_VMPI3S evitar_VLINF;se_SE la_ARTDFS
inclusión_NCFS de_PREP dos_CARDXP enlaces_NCMP por_PREP
satélite_NCMS en_PREP una_ARCAFS conexión_NCFS,_,
salvo_ADVN en_PREP casos_NCMP excepcionales_ADJGMP._. A_PREP fin_NCMS
de_PREP facilitar_VLINF el_ARTDMS cumplimiento_NCMS de_PREP esa_DMDXFS
Recomendación_NCFS,_, conviene_VLPI3S informar_VLINF a_PREP
los_ARTDMP centros_NCMP de_PREP tránsito_NCMS
subsiguientes_ADJGMP,_, mediante_PREP señalización_NCFS,_,
de_PREP que_CQUE ya_ADVT existe_VLPI3S un_ARCAMS enlace_NCMS por_PREP
satélite_NCMS en_PREP la_ARTDFS conexión_NCFS.
Durante_PREP el_ARTDMS siguientes_ADJGMS proceso_NCMS de_PREP
encaminamiento_NCMS,_, el_ARTDMS centro_NCMS o_CC los_ARTDMP
centros_NCMP de_PREP tránsito_NCMS deberán_VMFI3P
elegir_VLINF un_ARCAMS enlace_NCMS terrenal_ADJGMS._.
```

Figure 2.7 Example of part-of-speech tagging of Spanish, from the CRATER corpus

.	punctuation tag, full stop
ADJGMS	general adjective, masculine singular
ADVT	temporal adverb
ARTDMP	article/determiner masculine plural
ARTDMS	article/determiner masculine singular
CARDXP	cardinal number, plural
CC	coordinating conjunction
CQUE	*que* conjunction
NCFS	feminine singular common noun
NCMS	masculine singular common noun
PREP	preposition
VLINF	infinitive form of lexical verb
VLPI3S	third person singular indicative present of lexical verb

Part-of-speech annotation was one of the first types of annotation to be performed on corpora and is today by far the most common. One of the reasons for this is that part-of-speech annotation is a task which can be carried out by a computer to a high degree of accuracy without manual intervention, since the correct part of speech for any given word is highly predictable from the surrounding context, given some very basic information about the language (e.g. common word suffixes and their possible parts of speech). Working at Brown University in the United States, Greene and Rubin (1971), with one of the earliest part-of-speech tagging programs (TAGGIT), achieved a success rate of 77 per cent correctly tagged words. Their program made use of rule-based templates for disambiguation. In the early 1980s, the UCREL team at Lancaster University reported a success rate in excess of 95 per cent using their program CLAWS, which is based on probabilistic methodologies rather than rule-based templates (see Chapter 5). Similar degrees of success are now being achieved by most research teams working on part-of-speech annotation, and these results are no longer confined solely to probabilistic taggers (cf. Brill 1992).

But part-of-speech annotation should not be thought of as a trivial task. In programming a computer to annotate parts of speech, there are a number of very important a priori considerations.

One problem that the Lancaster team which developed CLAWS had to deal with was the issue of idiomatic sequences of words. In this context, 'idiomatic' does not refer to phrases such as *up the creek without a paddle*, whose senses are idiomatic (in this case, 'in difficulties') but which are easy to analyse in terms of parts of speech: rather, it refers to sequences of words which are difficult to break down into single units of word-plus-part-of-speech. Whilst it is relatively easy to assign part-of-speech tags to a sentence such as:

Lyddy had left the room to polish her boots. (BNC)

it is not so easy to assign them in sentences such as the following:

You brought me here *so that* I'd be safe. (BNC)

The reason for this is that the italicised word sequence *so that* cannot be broken down into two functionally distinct component parts: despite the fact that it is made up of two separate words, it functions as a single unit. The way that the Lancaster team handled this was to define what they called **ditto tags**. Ditto tagging involves assigning the same part-of-speech to each word in an idiomatic sequence such as the one above, together with markers to indicate that they belong to a single phraseological unit. Thus, *so that*, which functions as a subordinating conjunction (CS in the CLAWS tagset), would be tagged:

so_CS21 that_CS22

with both words receiving the tag for subordinating conjunction, followed by (a) a number indicating the number of words in the phraseological unit (in this case 2); and (b) a number indicating the position of word x in that unit. Hence *so* is the first part of a two-part unit (CS21) and *that* is the second part of a two-part unit (CS22).

One of the main design specifications for linguistic annotation schemes, as mentioned above, is recoverability, that is, the possibility for the user to be able to recover the basic original text from any text which has been annotated with further information. This means that the linguistic content of texts themselves should not be manipulated, or if it is, it should be made explicit how this was done so that the original text can be reconstructed. One of the problems for recoverability in the context of part-of-speech annotation is that of contracted forms such as *don't*. Clearly, these are made up of two separate part-of-speech units: a verbal part (*do*) and a negative particle (*not*). Although it is possible to expand out such forms to, for example, *do not*, this makes recoverability impossible. One alternative possibility is to assign two parts of speech to the one orthographic unit, so that *don't* might be tagged:

don't_VD0+XX

This is, however, far from ideal as it is the basic aim of part-of-speech annotation that there should be only one part of speech per unit. What the CLAWS system did, therefore, was to expand out the forms for tagging purposes but also to mark clearly where this had been done using angled brackets to mark the interdependency of the two forms. In this way, each unit could receive a single part-of-speech tag, but it would also be clear where the text had been expanded so that the original contracted form could be recovered, for example:

0000117 040	I		03 PPIS1
0000117 050	do	>	03 VD0
0000117 051	n't	<	03 XX
0000117 060	think		99 VVI

One design consideration in annotation has been that of ease of use. This has come partly to be reflected in the ways that tagsets often strive for mnemonicity, that is the ability to see at a glance from a tag what it means rather than having to look it up in a table. So, for example, a singular proper noun might be tagged NP1 (where the N clearly stands for 'noun', the P stands for 'proper', and the 1 indicates singularity) rather than, say, 221, a number which only makes sense when it is looked up in a tag table. A further usability precept which has become commonplace is divisibility, the idea that each element in each tag should mean something in itself and add to the overall 'sense' of that tag. In the tagsets for the Brown and, subsequently, the LOB corpora, divisibility was only partly present. Whilst distinctions were made between, for example, present participles (VBG) and past participles (VBN), which both belonged to the verb class (VB-), modal verbs had their own tag of MD which had no visible relation with the other verbal tags, which all began with V. In later versions of the CLAWS tagset, the concept of divisibility has been more rigorously applied. In the current tagset (known as C7), all verb tags begin with V. The second element in the tag indicates what class of verb they belong to: lexical (V), modal (M), or one of the irregular verbs *be* (B), *do* (D) or *have* (H). The third element indicates the verb form, for example N (past participle) or G (present participle). Similar hierarchies apply to the other parts of speech such as nouns and adjectives.

As commented earlier, there is a conflict in annotation between retaining fine distinctions for maximal utility to the end user and removing difficult distinctions to make automatic annotation more accurate. Some annotation projects have considerably reduced the number of part-of-speech distinctions which are made in the tagset. Amongst those projects which employ such reduced tagsets is the Penn treebank project at the University of Pennsylvania.

Whereas the CLAWS tagset used at Lancaster distinguishes lexical verbs, modal verbs and the irregular verbs *be, do* and *have*, the Penn tagset uses the same base tag for all verbs – namely VB – and distinguishes only the morphosyntactic forms of the verb. This reduction is made on the perfectly justifiable grounds that these distinctions are lexically recoverable and do not need additional annotation. Whilst, for example, one cannot easily separate out the verbal uses of *boot* from the nominal uses, one can separate out the modal verbs from other verbs, since they form a lexically closed set: the only important thing for annotation is that they are actually identified as verbs rather than nouns. Explicit annotation makes it a bit quicker to extract all the modals, but this particular distinction is not as essential as others.

2.2.3(b) Lemmatisation Closely allied to the identification of parts of speech is the issue of lemmatisation. Lemmatisation involves the reduction of the words in a corpus to their respective lexemes – the head word form that one would look up if one were looking for the word in a dictionary. Thus, for example, the forms *kicks, kicked* and *kicking* would all be reduced to the lexeme KICK. These variants are said to form the **lemma** of the lexeme KICK.[3] Lemmatisation applies equally to morphologically irregular forms, so that *went* as well as *goes, going* and *gone*, belongs to the lemma of GO.

Lemmatisation is an important procedure in corpus-based research. In vocabulary studies and lexicography, for instance, it allows the researcher to extract and examine all the variants of a particular lexeme without having to input all the possible variants, and to produce frequency and distribution information for the lexeme. However, although quite accurate software has been produced for the purpose (e.g. Beale 1987), lemmatisation has not been applied to many of the more widely available corpora. One corpus which does include such information is the SUSANNE corpus, produced by Geoffrey Sampson and his team: here the lemmatised forms of the corpus words are displayed parallel to them in a verticalised format, alongside part-of-speech and syntactic information (see Figure 2.8). Other lemmatised corpora are also now being produced: for example, the trilingual parallel CRATER corpus of English, French and Spanish, which is currently being built at Lancaster University, the Universidad Autónoma de Madrid, and C2V Paris, will be lemmatised for all three languages.

In Figure 2.8, the important columns for our present purpose are the third column (the actual words of the text) and the fourth column (which shows the lemma of each text word). For example we can see that *studied* belongs to the lemma STUDY. The other columns need not detain us here, but they are: column 1 – text reference; column 2 – part of speech; and column 5 – syntactic parse.

2.2.3(c) Parsing Once basic morphosyntactic categories have been identified in a text, it is then possible to consider bringing these categories into higher-level syntactic relationships with one another. The procedure of doing

```
N12:0510g  -  PPHS1m   He        he        [O[S[Nas:s.Nas:s]
N12:0510h  -  VVDv     studied   study     [Vd.Vd]
N12:0510i  -  AT       the       the       [Ns:o.
N12:0510j  -  NN1c     problem   problem   .Ns:o]
N12:0510k  -  IF       for       for       [P:t.
N12:0510m  -  DD221    a         a         [Np[DD2=.
N12:0510n  -  DD222    few       few       .DD2=]
N12:0510p  -  NNT2     seconds   second    .Np]P:t]
N12:0520a  -  CC       and       and       [S+.
N12:0520b  -  VVDv     thought   think     [Vd.Vd]
N12:0520c  -  IO       of        of        [Po:u.
N12:0520d  -  AT1      a         a         [Ns:135.
N12:0520e  -  NNc      means     means     .
N12:0520f  -  IIb      by        by        [Fr[Pb:h.
N12:0520g  -  DDQr     which     which     [Dq:135.Dq:135]Pb:h]
N12:0520h  -  PPH1     it        it        [Ni:S.Ni:S]
N12:0520i  -  VMd      might     may       [Vdcp.
N12:0520j  -  VB0      be        be        .
N12:0520k  -  VVNt     solved    solve     .Vdcp]Fr]Ns:135]Po:u]S+]S]
N12:0520m  -  YF       +.        -         .
```

Figure 2.8 Example of lemmatisation from the SUSANNE corpus

this is generally known as **parsing**. Parsing is probably the most commonly encountered form of corpus annotation after part-of-speech tagging. Corpora which have been parsed are sometimes known as 'treebanks'. This term alludes to the tree diagrams or 'phrase markers' which will be familiar from most introductory syntax textbooks. For example, the structure of the sentence *Claudia sat on a stool* (BNC) might be represented by the following tree diagram:

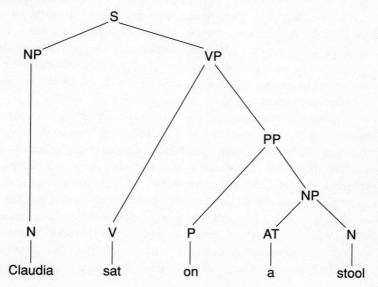

where S = sentence, NP = noun phrase, VP= verb phrase, PP = prepositional phrase, etc. Such visual diagrams are only quite rarely encountered in corpus annotation, but nevertheless the image sticks. More often the identical information is represented using sets of labelled brackets. Thus, for example, the above parsed sentence might appear in a treebank in a form something like this:

[S [NP Claudia_NP1 NP] [VP sat_VVD [PP on_II [NP a_AT1 stool_NN1 NP] PP] VP] S]

The constituents here are indicated by opening and closing square brackets annotated with the phrase type, using the same abbreviations as in the tree diagram; morphosyntactic information is attached to the words by underscore characters in the form of part-of-speech tags. Sometimes such bracket-based annotations are displayed with indentations so as to capture some of the visual properties of a tree diagram: for instance, the example above could be displayed like this:

```
[S

    [NP Claudia NP]
    [VP sat
        [PP on
            [NP a stool NP]
        PP]
    VP]
S]
```

A form of indented layout similar to this is used by the Penn Treebank project.

Different parsing schemes are employed by different annotators. These schemes differ both in the number of constituent types which they employ (as with part-of-speech tagging) and in the way in which constituents are permitted to combine with one another. To give an example of the latter, with sentences such as *Claudia sat on a stool,* some annotators have the prepositional phrase governed by the verb phrase (as shown above) whilst others have it as a sister of the noun phrase and the verb phrase, governed only by the sentence (S) node, as in the diagram opposite.

However, despite differences such as these, the majority of parsing schemes have in common the fact that they are based on a form of context-free phrase structure grammar. Within this broad framework of context-free phrase structure grammars, an important distinction which is made is between **full parsing** and **skeleton parsing**. Full parsing on the one hand aims to provide as detailed as possible an analysis of the sentence structure. Skeleton parsing on the other hand is, as its name suggests, a less detailed approach which tends to use a less finely distinguished set of syntactic constituent types and ignores, for example, the internal structure of certain constituent types. The difference between full and skeleton parsing will be evident from the Figures 2.9 and 2.10.

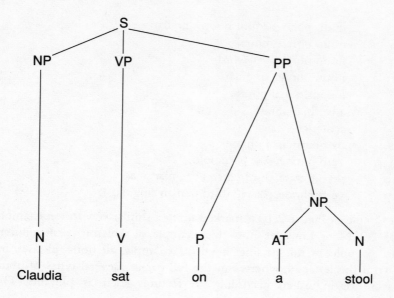

```
[S[Ncs another_DT new_JJ style_NN feature_NN Ncs] [Vzb is_BEZ Vzb]
[Ns the_ATI [NN/JJ& wine-glass_NN [JJ+ or_CC flared_JJ JJ+]NN/JJ&]
heel_NN ,_, [Fr[Nq which_WDT Nq][Vzp was_BEDZ shown_VBN Vzp]
[Tn[Vn teamed_VBN Vn] [R up_RP R][P with_INW
[Np[JJ/JJ/NN& pointed_JJ ,_, [JJ- squared_JJ JJ-] ,_,
[NN+ and_CC chisel_NN NN+]JJ/JJ/NN&] toes_NNS Np]P]Tn]Fr]Ns] ._. S]
```

Figure 2.9 Example of full parsing from the Lancaster-Leeds treebank

```
[S&[P For_IF [N the_AT members_NN2 [P of_IO [N this_DD1
university_NNL1 N]P]N]P][N this_DD1 charter_NN1 N][V enshrines_VVZ [N
a_AT1 victorious_JJ principle_NN1 N]V]S&] ;_; and_CC [S+[N the_AT
fruits_NN2 [P of_IO [N that_DD1 victory_NN1 N]P]N][V can_VM
immediately_RR be_VB0 seen_VVN [P in_II [N the_AT international_JJ
community_NNJ [P of_IO [N scholars_NN2 N]P][Fr that_CST [V has_VHZ
graduated_VVN here_RL today_RT V]Fr]N]P]V]S+] ._.
```

Figure 2.10 Example of skeleton parsing from Spoken English Corpus

In the example in Figure 2.9, the syntactic constituent structure is indicated using nested pairs of labelled square brackets. The words themselves have part-of-speech tags attached to them. The syntactic constituent labels are:

&	whole coordination
+	subordinate conjunct, introduced
-	subordinate conjunct, not introduced
Fr	relative phrase
JJ	adjective phrase

Ncs	noun phrase, count noun singular
Np	noun phrase, plural
Nq	noun phrase, *wh*-word
Ns	noun phrase, singular
P	prepositional phrase
R	adverbial phrase
S	sentence
Tn	past participal phrase
Vn	verb phrase, past participle
Vzb	verb phrase, third person singular *to be*
Vzp	verb phrase, passive third person singular

The example in Figure 2.10 is marked up in a similar way to the example in Figure 2.9. Note, however, how this example of skeleton parsing differs from the example of full parsing: here, for example, all noun phrases are labelled with the letter N, whereas in the full parsing several types of noun phrase were distinguished according to features such as plurality. The constituent labels here are:

Fr	relative clause
N	noun phrase
P	prepositional phrase
S&	1st main conjunct of a compound sentence
S+	2nd main conjunct of a compound sentence
V	verb phrase

But it is by no means always the case that a corpus is parsed using a context-free phrase structure grammar. Some annotators have used other types of grammars such as dependency grammars or functional grammars.[4] The Birmingham Bank of English has been part-of-speech tagged and parsed at the University of Helsinki using a form of dependency grammar known as **constraint grammar** (Karlsson *et al.* 1995). The constraint grammar, rather than identifying hierarchies of constituent phrase types in the way that we have already seen in Figures 2.9 and 2.10, marks instead the grammatical functions of words within a sentence and the interdependencies between them. For example, a code AN> (with a forward pointing arrowhead) indicates a premodifying adjective whilst <NOM-OF (with a backward pointing arrow-head) indicates a postmodifying *of.* Figure 2.11 shows an example of parsing using the Helsinki constraint grammar for English.[5]

In Figure 2.11, the words of the text are enclosed in " < >" symbols and begin at the left-hand margin. On the next line to each text word, indented, are three or sometimes more pieces of information. The first item, contained in double quotes, is the lemma of the word; following that, in most cases, is a part-of-speech code (unlike earlier examples which we have seen, this can include more than one string, e.g. N NOM PL); and at the right-hand end of

Isolated by its relative inaccessibility, Switzerland was able to develop
    without major hindrance, after its founding in 1291, from a tiny
    confederation of 3 cantons to a nation of 23 member states. It has
    maintained its independence and present boundaries intact since 1815.

```
"<*isolated>"
        "isolate" <*> <SVO> <DER:ate> PCP2 @-FMAINV
"<by>"
        "by" PREP @ADVL
"<its>"
        "it" PRON GEN SG3 @GN>
"<relative>"
        "relative" <DER:ive> A ABS @AN>
"<inaccessibility>"
        "inaccessibility" <DER:bility> <-Indef> N NOM SG @<P
"<$,>"
"<*switzerland>"
        "switzerland" <*> <Proper> N NOM SG @SUBJ
"<was>"
        "be" <SV> <SVC/N> <SVC/A> V PAST SG1,3 VFIN @+FMAINV
"<able>"
        "able" A ABS @PCOMPL-S
"<to>"
        "to" INFMARK> @INFMARK>
"<develop>"
        "develop" <SVO> <SV> V INF @<NOM-FMAINV
"<without>"
        "without" PREP @ADVL
"<major>"
        "major" <Title> <Nominal> A ABS @AN>
"<hindrance>"
        "hindrance" N NOM SG @<P
"<$,>"
"<after>"
        "after" PREP @ADVL
"<its>"
        "it" PRON GEN SG3 @GN>
"<founding>"
        "found" <SVO> <P/on> PCP1 @<P
"<in>"
        "in" PREP @<NOM @ADVL
"<1291>"
        "1291" NUM CARD @<P
"<$,>"
"<from>"
        "from" PREP @ADVL
"<a>"
        "a" <Indef> DET CENTRAL ART SG @DN>
"<tiny>"
        "tiny" A ABS @AN>
"<confederation>"
        "confederation" N NOM SG @<P
"<of>"
        "of" PREP @<NOM-OF
"<3>"
        "3" NUM CARD @QN>
"<cantons>"
```

```
        "canton" N NOM PL @<P
"<to>"
        "to" PREP @<NOM @ADVL
"<a>"
        "a" <Indef> DET CENTRAL ART SG @DN>
"<nation>"
        "nation" N NOM SG @<P
"<of>"
        "of" PREP @<NOM-OF
"<23>"
        "23" NUM CARD @QN>
"<member>"
        "member" N NOM SG @NN>
"<states>"
        "state" N NOM PL @<P
"<$.>"
"<*it>"
        "it" <*> <NonMod> PRON NOM SG3 SUBJ @SUBJ
"<has>"
        "have" <SVO> <SVOC/A> V PRES SG3 VFIN @+FAUXV
"<maintained>"
        "maintain" <Vcog> <SVO> <SVOC/A> PCP2 @-FMAINV
"<its>"
        "it" PRON GEN SG3 @GN>
"<independence>"
        "independence" <-Indef> N NOM SG @OBJ @NN>
"<and>"
        "and" CC @CC
"<present>"
        "present" <SVO> <P/in> <P/with> V INF @-FMAINV
        "present" A ABS @AN>
"<boundaries>"
        "boundary" N NOM PL @OBJ
"<intact>"
        "intact" A ABS @PCOMPL-O @<NOM
"<since>"
        "since" PREP @<NOM @ADVL
"<1815>"
        "1815" <1900> NUM CARD @<P
"<$.>"
```

Figure 2.11 Example of parsing using the Helsinki constraint grammar

the line is a tag indicating the grammatical function of the word. Grammatical function tags used in Figure 2.11 above are:

@+FMAINV	finite main predicator
@-FMAINV	non-finite main predicator
@<NOM-OF	postmodifying *of*
@<NOM-FMAINV	postmodifying non-finite verb
@<NOM	other postmodifier
@<P	other complement of preposition
@ADVL	adverbial
@AN>	premodifying adjective

@CC	coordinator
@DN>	determiner
@GN>	premodifying genitive
@INFMARK>	infinitive marker
@NN>	premodifying noun
@OBJ	object
@PCOMPL-O	object complement
@PCOMPL-S	subject complement
@QN>	premodifying quantifier
@SUBJ	subject

Unlike part-of-speech annotation, which is almost always performed automatically by computer (occasionally with human post-editing), parsing is performed by a greater variety of means. This reflects the fact that at the present time, with a very small number of exceptions, automatic parsing software has a lesser success rate than automated part-of-speech tagging. Parsing may be carried out fully automatically (again perhaps with human post-editing); it may be carried out by human analysts aided by specially written parsing software; or it may be carried out completely by hand. The Lancaster-Leeds treebank, a fully parsed subset of the LOB corpus, was parsed manually by Geoffrey Sampson (now at the University of Sussex) and the parses then entered into the computer. By contrast, the Lancaster Parsed Corpus, also a subset of the LOB corpus, was parsed by a fully automated parser, and then substantially corrected by hand. In between these two approaches, it is also common for human analysts to parse corpora with the aid of specially written intelligent editors. At Lancaster University, for example, an editor known as EPICS (Garside 1993a) has been used by analysts to parse several corpora, including a subset of the BNC. Sometimes two approaches to parsing may be combined. At the Catholic University of Nijmegen, a hybrid approach was used to parse the Nijmegen corpus: parts of speech and constituent boundaries were identified by human annotators, and then full parse trees were assigned using an automatic parser. At the present time, human parsing or correction cannot completely be dispensed with. The disadvantage of manual parsing, however, in the absence of extremely strict guidelines, is inconsistency. This is particularly true where more than one person is parsing or editing the corpus, which is often the case on large corpus annotation projects. But even with guidelines, there also frequently occur ambiguities where at the level of detailed syntactic relations more than one interpretation is possible.

2.2.3(d) Semantics Two broad types of semantic annotation may be identified:

1. the marking of semantic relationships between items in the text, for example the agents or patients of particular actions;

2. the marking of semantic features of words in a text, essentially the annotation of word senses in one form or another.

The first type of annotation has scarcely begun to be widely applied to corpora at the time of writing, although forms of parsing which use dependency or functional grammars (see above) capture much of its import.

The second type of semantic annotation, by comparison, has quite a long history. The machine-aided annotation of lexical meanings has previously spent much of its history within the social scientific research methodology of content analysis, a technique which, to simplify greatly, uses frequency counts of groups of related words (e.g. words connected with death) in texts to arrive at conclusions about the prominence of particular concepts. Despite the fact that reasonable quality automatic annotation of this type was being carried out in the late 1960s within the content analysis paradigm, pre-dating much of the research on the arguably easier task of part-of-speech annotation (see e.g. Stone *et al.* 1966), it is only recently that it has become prominent in mainstream corpus linguistics. Few of these older tagged texts have survived, or at least they have not been made more widely available, and, at the time of writing, few semantically analysed corpora exist: to the best of our knowledge, the only publicly available word-sense-tagged *corpus* is a subset of the Brown corpus which is distributed as a component of WORDNET, a piece of software which provides access to a semantic network of English words (Miller *et al.* 1990/93).

As with part-of-speech annotation, there is no universal agreement in semantics about which features of words should be annotated. In the past, owing to the practical orientation of word sense annotation in content analysis, much of the annotation was not in fact motivated by notions of linguistic semantics at all, but by social scientific theories of, for instance, social interaction or political behaviour. An exception to this was the work of Sedelow and Sedelow (e.g. 1969), who made use of *Roget's Thesaurus* – in which words are organised into general semantic categories – for text annotation, but they represent only a small minority. However, there has been a recent resurgence of interest in the semantic analysis of corpora in general, as well as from the standpoint of content analysis. At the University of Amsterdam, for instance, some preliminary work has been carried out on the enrichment of parsed corpora with semantic information. This work has focused on the automatic disambiguation of word senses and the assignment of semantic domains to the words in the text using the 'field codes' from the machine-readable *Longman Dictionary of Contemporary English* (Janssen 1990).

Other projects on semantic text analysis are also underway. For example, a joint project between the Bowling Green State University in Ohio and the Christian-Albrechts-Universität Kiel, directed by Klaus Schmidt, is carrying out the semantic analysis of a body of mediaeval German epic poetry (see also 4.3). One of the present authors is carrying out a similar analysis of a Latin biblical text (Wilson, forthcoming). Figure 2.12 shows an English example based on the latter work and gives an idea of the sorts of semantic categories

And	00000000
the	00000000
soldiers	23241000
platted	21072000
a	00000000
crown	21110400
of	00000000
thorns	13010000
and	00000000
put	21072000
it	00000000
on	00000000
his	00000000
head	21030000
and	00000000
they	00000000
put	21072000
on	00000000
him	00000000
a	00000000
purple	31241100
robe	21110321

Key:

00000000	Low content word
13010000	Plant life in general
21030000	Body and body parts
21072000	Object-oriented physical activity
21110321	Men's clothing: outer clothing
21110400	Headgear
23241000	War and conflict: general
31241100	Colour

Figure 2.12 Example of semantic text analysis, based upon Wilson (forthcoming)

which are often used in this type of work. Such projects frequently store their data in a relational database format, but the illustrative example here is read vertically, with the text words on the left and the semantic categories, represented by 8-digit numbers, on the right. The category system exemplified here, which is based on that used by Schmidt (e.g. 1993), has a hierarchical structure, that is, it is made up of three top-level categories, each of which is sub-divided into further categories, which are themselves further subdivided, and so on. For example, it will be seen that the word "thorns" has a category which begins with a number 1 (indicating the top-level category of "Universe", "purple" has a category which begins with a number 3 (indicating the top-level category of "Man and the World"), and other words have categories beginning with a number 2 (indicating the top-level category of "Man"). The finer levels of sub-division can be exemplified by looking at the word "crown": this belongs in the category 211104, where 2, as already stated, indicated the top-level category of "Man"; the first 1 indicates the first sub-division of that category "Bodily Being"); the second two 1s indicate the eleventh sub-division of *this* category ("General Human Needs"); and the 4 in turn marks the fourth sub-division of "General Human Needs" ("Headgear"). Words with a lower degree of semantic importance (for example pronouns and articles) are placed in a completely separate category of 00000000.

2.2.3(e) Discoursal and text linguistic annotation With the exception of purely structural categories such as paragraphs or overlapping speech, aspects of language at the levels of text and discourse are probably the least frequently encountered annotations in corpora. Nevertheless, such annotations have sometimes been applied.

Stenström (1984b) describes her work on annotating the London-Lund spoken corpus with what she calls *discourse tags*. These tags were used to anno-tate items whose role in the discourse was primarily to do with discourse management rather than with the propositional content. There were sixteen categories in Stenström's system, which were derived empirically from an initial analysis of a subsample of the corpus. These included categories such as 'apologies' (e.g. *sorry, excuse me*), 'hedges' (e.g. *kind of, sort of things*), 'greetings' (e.g. *hello, good evening*), 'politeness' (e.g. *please*), and 'responses' (a category of 'general purpose' responses such as *really, that's right* etc.). Each category was subdivided according to how many lexical items there were in each phrase. However, despite their potential role in helping to quantify the study of discourse, these kinds of annotation have never become widely used in corpus linguistics. It seems likely that this has been the case not because of the manu-ally intensive nature of such annotations (that is also true of prosodic annota-tion) but because linguistic categories such as politeness are necessarily context-dependent and their identification in texts is a greater source of dispute between different linguists than the identification of other linguistic phenomena.

Another form of discourse and text level annotation which has been carried out on corpora is the marking of pronoun reference (**anaphoric annotation**). Halliday and Hasan's (1976) book *Cohesion in English* may perhaps be considered a turning point in text linguistics. Although theirs is not the only, and was not the first, account of cohesion, it has certainly been the most influential. Cohesion – the vehicle by which elements in texts are inter-connected through the use of pronouns, repetition, substitution, and other devices – is a crucial factor in our understanding of the processes involved in reading, producing and comprehending discourse, but in the field of natural language processing it has a particularly important place: given that a large amount of the conceptual content of a text is carried by pronouns, it is impor-tant to be able to determine to what or whom those pronouns are referring.

The full complexity of a pronoun system such as that of English can, however, only be realised and understood by reference to large amounts of empirical data – in other words, corpora. To be of greatest utility in generating

```
A039 1 v
(1 [N Local_JJ atheists_NN2 N] 1) [V want_VV0 (2 [N the_AT (9
Charlotte_NP1 9) Police_NN2 Department_NNJ N] 2) [Ti to_TO get_VV0
rid_VVN of_IO [N (3 <REF=2 its_APP$ chaplain_NN1 3) ,_, [N {{3 the_AT
Rev._NNSB1 Dennis_NP1 Whitaker_NP1 3} ,_, 38_MC N]N]Ti]V] ._.
```

Figure 2.13 Example of anaphoric annotation from Lancaster anaphoric treebank

and testing hypotheses, such corpora need to be already marked up to demonstrate the anaphoric references which are implicit within them. But in fact few such corpora exist. One of these corpora is the Lancaster/IBM anaphoric treebank, developed at Lancaster University in 1989–92 in collaboration with IBM T. J. Watson Research Center, New York. The importance of such anaphorically annotated corpora is certainly realised by the research community, and further corpora of this kind are already being developed, including corpora in languages other than English (e.g. Aone and Bennett 1994).

Anaphoric annotation is a form of annotation which can only be carried out by human analysts, since it is actually one of the aims of the annotation to provide the data on which to train computer programs to carry out this task. (This situation in corpus linguistics, where information has to be put in manually before a computer can be trained to do it automatically, has been called the 'bootstrapping problem'.) To help the Lancaster analysts in this task, Roger Garside developed a special editing program called Xanadu which enabled the analyst to highlight an anaphor and its antecedent and select the reference type from a menu (Garside 1993b). The set of possible reference types was based on Halliday and Hasan's theory, but excluded what they call *collocational cohesion*, that is, the use of words with different senses but within the same semantic domain. The marking of this latter form of cohesion is implicit within word sense annotation, discussed above. Figure 2.13 shows an extract from the anaphoric treebank with the categories of cohesion which are present

The text in Figure 2.13 has been part-of-speech tagged and skeleton parsed using the scheme demonstrated in Figure 2.10. Further annotation has been added to show anaphoric relations. The following are the anaphoric annotation codes used in this example:

(1 1) etc.   noun phrase which enters into a relationship with anaphoric elements in the text

<REF=2   referential anaphor; the number indicates the noun phrase which it refers to – here it refers to noun phrase number 2, *the Charlotte Police Department*)

{{3 3} etc.   noun phrase entering in equivalence relationship with preceding noun phrase; here *the Rev. Dennis Whitaker* is identified as being the same referent as noun phrase number 3, *its chaplain*.

2.2.3(f) Phonetic transcription Corpora of spoken language may, in addition to being transcribed orthographically, also be transcribed using a form of phonetic transcription. For the reasons discussed above under the heading of character sets, such transcription is unlikely to use the standard International Phonetic Alphabet (IPA) characters, but rather will employ methods by which the content of the IPA system may be represented using the basic characters available on the computer or TEI conventions. Not many examples of publicly available fully phonetically transcribed corpora exist at the present time. However, the Lancaster/IBM Spoken English Corpus, which was originally transcribed only orthographically and prosodically, has been manipulated at the Universities of Lancaster and Leeds into the form of a relational database (the MARSEC corpus). This process has involved the extension of the amount of information available within the corpus, and the completed MARSEC corpus will also include a phonetic transcription.

Phonetic transcription is a form of annotation which needs to be carried out by human beings rather than computer programs, and moreover these need to be human beings who are well skilled in the perception and transcription of speech sounds. It follows that the task of phonetic transcription is a very time-consuming one and this helps to explain the paucity of such annotated corpora. Furthermore, the limitations of phonetic transcription are well known. Such transcription assumes that the speech signal may be divided into single, clearly demarcated 'sounds', whilst in fact the 'sounds' often do not have clear boundaries and what phonetic transcription takes to be the same sound may differ considerably according to its context, since the exact positions of the articulators vary because they are moving from and to the necessary positions for articulating the neighbouring 'sounds'. Also, the exact phonetic properties of sounds (such as frequency) vary from individual to individual, a fact which is the basis of forensic phonetics. Nevertheless, phonetically transcribed corpora are a useful addition to the battery of annotated corpora, especially for the linguist who lacks the technological tools and expertise for the laboratory analysis of recorded speech.

2.2.3(g) Prosody Although phonetic transcription has not been employed until very recently on a large scale in corpus annotation, prosodic annotation has a much longer history. The spoken parts of Randolph Quirk's Survey of English Usage, collected in the early 1960s, were prosodically annotated and later computer encoded as the London-Lund corpus. More recently, a major component of the analysis of the Lancaster/IBM Spoken English Corpus was the production of a prosodically annotated version of the corpus.

Prosodic annotation aims to capture in a written form the suprasegmental features of spoken language – primarily stress, intonation and pauses. The annotations in prosodically annotated corpora typically follow widely accepted descriptive frameworks for prosody such as that of O'Connor and Arnold (1961). Rather than attempting to indicate the intonation of every syllable in

```
1 8 14 1470 1 1 A 11   ^what a_bout a cigar\ette# .                    /
1 8 14 1480 1 1 A 20   *((4 sylls))*                                  /
1 8 14 1490 1 1 B 11   *I ^w\on't have one th/anks#* - - -            /
1 8 14 1500 1 1 A 11   ^aren't you •going to sit d/own# -             /
1 8 14 1510 1 1 B 11   ^[/\m]# -                                      /
1 8 14 1520 1 1 A 11   ^have my _coffee in p=eace# - - -              /
1 8 14 1530 1 1 B 11   ^quite a nice •room to !s\it in ((/actually))#/
1 8 14 1540 1 1 B 11   *^\isn't* it#                                  /
1 8 15 1550 1 1 A 11   *^y/\es#* - - -                                /
```

Figure 2.14 Example of prosodic annotation from London-Lund corpus

the corpus, it is more usual for only those which are most prominent to be annotated and the intonation of others left to be inferred from the direction of the intonation on neighbouring prominent syllables. Figure 2.14 shows an example of prosodic annotation from the London-Lund corpus. The codes in Figure 2.14 are:

#	end of tone group
^	onset
/	rising nuclear tone
\	falling nuclear tone
/\	rise-fall nuclear tone
_	level nuclear tone
[ ]	enclose partial words and phonetic symbols
'	normal stress
!	booster: higher pitch than preceding prominent syllable
=	booster: continuance
(())	unclear
★ ★	simultaneous speech
–	pause of one stress unit

The main difficulties of producing prosodically annotated corpora revolve around the impressionistic nature of the judgements which are made, and the specialist ear training required for making those judgements. Prosodic transcription is a task which requires the manual involvement of highly skilled phoneticians: unlike part-of-speech analysis, it is not a task which can be delegated to the computer, and unlike the construction of an orthographically transcribed corpus, it cannot be delegated to clerical staff.

The level of a tone movement or the salience of a pause is a difficult matter to agree upon. Some listeners may perceive only a fall in pitch, whereas others may notice a slight rise at the end of the fall; and there may be a difference in perception as to whether the tone has a high or a low pitch. It is therefore difficult to maintain consistency of judgement throughout a corpus if the corpus is prosodically transcribed by two or more persons, which is

commonly the case given how laborious this task is. What the compilers of the
Spoken English Corpus did to help alleviate this problem, or at least turn the
observation to some academic advantage, was to have a small part of the
corpus (approximately 9 per cent) transcribed by *both* the transcribers. These
so-called 'overlap passages' can then be, and have been, used to study the
differences in transcription practices between two transcribers (in fact these
have turned out to be quite significant).

Prosodic corpora are perhaps the most problematic corpora for the principle of recoverability, since prosodic features are carried by syllables rather
than whole words. This means that annotation has to be introduced within
words themselves, thus making it more difficult for software to retrieve the
raw corpus. It has also tended to be the case up to now that prosodic annotation aims to provide something of a graphic representation of pitch changes
and so on. The London-Lund corpus used punctuation marks for this – for
example / indicated a rising tone – and this compounds the problem of
recoverability, since the extent of the annotation is not clearly demarcated
from the text. The Lancaster/IBM Spoken English Corpus presents a different
problem. With this corpus, rather than using characters from the standard
computer character set, special graphic characters were introduced. But not all
computers and printers can handle these characters, and so the utility of the
corpus is somewhat reduced. It is to be hoped that the TEI guidelines for text
encoding will help to alleviate the difficulties which prosodic annotation
presents. Certainly, an extension of the markup scheme for the International
Corpus of English has suggested a form of TEI conformant markup which eases
the problems of non-standard characters and split words: in this corpus, tone
direction is indicated by an abbreviation within angled brackets immediately
preceding the relevant word, and the accented syllable is simply capitalised
within that word (Johansson *et al.* 1991). Thus a rising tone on the third
syllable of *university* would be represented as:

<% R> uniVERsity

This means that the annotation can use the standard alphabet, and is clearly
marked off as being annotation rather than a part of the text; the fact that the
annotation precedes the word, with the syllable merely capitalised, means that
the raw text can easily be recovered, since this only entails making the retrieval
program insensitive to the difference between upper- and lower-case characters.

2.2.3(h) Problem-oriented tagging The above sections have summarised
the major widely performed types of linguistic corpus annotation. But one
type of annotation remains to be considered. This is what de Haan (1984) has
referred to as *problem-oriented tagging*. Most of the annotation types considered
up to now are intended to be useful for a very broad range of applications, and
attempt to employ widely agreed criteria. For instance, as we shall see in
Chapters 4 and 5, a corpus parsed with a basic context-free phrase structure

grammar may be of use not only in studies of descriptive syntax, but also in the teaching of grammar and in the training of automatic parsers for various purposes. But such types of annotation are not always the most useful for the end user of a corpus who wants to make more specific distinctions between certain features. Occasionally, therefore, users will take a corpus, either unannotated or annotated, and add to it their own form of annotation, oriented particularly towards their research goal. Problem-oriented tagging differs in two fundamental ways from most of the annotations which we have considered in this chapter. First, it is not exhaustive. Rather than annotating the entire contents of the corpus or text (each word, each sentence, etc.), only the phenomena directly relevant to the research are annotated: Meyer and Tenney (1993), for instance, use as an example the annotation of just the cases of apposition within a corpus. This is something which problem-oriented tagging has in common with anaphoric annotation, but not with the ordinary kind of parsed corpus where all phrasal types are parsed, and not just, for example, prepositional phrases. Second, problem-oriented tagging uses an annotation scheme which is selected not for its broad coverage and consensus-based theory-neutrality but for the relevance of the distinctions which it makes to the specific questions which each analyst wishes to ask of his or her data. In view of this dependence on individual research questions, it is not possible to generalise further about this form of corpus annotation, but it is a very important type to keep in mind in the context of practical research using corpora.

3. MULTILINGUAL CORPORA

So far in this chapter, corpora have been considered as if they are entities which contain texts in only one particular language, and indeed for the most part this is a true representation of corpora at the present time. However, not all corpora are monolingual, and an increasing amount of work is being carried out on the building of multilingual corpora, which contain texts in several different languages.

In practice, some multilingual corpora might more truly be described as small collections of individual monolingual corpora in the sense that they use the same or similar sampling procedures and categories for each language but contain completely different texts in those several languages. Thus, for example, the Aarhus corpus of Danish, French and English contract law actually consists of a set of three monolingual contract law corpora, sampled broadly according to the same criteria but not comprised of translations of the same texts. Such corpora may be compared with the International Corpus of English, which also consists of a number of individual subcorpora, sampled according to the same procedures.

Another type of multilingual corpus, which is arguably the more useful type, is the parallel corpus. Parallel corpora are corpora which, rather than simply employing the same sampling procedures, actually hold the same texts in more than one language.[6] The basic notion of a parallel corpus pre-dates computer corpus linguistics by several centuries. From mediaeval times onwards, so-called 'polyglot' bibles were produced which contained the biblical texts side by side in Hebrew, Greek, Latin, and sometimes vernacular versions. In an almost identical way, a machine-readable parallel corpus presents the user with different translations of the same text. However, a corpus which simply contains two or more parallel subcorpora is not immediately user-friendly. For the corpus to be of maximum utility, it is necessary to go further and identify which sentences in these subcorpora are translations of each other, and, below that level, which words are translations of each other. In order to bring the parallel subcorpora into this more specific relationship with one another they need to be *aligned*. An aligned corpus tackles the problem of equivalence by aligning – that is making an explicit link between – those elements which are mutual translations of one another. For example, within a corpus we may see the sentences *Das Buch ist auf dem Tisch* and *The book is on the table* aligned together; below that level, we may also see further alignments of words which are translations of one another: for instance, *das* may be aligned with *the*, *Buch* may be aligned with *book*, *ist* may be aligned with *is*, and *auf* may be aligned with *on*. It should be observed, however, that such alignments are not always simple one-to-one relationships and we may sometimes find, for example, that one word in one language is aligned with more than one word in the other language. In English, for instance, the present continuous is made up using two words (the simple present of *to be* and the *-ing* form of the relevant verb) whereas in German only the simple present of the relevant verb is used; thus in the pair of sentences *Die Frau raucht eine Zigarette* and *The woman is smoking a cigarette*, the single German word *raucht* would be aligned with the two English words *is smoking*. Nevertheless, sentence and word alignment may be achieved with a high degree of accuracy automatically, using such statistical techniques as mutual information (see Chapter 3, section 4.4), and work in several major projects is currently aiming to refine the techniques available for alignment and storage. Figure 2.15 shows an extract from a parallel French–English corpus, aligned at the sentence level.

Typically, at present, parallel corpora tend to be bilingual rather than multi-lingual. However, this situation is beginning to change: for example, work on two major EU-funded projects (CRATER and MULTEXT) is aiming to produce genuinely multilingual parallel corpora. Furthermore, there is a general paucity of *annotated* parallel corpora. A very few do exist, such as the Canadian Hansard (a parallel corpus in French and English of the proceedings of the Canadian Parliament) and a corpus of IBM technical manuals (English and French), but their availability is somewhat limited and they only cover a restricted range of domains and text types. However, multilingual corpus linguistics is very much a growth area at present, and this situation is likely to

```
sub d = 22 ----------&
```

```
the location register should as a minimum contain the following infor-
mation about a mobile station :
-----&
l ' enregistreur de localisation doit contenir au moins les renseigne-
ments suivants sur une station mobile :
sub d = 386 ----------&
handover is the action of switching a call in progress from one cell to
another ( or radio channels in the same cell ) .
-----&
le transfert intercellulaire consiste à commuter une communication en
cours d ' une cellule à une autre cellule ( ou d ' une voie radioélec-
trique à l ' autre à l ' intérieur de la même cellule ) .
sub d = 380 ----------&
the location register , other than the home location register used by
an msc to retrieve information for , for instance , handling of calls
to or from a roaming mobile station , currently located in its area .
-----&
enregistreur de localisation , autre que l ' enregistreur de localisa-
tion nominal , utilisé par un ccm pour la recherche d ' informations en
vue , par exemple , de l ' établissement de communication en provenance
ou à destination d ' une station mobile en déplacement , temporairement
située dans sa zone .
```

Figure 2.15 Example of French–English aligned sentences from the CRATER corpus

change dramatically in the near future with the encouragement and sponsor-ship of bodies such as the Commission of the European Communities. For example, the corpus being produced in the CRATER project will be annotated with part-of-speech information in all three of its languages (English, French and Spanish). Such multilingual corpora have important applications in a number of areas, for example in the development of machine translation systems (see Chapter 5, section 7) and in the teaching of translation skills (see Chapter 4, section 9 and, for a more detailed idea of this application, Zanettin 1994).

4. CHAPTER SUMMARY

In this chapter, we have seen what the term 'corpus' entails within modern linguistics, and what kinds of transcription and annotation one might expect to find within a corpus. We saw first of all that a corpus typically implies a finite body of text, sampled to be maximally representative of a particular variety of a language, and which can be stored and manipulated using a computer. However, we also saw that there can be exceptions to this prototype, notably the open-ended collection of text known as a monitor corpus. A basic distinction was then made between an unannotated corpus and an annotated corpus, which is enriched with various kinds of additional information. We saw how this practice of corpus annotation has evolved from a range of different systems for representing such information to the present-day situation where guidelines and international standards are being sought through consensus by the scholarly community. The various kinds of corpus annotation and encoding – orthographic representation, textual and extra-textual information, part-of-speech tagging, parsing, semantic annotation, anaphoric annotation, phonetic and prosodic transcription, and problem-oriented tagging – were presented in turn, along with the problems and decisions which each entails. Finally, it was shown that corpora need not be monolingual and that the concept of a multilingual parallel corpus is an increasingly important one.

5. STUDY QUESTIONS

1. What are the advantages and disadvantages of standard representations (such as the TEI guidelines) for encoding information in corpora?

2. Look critically at any linguistic annotation scheme or schemes to which you have access. Using Leech's desiderata and your own ideas about what features an annotation scheme should demonstrate, consider carefully the positive and negative features of each scheme for the purpose of corpus annotation and analysis. If possible, try to compare two or more systems.

    (Note: if you do not have easy access to any corpus annotation schemes, and your tutor is not able to provide samples, you will find some part-of-speech tagsets in the appendices to Garside *et al.* 1987.)

3. Ready-annotated corpora are now widely available. How far does the use of such corpora constrain the end user and to what extent is such constraint a serious problem? Are there any aspects of language for which you consider pre-encoded annotation to be unsuitable? Explain your answer.

6. FURTHER READING

Leech (1993) discusses the formal desiderata of corpus annotation in somewhat more detail than in this chapter. Various syntactic parsing schemes are discussed by Sampson (1991) and Souter (1993). The most recent TEI text annotation guidelines (P3) can be found in Sperberg-McQueen and Burnard (1994). These replace the earlier P2 guidelines on which the examples in this chapter are based.

NOTES

1. Here and elsewhere, (BNC) = example taken from British National Corpus.
2. However, 'intelligent' text retrieval programs can replace the TEI markup with the original graphic character.
3. Sometimes the lexeme itself is also referred to as the lemma.
4. For the latter, see e.g. Souter (1990).
5. Constraint grammars also exist for other languages.
6. Note, however, that some corpus linguists employ a different terminology for multilingual corpora: they refer to what we have termed 'parallel corpora' as *translation corpora* and use the term 'parallel corpus' instead to refer to the other kind of multilingual corpus which does not contain the same texts in different languages.

Quantitative data

1. INTRODUCTION

The notion of a form of linguistics based firmly upon empirical data is present throughout this book. But, as the warnings of scholars such as Chomsky (which we reviewed in Chapter 1) suggest, empirical data can sometimes be deceptive if not used with appropriate caution. Chomsky's argument against corpora was based upon the observation that when one derives a sample of a language variety it will be skewed: chance will operate so that rare constructions may occur more frequently than in the variety as a whole, and some common constructions may occur less frequently than in the variety as a whole. It was suggested briefly in Chapter 2 that, whilst these criticisms are serious and valid ones, the effects which they describe can at least partially be countered through better methods of achieving representativeness. This is one of the themes of this chapter. But there is also another issue implicit in Chomsky's criticism, and that is the issue of frequency. Chomsky's concentration on rarity and commonness appears to assume that corpus linguistics is a quantitative approach. This is at least partly true: a corpus, considered to be a maximally representative finite sample, enables results to be quantified and compared to other results in the same way as any other scientific investigation which is based on a data sample. The corpus thus stands in contrast to other empirical data sets which have not been sampled to be maximally representative and from which broader conclusions cannot therefore be extrapolated. But it is not essential that corpus data be used solely for quantitative research, and in fact many researchers have used it as a source of qualitative data. Before moving on to consider the various quantitative issues which arise in corpus linguistics, therefore, we shall look in the next section at the relationship between quantitative and qualitative approaches to corpus analysis.

2. QUALITATIVE VS. QUANTITATIVE ANALYSIS

The difference between qualitative and quantitative corpus analysis, as the terms themselves imply, is that in qualitative research no attempt is made to assign frequencies to the linguistic features which are identified in the data. Whereas in quantitative research we classify features, count them, and even construct more complex statistical models in an attempt to explain what is observed, in qualitative research the data are used only as a basis for identifying and describing aspects of usage in the language and to provide 'real-life' examples of particular phenomena.

As Schmied (1993) has observed, a stage of qualitative research is often a precursor for quantitative analysis, since, before linguistic phenomena are classified and counted, the categories for classification must first be identified.[1] But it is more useful to consider these two as forming two different, but not necessarily incompatible, perspectives on corpus data.

Qualitative forms of analysis offer a rich and detailed perspective on the data. In qualitative analyses, rare phenomena receive, or at least ought to receive, the same attention as more frequent phenomena, and, because the aim is complete detailed description rather than quantification, delicate variation in the data is foregrounded: qualitative analysis enables very fine distinctions to be drawn since it is not necessary to shoehorn the data into a finite number of classifications. The fact that qualitative analysis is not primarily classificatory also means that the ambiguity which is inherent in human language – not only by accident but also through the deliberate intent of language users – can be fully recognised in the analysis: qualitative research does not force a potentially misleading intepretation. For instance, in a quantitative stylistic analysis it might be necessary to classify the word *red* as either simply a colour or as a political categorisation (signifying socialism or communism): in a qualitative analysis both the senses of *red* in a phrase such as *the red flag* could be recognised – the physical property of the flag's colour and its political significance. However, the main disadvantage of qualitative approaches to corpus analysis is that their findings cannot be extended to wider populations with the same degree of certainty with which quantitative analyses can, because, although the corpus may be statistically representative, the specific findings of the research cannot be tested to discover whether they are statistically significant or more likely to be due to chance.

In contrast to qualitative analysis, the quantititative analysis of a sampled corpus does allow for its findings to be generalised to a larger population, and, furthermore, it means that direct comparisons may be made between different corpora, at least so long as valid sampling and significance techniques have been employed. Quantitative analysis thus enables one to separate the wheat from the chaff: it enables one to discover which phenomena are likely to be genuine reflections of the behaviour of a language or variety and which are merely chance occurrences. In the more basic task of looking non-comparatively at a single language variety, quantitative analysis enables one to get a precise picture of the frequency and rarity of particular phenomena and hence, arguably, of their relative normality or abnormality. However, the picture of the data which emerges from quantitative analysis is necessarily less rich than that obtained from qualitative analysis. Quantification, as suggested above, entails classification. For statistical purposes, these classifications have to be of the hard-and-fast (so-called 'Aristotelian') type, that is an item either belongs in class *x* or it doesn't: to take our example of *red* again we would have to decide firmly whether to put the word in the category 'colour' or the category 'politics'. In practice, however, many linguistic items and phenomena do not fit this Aristotelian model: rather, they are consistent with the more recent notions of 'fuzzy sets', where some phenomena may clearly belong in class *x* but others have a more dubious status and may belong in potentially more than one class, as was the case above with the word *red* above. Quantitative analysis may therefore entail in some circumstances a certain idealisation of the data: it forces the analyst to make a decision which is perhaps not a 100 per cent accurate reflection of the reality contained in the data. At the same time, quantitative analysis also tends to sideline rare occurrences. To ensure that certain statistical significance tests (such as the chi-squared test which we shall meet later in Section 4.3 of this chapter) provide reliable results, it is essential that specific minimum frequencies are obtained and this can mean that fine distinctions have to be deliberately blurred to ensure that statistical significances can be computed, with a resulting loss of data richness.

It will be appreciated from this brief discussion that both qualitative and quantitative analyses have something to contribute to corpus study. Qualitative analysis can provide greater richness and precision whereas quantitative analysis can provide statistically reliable and generalisable results. There has recently been a move in social science research towards multi-method approaches which largely reject the narrow analytical paradigms in favour of the breadth of information which the use of more than one method may provide. Corpus linguistics could, as Schmied (1993) demonstrates, benefit as much as any field from such multi-method research, combining both qualitative and quantitative perspectives on the same phenomena.

3. CORPUS REPRESENTATIVENESS

Although quantitative analyses may be carried out on any sample of text, these can be misleading if one wants to generalise the findings on that sample to some larger population, for example a genre as a whole. This, as we have already seen in Chapter 1, was essentially the foundation of Chomsky's criticism of early corpus linguistics. Chomsky took the view that because a corpus *did* constitute only a small sample of a large and potentially infinite population – namely the set of possible sentences of a language – it would be skewed and hence unrepresentative of the population as a whole. This is a valid criticism –

it is true with any kind of sample that rare elements *may* occur in higher proportions and frequent elements in lesser proportions than in the population as a whole – and this criticism applies not only to linguistic corpora but to any form of scientific investigation which is based on sampling rather than on the exhaustive analysis of an entire and finite population: in other words, it applies to a very large proportion of the scientific and social scientific research which is carried out today. However, the effects of Chomsky's criticism are not quite so drastic as it appears at first glance, since there are many safeguards which may be applied in sampling for maximal representativeness.

The reader will recall from Chapter 1 that at the time when Chomsky first made his criticism in the 1950s, most corpora were very small entities. This was due as much to necessity as to choice: the development of text analysis by computer had still to progress considerably and thus corpora had still largely to be analysed by hand. Hence these corpora had to be of a manageable size for manual analysis. Although size – short of including the whole target population – is not a guarantee of representativeness, it does enter significantly into the factors and calculations which need to be considered in producing a maximally representative corpus. Small corpora tend only to be representative for certain high frequency linguistic features, and thus Chomsky's criticism was at least partly true of these early corpora. But since today we have powerful computers which can readily store, search and manipulate many millions of words, the issue of size is no longer such a problem and we can attempt to make much more representative corpora than Chomsky could dream of when he first criticised corpus-based linguistics.

In discussing the ways of achieving the maximal degree representativeness, it should first be emphasised once again that in producing a corpus we are dealing with a **sample** of a much larger **population**. Random sampling techniques in themselves are standard to many areas of science and social science, and these same techniques are also used in corpus building. But there are particular additional caveats which the corpus builder must be aware of.

Biber (1993b), in a detailed survey of this issue, emphasises as the first step in corpus sampling the need to define as clearly as possible the limits of the population which we are aiming to study before we can proceed to define sampling procedures for it. This means that we should not start off by saying vaguely that we are interested in, for instance, the written German of 1993, but that we must actually rigorously define what the boundaries of 'the written German of 1993' are for our present purpose, that is, what our **sampling frame** – the entire population of texts from which we will take our samples – is. Two approaches have been taken to this question in the building of corpora of written language. The first approach is to use a comprehensive bibliographical index. So, for 'the written German of 1993', we might define our sampling frame as being the entire contents of an index of published works in German for that year, for example the *Deutsche National-Bibliographie*.

This is the approach which was taken by the Lancaster-Oslo/Bergen corpus, using the *British National Bibliography* and *Willings' Press Guide* as the indices. The second possible approach is to define the sampling frame as being the holdings of a given library which belong to the variety and period in which we are interested. So, for our example, we might define the sampling frame as being all the German-language books and periodicals in Lancaster University Library which were published in 1993. This latter approach is the one which was taken in building the Brown corpus and also the Guangzhou Petroleum English Corpus.

These approaches are all well and good with published works such as books or newspapers, but it is not possible to use them with informal language such as conversations or private correspondence, since such kinds of language are not formally indexed or stored in a library. In these cases, therefore, instead of basing the sampling frame on an index it is usual to employ demographic sampling of the kind which will be familiar from its use in public opinion research, that is, selecting informants on the basis of their age, sex, region, social class, and so on. This is a method which was used in collecting the spoken parts of the British National Corpus: informants were selected on the basis of demographic sampling and were then given personal-stereo cassette recorders on which they recorded their everyday spoken interactions for a period of two to seven days (Crowdy 1993). However, as Crowdy notes, this kind of demographic sampling can miss out on many important language types and hence it is often necessary to supplement the demographic sampling with a more context governed approach. Again, this is what was done in the BNC project. It was recognised that such important spoken activities as broadcast interviews and legal proceedings would probably not enter into the interactions recorded by the informants and so a selection of contextually determined linguistic activity types such as these were defined and sampled in addition to the demographically sampled corpus; the former make up approximately half of the entire spoken corpus.

In addition to defining the population itself, Biber (1993b) also emphasises the advantage of determining beforehand the hierarchical structure (or **strata**) of the population, that is, defining what different genres, channels, and so on, it is made up of. So, going back to our example of written German, we could say it is made up of genres such as newspaper reporting, romantic fiction, legal statutes, scientific writing, and so on. Biber observes that stratificational sampling is never less representative than pure probabilistic sampling, and is often more so, since it enables each individual stratum to be subjected to a full probabilistic sampling. But, to state the opposite case, it has to be said that these strata, like corpus annotation, are an act of interpretation on the part of the corpus builder because they are founded on particular ways of dividing up language into entities such as genres which it may be argued are not naturally inherent within it: different linguists may specify different genre groupings according to their theoretical perspectives on linguistic variation.

Having defined the population, one needs to determine which sample sizes are most representative of it, both in terms of the optimal *length* of each sample text and the optimal *number* of texts which should be included in the corpus. Both these figures are ultimately dependent on the distribution of linguistic features within the population, that is, what is the probability that y text samples of length n will contain proportionately the same number and distribution of examples of particular items as the total population? In a pilot study, Biber found that frequent items are stable in their distributions, and hence small samples are adequate for these. Rarer features on the other hand show more variation in their distributions and consequently require larger samples if they are to be fully represented in the corpus, as de Haan (1992) has also observed. In terms of such rarer features, therefore, we can perhaps admit that Chomsky's criticism of the small corpora of the 1950s was a valid one.

Biber notes that the standard statistical equations which are used to determine these optimal sample lengths and sample numbers are problematic for corpus building (1993b). This is because they require two statistical values which cannot be computed for a corpus as a whole: **standard deviations** which must be calculated for each individual feature, and **tolerable error** which will vary according to the overall frequency of a feature. These values are therefore problematic, since a corpus, unless collected for one specific purpose, is normally intended for use in research on many different features of language. Biber's suggestion in this situation is that the most conservative way of ensuring representative samples is to base the computations on the most widely varying feature. With regard to sample lengths, taking samples of sizes which are representative of that feature should mean that the samples are also representative of those features which show less variation in distribution. Similarly with the number of texts within each genre, the degree of variation on that feature which occurs within given genres is used to scale the number of texts required to represent each genre.

It will be appreciated, then, that corpus sampling is by no means a straightforward exercise. However, the constant application of strict statistical procedures should ensure that the corpus is as representative as possible of the larger population, within the limits imposed by practicality.

4. APPROACHING QUANTITATIVE DATA

In the preceding sections, we have seen the value of supplementing qualitative analyses of language with quantitative data. We have also seen why corpora in particular are of value for quantitative linguistic analysis. But it should be noted that the use of quantification in corpus linguistics typically goes well beyond simple counting: many sophisticated statistical techniques are used which can both provide a mathematically rigorous analysis of often complex data – one might almost say, colloquially, to bring order out of chaos – and be used to show with some degree of certainty that differences between texts, genres, languages, and so on, are real ones and not simply a fluke of the sampling procedure.

In this section we introduce briefly some of the quantitative methods which are of most value in working practically with corpora. But before we move on we must raise two notes of caution. First, this section is of necessity incomplete. There are very many statistical techniques which have been, or can potentially be, applied to corpora and space precludes coverage of all of them. Instead we have chosen to concentrate on those which we consider to be the most important and most widely used. Second, we do not aim here to provide a complete step-by-step 'how to do it' guide to statistics. Many of the statistical techniques used in corpus linguistics are very complex, and most require the use of computer software for them to be made manageable. To explain the mathematics fully we would need something approaching a full chapter for each technique. What we have done instead is to try to outline with as little mathematics as possible what each technique does and why it is of practical value to the corpus linguist. Other books in the Edinburgh Textbooks in Empirical Linguistics series – notably *Language and Computers* and *Statistics for Corpus Linguistics* – pick up again on these methods and present them in much more detail than we have space to do here. Our recommendation is that the student reads what we have to say here as a brief introduction to how the techniques may be used and then progresses to the more detailed treatments in the other texts for further explanation.

4.1. Frequency counts

The most straightforward approach to working with quantitative data is simply to classify items according to a particular scheme and to perform an arithmetical count of the number of items (or *tokens*) within the text which belong to each classification (or *type*) within the scheme. So, for instance, we might set up a classification scheme to look at the frequency of four major parts of speech – noun, verb, adjective and adverb. These four classes would constitute our types. Every time we met a word in the corpus which belonged to one of these categories – a token of one of the types – we would simply add 1 to the count for corresponding category type. Sometimes the classification scheme used in frequency counts may be a simple one-to-one mapping of form onto classification. This can be the case with word frequency analysis, where each graphical word form is equivalent to one type within the classification scheme. More often, however, the use of a classification scheme implies a deliberate act of categorisation on the part of the investigator. This is even sometimes the case with word frequency analysis, in that variant forms of the same lexeme may be lemmatised before a frequency count is made: for instance, *loved*, *loving* and *loves* might all be considered to be instances of the lexeme LOVE. Very often the classification scheme will correspond to the types of linguistic annotation which have already been introduced into the corpus at some earlier stage (see Chapter 2). An example of this might be an analysis of the incidence of different parts of speech in a corpus, where the parts of speech have been previously classified by automated or manual part-of-speech tagging.

4.2. Working with proportions

Simple frequency counts are a useful approach to quantifying linguistic data, and they have often been used in corpus-based research. However, they have certain disadvantages. The main disadvantage arises when one wishes to compare one data set with another – for example a corpus of spoken language with a corpus of written language. Arithmetical frequency counts simply count occurrences: they do *not* indicate the prevalence of a type in terms of a proportion of the total number of tokens within the text. This can be problematic when the two or more texts or corpora which are being compared are different in size. Where a disparity in size occurs, a simple frequency count of a type in one text, although it is larger than the count for the same type in another text, may actually indicate a smaller *proportion* of the type in that text than the smaller count indicates for the other text. For instance, assume that we have a corpus of spoken English with a size of 50,000 words and a corpus of written English with a size of 500,000 words. We may find that in the corpus of spoken English, the word *boot* occurs 50 times whereas in the corpus of written English it occurs 500 times. So it looks at first glance as if *boot* is more frequent in written than in spoken English. But let us now look at these data in a different way. This time we shall go one step further beyond the simple arithmetical frequency and calculate the frequency of occurrence of the type *boot* as a percentage of the total number of tokens in the corpus, that is, the total size of the corpus. So we do the following calculations:

spoken English: 50 / 50,000   x 100 = 0.1%
written English: 500 / 500,000 x 100 = 0.1%

Looking at these figures, we see that, far from being 10 times more frequent in written English than in spoken English, *boot* has the same frequency of occurrence in both varieties: it makes up 0.1 per cent of the total number of tokens in each sample. It should be noted, therefore, that if the sample sizes on which a count is based are different, then simple arithmetical frequency counts cannot be compared directly with one another: it is necessary in those cases to normalise the data using some indicator of proportion. Even where disparity of size is not an issue, proportional statistics are a better approach to presenting frequencies, since most people find it easier to understand and compare figures such as percentages than fractions of unusual numbers such as 53,000.

There are several ways of indicating proportion, but they all boil down to a ratio between the size of the sample and the number of occurrences of the type under investigation. The most basic involves simply calculating the ratio:

ratio = number of occurrences of the type / number of tokens in entire sample

The result of this calculation may be expressed as a fraction, or, more commonly, as a decimal. Usually, however, when working with large samples such as corpora and potentially many classifications, this calculation gives unwieldy looking small numbers. For example, the calculation we performed above would give a simple ratio of 0.0001. Normally, therefore, the ratio is scaled up to a larger, more manageable number by multiplying the result of the above equation by a constant. This is what we did with the example: in that case the constant was 100 and the result was therefore a percentage. Percentages are perhaps the most common way of representing proportions in empirical linguistics but, with a large number of classifications, or with a set of classifications in which the first few make up something like half the entire sample, the numbers can still look awkward, with few being greater than 1. It may sometimes be sensible, therefore, to multiply the ratio formula by a larger constant, for example 1,000 (giving a proportion *per mille* (‰)) or 1,000,000 (giving a proportion in parts per million (p.p.m.)). It is not crucial which option is selected: what is important is to indicate clearly which has been used.

4.3. Tests of significance

Let us suppose now that we are interested in examining the Latin versions of the Gospel of Matthew and the Gospel of John. We are interested in looking at how third person singular speech is represented and specifically in comparing how often the present tense form of the verb 'to say' is used (i.e. *dicit*) and how often the perfect form of the verb used (i.e. *dixit*). So we decide to make a simple count of each of these two verb forms in each of the two texts. Having done this, we arrive at the following frequencies:

	dicit	*dixit*
Matthew	46	107
John	118	119

From these figures, it looks as if John uses the present tense form (*dicit*) proportionally more often than Matthew does. But with what degree of certainty can we infer that this is a genuine finding about the two texts rather than a result of chance? From these figures alone we cannot decide: we need to perform a further calculation – a test of **statistical significance** – to determine how high or low the probability is that the difference between the two texts on these features is due to chance.

There are several significance tests available to the corpus linguist – the chi-squared test, the [Student's] t-test, Wilcoxon's rank sum test, and so on – and we will not try to cover each one here. As an example of the role of such tests we will concentrate on just one test – **the chi-squared test**. The chi-squared test is probably the most commonly used significance test in corpus linguistics and also has the advantages that (a) it is more sensitive than, for example, the t-test; (b) it does not assume that the data are 'normally distributed' – this is often not true of linguistic data; and (c) in 2 x 2 tables such as the one above – a common calculation in linguistics – it is very easy to calculate, even without a computer statistics package (see Swinscow 1983). The main disadvantage of chi-square is that it is unreliable with very small frequencies. It should also be noted that proportional data (percentages etc.) *cannot* be used with the chi-squared test: disparities in corpus size are unimportant, since the chi-squared test itself compares the figures in the table proportionally.

Very simply, the chi-squared test compares the difference between the actual frequencies which have been observed in the corpus (the *observed* frequencies) and those which one would expect if no factor other than chance had been operating to affect the frequencies (the *expected* frequencies). The closer the expected frequencies are to the observed frequencies, the more likely it is that the observed frequencies are a result of chance. On the other hand, the greater the difference between the observed frequencies and the expected frequencies, the more likely it is that the observed frequencies are being influenced by something other than chance, for instance a true difference in the grammars of two language varieties.

Let us for the present purpose omit the technicality of calculating the chi-square value and assume that it has already been calculated for our data. Having done this, it is then necessary (if not using a computer program which gives the information automatically) to look in a set of statistical tables to see how significant our chi-square value is. To do this one first requires one further value – the number of **degrees of freedom** (usually written **d.f.**). This is very simple to work out. It is simply:

(number of columns in the frequency table – 1) x (number of rows in the frequency table – 1)

We now look in the table of chi-square values in the row for the relevant number of degrees of freedom until we find the nearest chi-square value to the one which has been calculated, then we read off the probability value for that column. A probability value close to 0 means that the difference is very strongly significant, that is, it is very unlikely to be due to chance; a value close to 1 means that it is almost certainly due to chance. Although the interval between 1 and 0 is a continuum, in practice it is normal to assign a cut-off point which is taken to be the difference between a 'significant' result and an 'insignificant' result. In linguistics (and most other fields) this is normally taken to be a probability value of 0.05: probability values of less than 0.05 (written as *p < 0.05*) are assumed to be significant, whereas those greater than 0.05 are not.

Let us then return to our example and find out whether the difference which we found is statistically significant. If we calculate the chi-square value for this table we find that it is 14.843. We have two columns and two rows in the original frequency table, so the number of degrees of freedom in this case is $(2 - 1) \times (2 - 1) = 1$ d.f. For 1 d.f. we find that the probability value for this chi-square value is 0.0001. Thus the difference which we found between Matthew and John is significant at $p < 0.05$, and we can therefore say with quite a high degree of certainty that this difference is a true reflection of variation in the two texts and is not due to chance.

4.4. Significant collocations

The idea of **collocations** – the characteristic co-occurrence patterns of words – is an important one in many areas of linguistics. Kjellmer (1991), for instance, has argued that our mental lexicon is made up not only of single words but also of larger phraseological units, both fixed and more variable. The identification of patterns of word co-occurrence in textual data is particularly important in dictionary writing, since, in addition to identifying Kjellmer's phraseological units, the company which individual words keep often helps to define their senses and use (cf. the basis of probabilistic tagging, which is discussed in Chapter 5, section 3). This information is in turn important both for natural language processing and for language teaching. But in connected discourse every single word occurs in the company of other words. How, therefore, is it possible to identify which co-occurrences are *significant* collocations, especially if one is not a native speaker of a language or language variety so that introspection is not an available option?

Given a text corpus, it is possible to determine empirically which pairs of words have a statistically significant amount of 'glue' between them, and which are hence likely to constitute significant collocations in that variety rather than chance pairings. The two formulae which are most commonly used to calculate this relationship are **mutual information** and the **Z-score**.

Mutual information is a formula borrowed from the area of theoretical computer science known as information theory. The mutual information score between any given pair of words – or indeed any pair of other items such as, for example, part-of-speech categories – compares the probability that the two items occur together as a joint event (i.e. because they belong together) with the probability that they occur individually and that their co-occurrences are simply a result of chance. For example, the words *riding* and *boots* may occur as a joint event by reason of their belonging to the same multiword unit (*riding boots*) whereas the words *formula* and *borrowed* in the sentence above simply occur together in a relatively one-off juxtaposition: they do not have any special relationship to each other. The more strongly connected two items are, the higher will be the mutual information score. On the other hand, if the two items have a very low level of co-occurrence, that is, they occur more often in isolation than together, then the mutual information score will be a negative number. And if the co-occurrence of item 1 and item 2 is largely due to chance, then the mutual information score will be close to zero. In other words, pairs of items with high positive mutual information scores are are more likely to constitute characteristic collocations than pairs with much lower mutual information scores.[2]

The Z-score provides similar data to mutual information. For any given word (or other item) in a text, this test compares the actual frequency of all other words occurring within a specified size of context window (for example three words either side of the item) with their expected frequency of occurrence within that window if only chance were affecting the distribution. The higher the Z-score is for a given word or item in connection with the *node word* (i.e. the word whose associations we are looking at), the greater is its degree of collocability with that word. The Z-score is on the whole used rather less frequently than mutual information in corpus linguistics, but it is important to mention it since the TACT concordance package – one of the very few widely available packages which include a collocation significance function – does in fact use the Z-score rather than mutual information.

As suggested above, techniques such as mutual information and the Z-score are of particular use in lexicography. One of their uses is to extract what are known as **multiword units** from corpora, which include not only traditional idiomatic word groups such as *cock and bull* but also, for example, multiword noun phrases such as *temporal mandibular joint*. The extraction of this latter kind of terminology is useful not only in traditional lexicography but also particularly in specialist technical translation where a detailed knowledge of the terminology of a field, both at the level of individual words and at the level of multiword units, is an important step towards establishing an exhaustive database of translation equivalents.

A second use of mutual information and the Z-score is as aids to sense discrimination in corpus data. In this case, instead of trying to extract specific multiword units we are interested in the more general patterns of collocation for particular words. If we take the most significant collocates for a word, it is possible either (a) to group similar collocates together to help in semi-automatically identifying different senses of the word (for example, *bank* might collocate with geographical words such as *river* (indicating the landscape sense of *bank*) and with financial words such as *investment* (indicating the financial type of *bank*)); or (b) to compare the significant collocates of one word with those of another with the aim of discriminating differences in usage between two rather similar words. As an example of the latter we may consider one of the experiments carried out by Church *et al.* (1991), in which they looked at the different collocations of *strong* and *powerful* in a 44.3-million-word corpus of press reports. Although these words may be seen to have very similar meanings, the mutual information scores for their associations with other words in the corpus in fact revealed interesting differences. *Strong*, for example, collocated particularly with words such as *northerly, showings, believer, currents, supporter* and *odor*, whereas *powerful* had significant collocations with words such as *tool, minority, neighbor, symbol, figure, weapon* and *post*. Although these collocates do not form very generalisable semantic groups, such information about the delicate differences in collocation between the two words has a potentially important role, for example in helping students of English as a foreign language to refine their vocabulary usage.

One further application of mutual information should also be noted. Mutual information can be used not only to study associations within a corpus but also to help define associations between two parallel aligned corpora. Assuming that a bilingual parallel corpus has been aligned at the level of the sentence, so that for any given sentence in one language we know which sentence is its translation in the other language, we may then want to know which *words* in those sentences are translations of each other. If we were to take the two sentences, we could make a list of all the possible pairs of words which could be translations of each other. So with the two sentences

> Die Studentin bestand ihre Prüfung.
> The student passed her exam.

die could potentially be translated as *the, student, passed, her* or *exam*; and similarly *Studentin* could potentially be translated as *the, student, passed, her* or *exam*. Throughout the corpus, some words will be paired together more often than other words, but patterns of frequency distribution may result in a word's being paired less frequently with its correct translation than with some other word. However, if mutual information is used instead of pure frequencies to guide this process of pairing, then it is possible to discover which word pairs are the most statistically significant rather than simply the most frequent and hence to approximate more closely to the correct pairing of translation equivalents.

4.5. Examining relations between many variables

The kinds of statistical significance tests which we have already seen in this chapter are useful tools in that they can provide additional support for quantitative results by showing how high or low the probability is that any differences which are observed are due to chance. However, although they can pick up significant differences between particular **samples** (i.e. texts and corpora) on particular **variables** (i.e. linguistic features), they cannot provide a picture of the complex interrelationships of similarity and difference between a large number of samples and large number of variables. For example, it would not be possible using tests such as the chi-squared test to examine the vocabulary relations between five different genres, except on a word-by-word basis. To perform such holistic comparisons for large numbers of variables we need a different type of statistical technique – a **multivariat**e one.

	A	B	C	D	E	F	G	H	J	K	L	M	N	P	R
can	210	148	59	89	211	178	264	106	424	202	55	9	47	67	55
could	120	49	36	23	84	117	186	39	164	340	134	6	81	108	54
may	100	86	15	46	93	112	130	204	249	48	21	3	6	8	14
might	24	29	13	4	10	41	29	10	52	52	22	0	7	9	9
must	43	34	12	28	42	59	126	58	114	110	59	4	20	33	19
ought	3	4	0	1	4	5	12	2	5	4	2	0	0	1	0
shall	12	4	0	10	9	7	28	162	42	38	17	17	13	8	3
should	117	131	33	27	150	114	144	203	183	95	44	0	27	33	13
will	227	218	37	43	164	154	156	315	206	280	153	21	55	90	49
would	199	104	36	46	135	176	306	123	186	510	205	9	90	164	65

Table 3.1 A cross-tabulation of modal verbs across genres

The general heading of 'multivariate statistics' covers a number of different techniques. The most commonly encountered in linguistic research are: factor analysis; principal components analysis, often incorrectly referred to as 'factor analysis';[3] correspondence analysis; multidimensional scaling; and cluster analysis. Despite important mathematical distinctions, the basic aim of all these techniques is very similar, namely to summarise a large set of variables· in terms of a smaller set on the basis of statistical similarities between the original variables, whilst at the same time losing the minimal amount of information about their differences.

No attempt will be made here to explain the complex mathematics behind these techniques.[4] However, it is important to grasp roughly the stages by which the techniques work. All the techniques start off with a traditional basic **cross-tabulation** of the variables and samples. Table 3.1 shows an example of a hypothetical cross-tabulation of the frequencies of different modal verbs (the *variables*) across fifteen different genres (the *samples*) within 'the Kolhapur corpus of Indian English.

For **factor analysis**, an **intercorrelation matrix** is then calculated from the cross-tabulation, showing how statistically similar all pairs of variables in the table are in their distributions across the various samples. Table 3.2 shows the first seven columns of the intercorrelation matrix calculated from the data in Table 3.1. Here we see that the similarity of variables with themselves (e.g. *can* and *can*) is 1: they are, as we would expect, identical. But we can also see that some variables show a greater similarity in their distributions than others: for instance, *can* shows a greater similarity to *may* (0.798) than it does to *shall*. (0.118).

Factor analysis takes intercorrelation matrices such as that shown in Table 3.2 and attempts to 'summarise' the similarities between the variables in terms of a smaller number of reference factors which the technique extracts. The hypothesis is that the many variables which appear in the original frequency cross-tabulation are in fact masking a smaller number of variables (the *factors*) which can help explain better why the observed frequency differences occur.

	can	could	may	might	must	ought	shall
	PEARSON PRODUCT MOMENT CORRELATION COEFFICIENT						
can	1	0.544	0.798	0.765	0.796	0.717	0.118
could	0.544	1	0.186	0.782	0.807	0.528	0.026
may	0.798	0.186	1	0.521	0.637	0.554	0.601
might	0.765	0.782	0.521	1	0.795	0.587	0.032
must	0.796	0.807	0.637	0.795	1	0.816	0.306
ought	0.717	0.528	0.554	0.587	0.816	1	0.078
shall	0.118	0.026	0.601	0.032	0.306	0.078	1
should	0.761	0.290	0.918	0.531	0.644	0.638	0.582
will	0.557	0.521	0.683	0.609	0.628	0.454	0.621
would	0.501	0.974	0.217	0.736	0.812	0.582	0.138

Table 3.2 Sample intercorrelation matrix

Each variable receives a **loading** on each of the factors which are extracted, signifying its closeness to that factor. Different variables will have larger or smaller loadings on each of the hypothesised factors, so that it is possible to see which variables are most characteristic of a given factor: for example, in analysing a set of word frequencies across several texts, one might find that words in a certain conceptual field (e.g. religion) received high loadings on one factor, whereas those in another field (e.g. government) loaded highly on another factor.

Correspondence analysis is very similar in intention to factor analysis. It again tries to summarise the similarities between larger sets of variables and samples in terms of a smaller number of 'best fit' **axes**, rather like the factors in factor analysis. However, it differs from factor analysis in the basis of its calculations, though these details need not detain us here.

Multidimensional scaling (MDS) is another useful technique for visualising the relationships between different variables. MDS starts off with an intercorrelation matrix in the same way as factor analysis. However, this is then converted to a matrix in which the correlation coefficients are replaced with rank order values, that is the highest correlation value receives a rank order of 1, the next highest a rank order of 2, and so on. MDS then iteratively attempts to plot and arrange these variables in a (usually) two-dimensional space, so that the more closely related items are plotted closer to each other than the less closely related items, until the difference between the rank orderings on the plot and the rank orderings in the original table is minimised as far as possible.

These last two techniques may be thought of as **mapping techniques**, since their results are normally represented graphically on a set of axes.[5] The techniques attribute scores to each sample as well as to each variable on the same sets of axes. When the scores and axes are plotted, therefore, it is possible, by looking at the graphs of variables and samples side by side, to see not only how the variables group together but also where the samples fall on the same axes, and thus to attempt to explain the differences between the samples in terms of their closeness to and distance from particular variables.

In **cluster analysis** the idea is slightly different, namely to assemble variables into unique groups or **clusters** of similar items. Starting from the initial cross-tabulation, cluster analysis requires a matrix of statistics in the same way as factor analysis and the mapping techniques. This may be an intercorrelation matrix, as in factor analysis, or sometimes instead it may be a **distance matrix**, showing the degree of difference rather than similarity between the pairs of variables in the cross-tabulation. Using the matrix which has been constructed, cluster analysis then proceeds to group the variables contained within it. Several approaches to clustering may be encountered. The simplest one looks first for the two variables with the highest similarity or lowest distance value in the matrix and links these together, then it looks for the variable with the highest similarity to, or lowest distance from, any of the two members of *this* group, and so on. This is what is known as **single linkage** cluster analysis. More often, however, the method used is **average linkage** clustering, which uses the average of the similarity or distance between a given variable and all the other variables in the existing cluster. Cluster analyses can also be **hierarchical** or **non-hierarchical**. The hierarchical methods, which are the more common, link the individual clusters together so that each cluster is in turn a member of a higher level cluster, with the final highest-level cluster being the single cluster representing the entire set of variables. The results of this type of clustering are typically presented as a tree diagram or **dendrogram**, as we shall see in the example below. The alternative non-hierarchical methods do not attempt to link the smaller clusters together, but they do on the other hand allow items to belong to more than one cluster.

As stated, other books in this series will explain in much more detail the theory behind these multivariate techniques. For the moment, the main point that should be kept in mind from the brief introduction given above is this. Simple frequency tables of linguistic features in texts and corpora can often mask more general patterns of similarity and difference which may help to explain better why particular features, varieties and languages behave in the way that they do: multivariate statistical techniques can help the corpus linguist to extract these hidden patterns from the raw frequency data. With this point kept in mind, perhaps the best way to appreciate the role of these rather complex but extremely useful forms of analysis is by way of some examples.

Let us begin first of all with factor analysis. Biber (1993a) was interested in how one might go about identifying word senses and uses from large numbers of concordance lines extracted from corpora. Biber notes the basic importance in this area of collocational techniques such as mutual information (which we discussed above, section 4.4) but he also observes that these techniques cannot identify relationships between different collocations of the same word in order to identify its different senses. Thus, for instance, mutual information might identify *riding*, *cowboy*, *disk* and *PC* as significant collocates of *boot*, but it could not group together *cowboy* and *riding* into a group representative of one sense (footwear) and *disk* and *PC* into another sense group (start a computer). To help overcome this problem, Biber suggests the use of factor analysis. Biber demonstrates this application of factor analysis by looking at two words in an 11.66 million word sample of the Longman-Lancaster corpus. Let us here just consider one of his examples – that of the word *right*.

Biber counted the frequencies of all left-hand and right-hand collocates of *right* in his corpus and selected those occurring greater than 30 times as being the most important collocates. He then counted the frequencies of the collocations of each of these words with *right* in all the texts longer than 20,000 words in his corpus. Biber thus constructed a cross-tabulation from these data, from which he computed an intercorrelation matrix. This matrix was then factor analysed.

The factor analysis of the *right* data suggested that four factors accounted best for the data in the original table. It will be recalled from the brief description of factor analysis given above that in a factor analysis each item (in this case a collocation) receives a loading on each factor signifying its contribution to that factor. By looking down the lists of loadings, it is therefore possible to see which items receive the highest loadings on each factor and hence which are most characteristic of those individual factors. In this case, looking at the loadings of the different collocations on his four factors, Biber was able to see that each factor appeared to represent a different usage of the word *right*. Factor 1 gave high loadings to collocations such as *right hemisphere*, *right sided*, *right hander*, and so on: this factor thus appeared to identify the locational sense of *right*. Factor 2 gave high loadings to collocations such as *right now*, *right away* and *right here*, thus identifying the sense of 'immediately', 'exactly', and so on. Factor 3, with high loadings for such collocations as *that's right*, *you're right* and *not right*, seemed to signify the sense of 'correct', whereas Factor 4 appeared to mark a somewhat less clearly defined stylistic usage of *right* at the end of a clause.

This example shows the role that factor analysis can play in an investigation where a corpus linguist wishes to look for more general groupings and interpretations to explain a large number of ostensibly independent variables (such as the different collocations in the example). In such cases, factor analysis is useful in that it is able to reduce these variables to a much smaller number of reference factors, with loadings signifying the degree of association of each given variable with each reference factor. By looking at how the variables load on the different factors, the linguist is then able to identify the high-loading groups of items on each factor and interpret those factors in terms of more general properties underlying the variables in the high-loading groups (such as the word senses of the other collocate (*right*) in the example above).

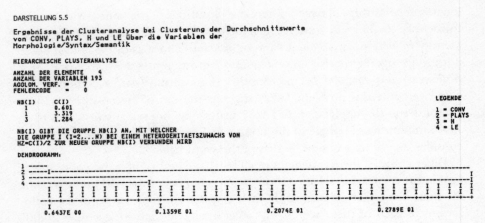

Figure 3.2 Cluster analysis dendrogram (Source: From Mindt 1992, reproduced by courtesy of Gunter Narr Verla)

Let us now look at an example of the use of cluster analysis. Mindt (1992) was interested in how far the English depicted in German textbooks of English as a foreign language constituted an accurate representation the language as used by native speakers. In this particular study he was interested in one specific area of English grammar, namely that of future time reference. Mindt took four corpora as the data for his study: the Corpus of English Conversation; a corpus of twelve modern plays; and the texts of two different German English courses. For each of these four corpora, Mindt made a count of a number of morphological, syntactic and semantic variables related to the expression of future time, for example the frequencies of individual verb lemmas and verb forms denoting futurity, the frequencies of different subjects of future time constructions (e.g. first person singular or third person plural), and so on. When this frequency analysis had been carried out, Mindt was left with a frequency table of values for 193 variables across each of the four corpora. Such a table is hard to interpret in its totality and so to try to make sense of this table in terms of the degrees of similarity and difference between the corpora Mindt carried out a hierarchical cluster analysis of the table. This, as we have seen, first required the calculation of a matrix of pairwise distance measures between the 4 corpora on the basis of the 193 variables and then proceeded to group the corpora into clusters according to how low the degree of dissimilarity was between them. The dendrogram which resulted from this analysis is reproduced in Figure 3.3.

If we look along the bottom of Mindt's dendrogram, we see a scale which represents the various distance values. On the left-hand side we see four digits, each representing one of the four corpora. Moving right from each digit, we see lines of dashes. At some point each line of dashes comes to an end with an 'I' character, which links it with the line for one of the other corpora or groups of corpora. Where this happens, we say that the two corpora or groups have formed a *cluster*, as we discussed above. The closer to the left of the diagram a cluster is formed, the less is the difference between the two corpora or groups in relation to the overall pattern of variables in the original table. In this dendrogram, we see that corpora 1 and 2 (the corpus of conversation and and the plays corpus) form a cluster very close to the left, that is, there is very little difference between them. Somewhat further on, but still within the left-hand half of the dendrogram, corpora 3 and 4 (the two textbooks) also form a cluster: there is thus also not a great deal of difference between these two samples, but they are not quite as closely related as the conversation and plays corpora. However, these two independent clusters which are formed by the corpus pairs do not themselves link together until the very right-hand side of the dendrogram, that is, there is a very large degree of difference between the cluster formed by corpora 1 and 2 and the cluster formed by corpora 3 and 4.

So what does this analysis tell us? Corpora 1 and 2, which form the first cluster, are both corpora of native-speaker English. Their clustering at the left-hand side of the dendrogram suggests that they have a close relationship to one another in their ways of expressing future time. Corpora 3 and 4, which form the second cluster, are both German textbooks of English. Again the cluster analysis shows them to be closely related in their future time usage. However, since the two clusters which are formed by the data are so dissimilar, we must conclude that there exist important differences between the patterns of usage which the textbooks present to the student and those which are actually used by native speakers.

What the cluster analysis has done for us in this case is to take the large number of variables in the original table, summarise them in terms of the overall amount of difference between the four corpora, and then use this information to automatically group the corpora. It is then up to us to interpret the empirical groupings in terms of what we already know about their members and to draw conclusions from them. As this example shows, cluster analysis is especially useful in corpus linguistics when we want to see in purely empirical terms whether the nature of a number of corpora or linguistic features can be accounted for in terms of a smaller number of broader but distinct groupings. In this case the four corpora could be so accounted for: the analysis reliably distinguished two groups representing native-speaker English and textbook English respectively.

Let us finally turn to an example of one of the mapping techniques. Nakamura (1993) was interested in exploring further an observation made by Hofland and Johansson (1982), namely that the frequencies of the modal verbs in the LOB and Brown corpora exhibit considerable variations between genre categories. To assist him in examining this two-way relationship between verbs and genres, Nakamura selected a statistical technique known as Hayashi's Quantification Method Type III, which is a very close cousin of correspondence

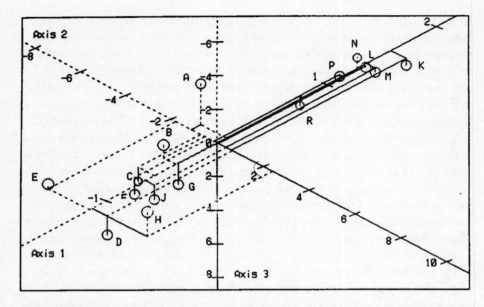

Figure 3.3 Hayashi's quantification method type III: three-dimensional distribution of genres in the Brown corpus (Source: Nakamura 1993, reproduced by courtesy of *ICAME Journal*)

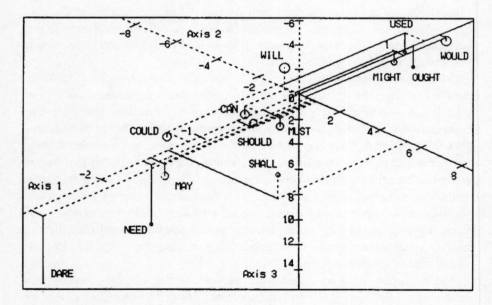

Figure 3.4 Hayashi's quantification method type III: three-dimensional distribution of modals in the Brown corpus (Source: Nakamura 1993, reproduced by courtesy of *ICAME Journal*)

analysis. Like correspondence analysis, this technique enables the analyst to look simultaneously at both the variables (in this case the modal verbs) and the samples (in this case the corpus genre categories). The first step in Nakamura's analysis was to make a cross-tabulation, similar to those which we have already met, of the frequencies of each modal verb in each genre category for each of the two corpora. This cross-tabulation was then subjected to Hayashi's quantification method type III.

The analysis produced three types of quantitative data for each corpus which was analysed: (a) a set of numerical scores for each genre category on each of n axes; (b) a set of numerical scores for each modal verb on each of the same n axes; and (c) a set figures denoting the proportion of the information in the original cross-tabulation which was accounted for by each of the n axes. The latter set of results showed that the first three axes extracted by the analysis accounted for approximately 90 per cent of the Brown corpus data and 84 per cent of the LOB corpus data. Nakamura was therefore able to select with some confidence just these three axes for further analysis. (It is in any case not possible to plot the results graphically in more than three dimensions.) He proceeded to plot the genres and modal verbs in the three-dimensional space formed by these three axes according to their scores on each axis, which can be considered as constituting three-dimensional coordinates. Nakamura performed three analyses – one for the Brown corpus, one for the LOB corpus, and one for the combined corpora – but for the purposes of illustrating the role of multivariate methods in corpus analysis it will suffice here only to look briefly at the analysis of the Brown corpus. The plots for this analysis are reproduced as Figures 3.3 and 3.4.

Axis 1 of the three Brown corpus axes (which runs diagonally from bottom left to top right in the figures) accounted for more than half of the total information in the original table (65 per cent). Looking at the points on this axis which represent the various genres (see Figure 3.3), Nakamura found that the axis reliably differentiated the 'informative' genres (such as learned writing) from the 'imaginative' genres (such as fiction): the informative genres (apart from press reportage) fell in the negative (bottom left) range of the axis, whereas the imaginative genres fell in the positive (top right) range. This distribution of points suggested that the informative/imaginative distinction was a major factor influencing the distribution of the different modal verbs and this conclusion corresponded well with previous studies of other linguistic categories which had suggested the importance of the informative/imaginative distinction. Looking next at the plots of the modal verbs themselves on the same set of axes (Figure 3.4), Nakamura was able to identify, by comparing the two graphs, which of the verbs were characteristic of the different genre types: *would*, *used*, *ought* and *might*, which fell in the positive range (top right of the diagram), could be seen to make up a group representative of imaginative prose, and *dare*, *need*, *may*, *shall* and *could*, which fell in the negative

range (bottom left of the diagram), could be seen to make up a group characteristic of informative prose. *Can, should* and *must* showed only a smaller
tendency towards a preferred use in informative prose (being situated closer to
zero than the other modals), and *will* was neutral between the two types,
falling as it did almost on the zero point on the axis.

Nakamura also looked at where the plots for verbs and genres fell on Axis
2 (which runs from top left to bottom right in the two figures). Here he was
able to see some more specific relationships between the individual modals
and the corpus categories. *Shall* was situated closest on this axis to category D
(religion) – most likely reflecting the frequency of *shall* in biblical quotation –
and category H (miscellaneous), which is mainly composed of government
documents; *could* was located closest to category G (skills and hobbies); and
will was located closest to category A (press reportage).

This sample analysis shows how the complex variations in frequency for
the thirteen modals across the fifteen genre categories of the Brown corpus
can be made more understandable by using a form of multivariate analysis to
statistically summarise these data. It is then possible to depict the statistical
summary data diagrammatically and to interpret an otherwise almost im-
possibly difficult matrix of numbers in terms of a broader distinction underlying those numbers which can be seen quite clearly on the graph, that is, a
distinction between informative and imaginative prose. The example also
demonstrates how plotting multivariate analysis scores for both variables and
samples – in this case modal verbs and genres – on the same set of axes can
facilitate the drawing of specific inferences about the connections between
one and the other: for example, in this study it could be concluded from a
comparison of the two graphs that the modal verb *shall* appeared to be
especially characteristic of government documents and religious prose.

4.6. Loglinear models

As we saw in the previous section, straightforward significance or association
tests, although important, cannot always handle the full complexity of the
data. The multivariate approaches which were presented there offer a way of
looking at large numbers of interrelated variables and discovering or confirm-
ing broader patterns within those variables. In this section we will consider a
different technique which deals with the interrelationships of several variables.

As linguists we typically want to go beyond the description of some
phenomenon and explain what it is that causes the data to behave in a particular way. The methodology known as **loglinear analysis** enables us to take
standard frequency cross-tabulations such as those which we have already met
in this chapter and to find out which variable or variables seem statistically
most likely to be responsible for a particular effect.

Let us imagine that we are interested in the factors which influence the presence or omission of the preposition *for* in phrases of duration such as *She studied [for] three years in Munich.* We may hypothesise several factors which could have an effect on this, for instance the text genre, the semantic category of the main verb, and whether or not the verb is separated by an adverb from the phrase of duration. It is plausible that any one of these variables may affect *for* omission. Alternatively, the omission of *for* may be influenced by a combination of more than one factor, or indeed by all the factors working together. In order to find out which model accounts best for the data, we must try them all out and see which ones give statistically significant results.

The way that we test the models in loglinear analysis is first to test the significance of associations in the most complex model, that is, the model which assumes that all the variables are working together. We then take away each variable at a time from that model and see whether significance is maintained in each case, and so on until we reach the model with the lowest possible number of dimensions. So if we were positing three variables (e.g. in the above example, genre, verb class, and separation by an adverb from the phrase of duration) we would first test the significance of the three-variable model, then each of the three two-variable models (taking away one of the variables in each case), and then each of the three one-variable models generated from the two-variable models. The best model would be taken to be the one with the fewest number of variables which still retained statistical significance.

This technique of loglinear analysis has a very close relationship with another technique known as **variable rule analysis** (VARBRUL). VARBRUL was pioneered in North American sociolinguistics by David Sankoff and others to study patterns of linguistic variation, but it is now slowly becoming more widely employed in corpus linguistics: John Kirk at the Queen's University Belfast, for example, has used VARBRUL to examine the factors influencing the uses of the modals in different corpora of modern English (Kirk 1993) and Gunnel Tottie has also used it in looking at negation in spoken and written English (Tottie 1991). VARBRUL uses an estimating procedure to calculate theoretical probability values which would maximise the likelihood of the same result that is embodied in the actual data, and this model is then used to generate predicted frequencies. The results of the model's predictions are then compared with those which actually occurred in the data (for example, using the chi-squared test, which we met earlier in this chapter, section 4.3) to find out how well the model accounts for the data.

4.7. Probabilistic language modelling

One of the most commonly encountered uses of frequency data from a corpus is that of probabilistic language modelling. Although until recently something of a minority taste in computational linguistics, probabilistic modelling techniques now being taken up with increasing enthusiasm as their success becomes more widely appreciated: probabilistic models have been shown time and again to perform more accurately and robustly than most purely rule-based systems. Such models play a wide variety of roles in natural language analysis, being used not only for part-of-speech annotation but also in syntactic parsing, in speech recognition and synthesis, and in word sense disambiguation. However, nothing more will be said on this topic here, since we shall return in detail to the issue of probabilistic language modelling in Chapter 5, section 3.

5. CHAPTER SUMMARY

This chapter has been concerned with the issue of corpora as sources of quantitative data. The important role of quantitative analysis and its interaction with qualitative analysis was first described. We then went on to look at how corpus builders attempt to make their corpora maximally representative of a language or language variety, so that quantitative results are of maximum utility to linguists, and the difficulties which this entails. Moving on from the notion of a representative corpus from which the results may be generalised to a language or variety, we looked at the various kinds of quantitative results which can be generated from such corpora. We saw first of all why it was desirable to supplement raw frequency counts with proportional data such as percentages, namely, to take account of different sample sizes and generally to make figures easier to compare. We saw, however, that intuitive comparisons cannot always be taken to tell us something significant about linguistic variation and so we considered the role of significance tests in telling us how far differences between samples may be due to chance. We also saw how it was possible to determine the significance of word co-occurrences in texts using mutual information or the Z-score. Returning to the issue of variation, we then looked at ways in which complex relationships between many different variables and samples could be examined using factor analysis, multivariate mapping techniques, cluster analysis, and loglinear modelling. Finally, we mentioned briefly an important computational application of corpus frequency data, namely that of probabilistic language modelling which is used for such tasks as part-of-speech annotation and parsing. This is discussed in detail in Chapter 5.

6. STUDY QUESTIONS

1. The language Shaf-ti is spoken on the island of Uvavu. Shaf-ti has two dialects – one from the mountainous region of the island and one from the coast. Harold Pennywise has collected corpora of the two dialects of Shaf-ti to look at relative clauses. He has tabulated these results and calculated a chi-square value.

	Mountain dialect	Coastal dialect
relativiser	124	85
no relativiser	30	36

Chi-square (1 d.f.) = 3.92, p = 0.0477

Interpret the results, commenting on their significance.

2. Is it really possible to achieve a representative corpus or was Chomsky right? How far does it matter?

3. Trudy Townley has been looking at verb frequencies in two different corpora. Corpus A contains 100,000 words; corpus B contains 500,000 words. Here are her results:

	Corpus A	Corpus B
BE	500	800
DO	80	400
HAVE	300	1500
GO	60	70
GIVE	40	30
TAKE	20	100

Which words have the same proportional frequency in both corpora?

4. Which of the statistical tests in this chapter would you use in the following situations:
   a) to find out how far the difference in frequency of two syntactic constructions in two corpora is due to something other than chance;
   b) to see how several texts are similar or different in respect of their total vocabularies;
   c) to discover which of several factors are influencing a variation in grammar.

7. FURTHER READING

Swinscow (1983) deals with the underlying assumptions of statistics and all the basic standard tests. We recommend it strongly as a paragon of brevity, clarity and simplicity in this complex and jargon-laden field. However, as one might guess from its publisher (the British Medical Association), the book is aimed fairly and squarely at medical statistics and it takes some imagination to make the examples correspond to linguistic problems. Other books deal more specifically with linguistic and textual (though mainly not corpus-oriented) statistics: see, for example, Kenny (1982), and Woods, Fletcher and Hughes (1986). On specific issues: Church *et al.* (1991) discuss mutual information in some detail; a discussion of loglinear modelling may be found in de Haan and van Hout (1986); and Alt (1990) provides a relatively accessible and non-mathematical introduction to factor analysis, cluster analysis, correspondence analysis and multidimensional scaling, although the discussion is not oriented towards linguistic problems.

NOTES

1. Schmied goes further in suggesting that this is necessarily the case, but he appears to overlook the possibility of deriving categories for quantification directly from theory. Furthermore, it is not always essential that categories should be pre-defined at all, though this is normally the case: in the study of lexis, for instance, 'categories' have sometimes been extracted empirically and quantitatively using statistical techniques on word frequency data.

2. More details about mutual information, including the formula, may be found in Church *et al.* (1991). It should be observed, however, that recently Daille (1995) has shown that mutual information can sometimes carry with it an unwanted effect which gives less frequent pairings more significance than frequent ones. One possible alternative measure that is suggested in her paper (IM3) is based on mutual information but cubes the enumerator of the formula.

3. Genuine factor analysis is somewhat different from principal components analysis. Its overall aims, however, are the same. The term 'factor analysis' is so widely used that it is difficult to distinguish the two in research reports unless one is well versed in their statistical foundations.

4. For a clear and relatively non-mathematical explanation of the details of these techniques, the reader is referred to the work by Alt (1990), cited in the Bibliography and in the further reading for this chapter.

5. Factor analyses can also be plotted graphically, though this happens much less often than with correspondence analysis and MDS.

The use of corpora in language studies

1. CORPORA AS SOURCES OF EMPIRICAL DATA

In this and the following chapter we examine the roles which corpora may play both in the study of language itself and in the development of computational tools for processing natural language. This chapter is concerned with their roles in the study of language.

The importance of corpora in language study is closely allied to the importance more generally of empirical data. Empirical data enable the linguist to make statements which are objective and based on language as it really is rather than statements which are subjective and based upon the individual's own internalised cognitive perception of the language. The use of empirical data also means that it is possible to study language varieties such as dialects or earlier periods in a language for which it may not be possible to use a rationalist approach. But empirical linguistic research may be carried out without using a corpus. Although many researchers will refer to their data as a corpus, frequently these data do not fit the definition of a corpus in the sense that we have tended to use that term in this book – as many other corpus linguists have – for a body of text which is carefully sampled to be maximally representative of a language or language variety. These other data should more properly be thought of collections of texts. Corpus linguistics proper, therefore, should be seen as a subset of the activity within an empirical approach to linguistics: corpus linguistics necessarily entails an empirical approach, but empirical linguistics need not entail the use of a corpus.

In the sections which follow, we consider the roles which corpora may play in a number of different fields of study in which language is the central object. In these brief discussions we focus on the conceptual issues of why corpus data are important in particular areas and how they can contribute to the advancement of knowledge in those areas, also providing real examples of the use of corpora in each area. In view of the huge amount of corpus-based linguistic research, the examples given are necessarily selective, and the student should consult the further reading for additional examples.

2. CORPORA IN SPEECH RESEARCH

The basic importance of corpora in speech research revolves around two main features. The first is that the corpus provides a *broad sample* of speech, that is, one which extends over a wide selection of variables (such as speaker age, sex and class) and across a variety of genres or activity types (such as conversation, news reading, poetry reading, liturgy, legal proceedings and so on). This breadth of coverage has two benefits. First, taking the corpus as a whole, it means that generalisations about spoken language can be made, which simply would not be possible with more restricted samples: in the case of the corpus, one is looking at features across as wide and representative a sample of the entire spoken language as it was feasible to collate. Second, by taking the constituent sections of the corpus either individually or together in the form of smaller subcorpora, it is possible to use the texts representing various variables, genres and activity types to study speech *variation* within a language.

The second important benefit of a spoken corpus is that − with a few exceptions − it provides a sample of *naturalistic* speech rather than speech which has been elicited under artificial conditions. The naturalistic nature of such data means that findings from the corpus are more likely to reflect language as it is actually used in 'real life', since these data are much less likely to be subject to additional production monitoring by the speaker, for example, trying to suppress a regional/social accent.[1]

On a more purely practical level, because the (transcribed) corpus has usually been enhanced with prosodic and other annotations, it is easier to carry out large scale quantitative analyses than with fresh raw data. Where the data have been enriched with other annotations such as parts of speech and syntactic structure, it is also possible to bring these into relationship with the phonetic annotations to study the interrelationships of linguistic levels. Furthermore, it is increasingly the case that the actual spoken data are also made available in high-quality form, so that instrumental analyses of the corpus may be carried out.

At least partly as a result of the fact that much phonetic corpus annotation has been at the level of prosody (see Chapter 2, section 2.2.3(g)), most phonetic and phonological research using corpora has, as one might expect, tended to focus upon issues of prosody rather than upon other levels of speech. The work in these areas which has been carried out to date on spoken corpora can be broadly divided into three types.

The first type of work has used the corpus to look at the nature of prosody and how the prosodic elements of speech relate to other linguistic levels. In the past many theories have been adduced about how such constructs as the boundaries of intonation groups are motivated. The use of a spoken corpus enables the researcher either (a) quantitatively to test out such hypotheses on real data to see whether or not they appear to hold, or (b) to generate hypotheses inductively from the corpus which may then be tested on further data.

An example of the first of these research paradigms is Wilson's (1989) study of prepositional phrases and intonation group boundaries. He hypothesised that postmodification of a noun by a prepositional phrase (e.g. *the man with the telescope*) would constitute a barrier to the placing of an intonation group boundary between the head noun and the preposition, since the prepositional phrase forms part of a larger noun phrase: an intonation group boundary would on the other hand be more likely to occur between a verb and a preposition where a prepositional phrase functions as an adverbial (e.g. *She ran with great speed*). These hypotheses were tested on a subsample of the Lancaster/IBM Spoken English Corpus and were found generally to hold, suggesting that there is indeed a relationship between the syntactic cohesiveness of a phrase and the likelihood of a prosodic boundary.

An example of the second paradigm is the work of Altenberg (1990), also on intonation group boundaries. Unlike Wilson, Altenberg did not start off with a hypothesis but instead generated a detailed account of the relationships between intonation group boundaries and syntactic structures from a monologue from the London–Lund corpus. From the results of this analysis he devised a set of rules for predicting the location of such boundaries, which were then applied by a computer program to a sample text from outside the corpus (a text from the Brown written corpus). When the sample text was read aloud, the predictions were found to identify correctly 90 per cent of the actual intonation group boundaries. In Altenberg's case, therefore, the research progressed from *analysing corpus data* to the generation of hypotheses to the testing of the hypotheses on more corpus data, rather than progressing from *theory* to the generation and testing of hypotheses.

A second type of work has looked at the basis of the prosodic transcriptions which are typically encoded within spoken corpora and used by researchers. Prosodic transcription raises the question of how far what is perceived and transcribed relates to the actual acoustic reality of the speech. Looking at the overlap passages of the Lancaster/IBM Spoken English Corpus, where the same passages were prosodically transcribed independently by two different phoneticians, Wilson (1989) and Knowles (1991) both found significant differences in the perception of intonation group boundaries, which suggested either that individual perception of the phonetic correlates of such boundaries differed or that other factors were affecting the placement of boundaries in the transcription. Wichmann (1993) looked more closely at the differences in the transcription of tones rather than boundaries. Looking at the transcription of falling tones in the corpus, she found that in the overlap passages there were major discrepancies in the perception of such tones. The transcribers seemed to have different notions of pitch height in relation to preceding syllables which was also sometimes overridden according to the level of a given tone in the speakers' overall pitch range, and the results of a perception experiment by Wichmann suggested that there is in fact no real *perceptual* category of high and low. Such studies seem to suggest, therefore, that in comparison to other forms of annotation such as part of speech, prosodic annotation is a much less reliable guide, at least to what it claims to depict.

The third type of work with speech corpora has looked at the typology of texts from a prosodic perspective. A good example of this is Wichmann's (1989) prosodic analysis of two activity types in the Lancaster/IBM Spoken English Corpus – poetry reading and liturgy. Considering Crystal and Davy's (1969) suggestion that a high frequency of level tones is especially characteristic of liturgy, she made a count of the distribution of level tones in all the text categories in the corpus. This count showed that whilst liturgy did have a high proportion of level tones this was not markedly the case and in fact the highest number of level tones was to be found in poetry reading. Looking in more detail at poetry reading and liturgy, Wichmann found that in the liturgical passages the highest concentration of level tones was in the prayer, whilst in the poetry reading the level tones tended to cluster in a final lyrical section of the poem which was included in the corpus. Wichmann suggests that in the context of the prayer reading, the listener may be assumed to constitute an audience rather than the addressee (which is God), whilst in the case of the lyric poetry the reading is more of a performance than an act of informing. In contrast, the narrative section of the same poem could be considered to be an act of informing and this in fact showed a much more conversational typology of tones. Wichmann links these observations about the nature of the speaker/hearer roles to the prosodic patterns which were discovered and, on the basis of these results, argues that, contrary to the generalisation proposed by Crystal and Davy, the intonation patterns are not related to activity type (such as liturgy) but rather to the discourse roles of the hearer such as audience and addressee. In this study, therefore, we see clearly how corpus data can be of value in challenging and amending existing theories.

3. CORPORA IN LEXICAL STUDIES

Lexicographers made use of empirical data long before the discipline of corpus linguistics was invented. Samuel Johnson, for example, illustrated his dictionary with examples from literature, and in the nineteenth century the *Oxford English Dictionary* made use of citation slips to study and illustrate word usage. The practice of citation collecting still continues, but corpora have changed the way in which lexicographers – and other linguists interested in the lexicon – can look at language.

Corpora, and other (non-representative) collections of machine readable text, now mean that the lexicographer can sit at a computer terminal and call up all the examples of the usage of a word or phrase from many millions of words of text in a few seconds. This means not only that dictionaries can be produced and revised much more quickly than before – thus providing more up-to-date information about the language – but also that the definitions can (hopefully) be more complete and precise, since a larger sample of natural examples is being examined. To illustrate the benefits of corpus data in lexicography we may cite briefly one of the findings from Atkins and Levin's (1995) study of verbs in the semantic class of 'shake'. In their paper, they quote the definitions of these verbs from three dictionaries – *the Longman Dictionary of Contemporary English*, the *Oxford Advanced Learner's Dictionary*, and the *Collins COBUILD Dictionary*. Let us look at an aspect of just two of the entries they discuss – those for *quake* and *quiver*. Both the Longman and COBUILD dictionaries list these verbs as being solely intransitive, that is they never take a direct object; the Oxford dictionary similarly lists *quake* as intransitive only, but lists *quiver* as being also transitive, that is, it can sometimes take an object. However, looking at the occurrences of these verbs in a corpus of some 50,000,000 words, Atkins and Levin were able to discover examples of both *quiver* **and** *quake* in transitive constructions (for example, *It quaked her bowels*; *quivering its wings*). In other words, the dictionaries had got it wrong: both these verbs can be transitive as well as intransitive. This small example thus shows clearly how a sufficiently large and representative corpus can supplement or refute the lexicographer's intuitions and provide information which will in future result in more accurate dictionary entries.

The examples extracted from corpora may also be organised easily into more meaningful groups for analysis, for instance by sorting the right-hand context of a word alphabetically so that it is possible to see all instances of a particular collocate together. Furthermore, the corpora being used by lexicographers increasingly contain a rich amount of textual information – the Longman-Lancaster corpus, for example, contains details of regional variety, author gender, date and genre – and also linguistic annotations, typically part-of-speech tagging. The ability to retrieve and sort information according to these variables means that it is easier (in the case of part-of-speech tagging) to specify which classes of a homograph the lexicographer wants to examine and (in the case of textual information) to tie down usages as being typical of particular regional varieties, genres and so on.

It is in dictionary building that the concept of an open-ended monitor corpus, which we encountered in Chapter 2, has its greatest role, since it enables the lexicographer to keep on top of new words entering the language or existing words changing their meanings or the balance of their use according to genre, formality, and so on. But the finite sampled type of corpus also has an important role in lexical studies and this is in the area of quantification. Although frequency counts, such as those of Thorndike and Lorge (1944), pre-date modern corpus linguistic methodologies, they were based on smaller, less representative corpora than are available today and it is now possible to produce frequencies more rapidly and more reliably than before, and also to subdivide these across various dimensions according to the varieties of a language in which a word is used. Moreover, frequency data need not apply solely to word forms: West (1953), working with a number of human analysts and an early, non-machine-readable corpus, produced a dictionary of word *sense* frequencies which has not yet been superseded. There is now an increasing interest in the frequency analysis of word senses and it should only be a matter of time before corpora are being used to provide word sense frequencies in dictionaries. Indeed, a project has been underway for over a decade at the Christian-Albrechts-Universität Kiel and Bowling Green State University in Ohio, which aims ultimately at the production of a broadly sense-ordered frequency dictionary for mediaeval German epic (Schmidt 1991): although based on the accumulation of analyses of individual literary texts rather than on a sampled corpus, this project is representative of the kinds of information which are increasingly becoming an issue in lexicography.

The ability to call up word combinations rather than individual words, and the existence of tools such as mutual information for establishing relationships between co-occurring words (see Chapter 3, section 4.4), mean that it is also now feasible to treat phrases and collocations more systematically than was previously possible. These are important for a number of reasons, as we have already suggested in Chapter 3. For instance, a phraseological unit may constitute a piece of technical terminology or an idiom, and collocations are important clues to specific word senses. Techniques for identifying such combinations in text corpora mean that, like individual words, they can now be better treated in dictionaries and in machine-readable terminology banks for professional technical translators. The experiments of Church *et al.* (1991) and Biber (1993a), which we have already discussed in Chapter 3, are clear examples of how such technology may benefit lexicographers in crafting definitions from corpus data. Biber's study, for instance, shows how factor analysis of frequent collocates can help empirically to group together individual senses of words: this may enable the lexicographer to organise his or her concordance data more swiftly and usefully into sense groups, with the possible additional pay-off of being able more easily to provide the sorts of sense frequency data that we discussed in the previous paragraph. Church *et al.*'s study shows a further way in which co-occurrence data can perhaps be used, that is to add greater delicacy to definitions: *strong* and *powerful*, for example, are often treated in dictionaries almost as synonyms, but the identification of differences in collocation can enable the lexicographer to draw these important distinctions in their usage as well as identifying their broad similarity in meaning.

As well as word meaning, we may also consider under the heading of lexical studies corpus-based work on **morphology** (word structure). The fact that morphology deals with language structure at the level of the word may suggest that corpora do not have any great advantage here over other sources of data such as existing dictionaries or introspection. However, corpus data do have an important role to play in studying the frequencies of different morphological variants and the productivity of different morphemes. Opdhal (1991), for example, has used the LOB and Brown corpora to study the use of adverbs which may or may not have a *-ly* suffix (e.g. *low/lowly*), finding that the forms with the *-ly* suffix are more common than the 'simple' forms and that, contrary to previous claims, the 'simple' forms are somewhat less common in American than in British English. Bauer (1993) has also begun to use data from his new corpus of New Zealand English for morphological analysis. At the time that he wrote his paper his corpus was incomplete and so his results are suggestive rather than definitive, but they demonstrate the role which a corpus can play in morphology. One example which Bauer concentrates on is the use of strong and weak past tense forms of verbs (e.g. *spoilt* (strong) vs. *spoiled* (weak)). In a previous elicitation study amongst New Zealand students, Bauer had concluded that the strong form was preferred by respondents to the weak form, with the exceptions of *dreamed* and *leaned*. The written corpus data, on the other hand, suggested that the weak form, with the exception of *lit*, was preferred to a greater degree than the elicitation experiment had suggested. Bauer wonders how far this difference between the elicitation experiment and the texts of the written corpus may be due to editorial pressure on writers to follow the more regular spelling variant, a non-linguistic factor which was not present in his elicitation experiment, and he looks forward to testing this theory in relation to the New Zealand spoken corpus, which also lacks this editorial constraint. Here, then, we see how a corpus, being naturalistic data, can help to define more clearly which forms are most frequently used and begin to suggest reasons why this may be so.

4. CORPORA AND GRAMMAR

Grammatical (or syntactic) studies have, along with lexical studies, been the most frequent types of research which have used corpora. What makes corpora important for syntactic research is, first, their potential for the representative quantification of the grammar of a whole language variety, and second, their role as empirical data, also quantifiable and representative, for the testing of hypotheses derived from grammatical theory.

Until the last quarter of this century, the empirical study of grammar had to rely primarily upon qualitative analysis. Such work was able to provide detailed descriptions of grammar but was largely unable to go beyond subjective judgements of frequency or rarity. This is even the case with more recent classic grammars such as the *Comprehensive Grammar of the English Language* (Quirk *et al.* 1985), whose four authors are all well-known corpus linguists. But advances in the development of parsed corpora (see Chapter 2) and tools for retrieval from them means that quantitative analyses of grammar may now more easily be carried out. Such studies are important, because they can now at last provide us with a representative picture of what usages are most typical and to what degree variation occurs both within and across varieties. This in turn is important not only for our understanding of the grammar of the language itself but also in studies of different kinds of linguistic variation and in language teaching (see sections 7, 8, 9 and 11 in this chapter).

Most smaller-scale studies of grammar using corpora have included quantitative data analyses. Schmied's (1993) study of relative clauses, for example, provides quantitative information about many aspects of the relative clauses in the LOB and Kolhapur corpora. However, there is now also a greater interest in the more systematic treatment of grammatical frequency and at least one current project (Oostdijk and de Haan 1994a) is aiming to analyse the frequency of the various English clause types. Oostdijk and de Haan have already produced preliminary results based upon the syntactically parsed Nijmegen corpus and they plan to extend this work in the near future to larger corpora. The Nijmegen corpus is only a small corpus of some 130,000 words, but, with the completion of the British National Corpus and the International Corpus of English, the stage seems set for much more intensive treatments of grammatical frequency.

As explained in Chapter 1, there has since the 1950s been a division in linguistics between those who have taken a largely rationalist view of linguistic *theory* and those who have carried on *descriptive* empirical research with a view to accounting fully for all the data in a corpus. Often these approaches have been presented as competitors but they are in fact not always as mutually exclusive as some would wish to claim: there is a further, though not at present very large, group of researchers who have harnessed the use of corpora to the *testing* of essentially rationalist grammatical theory rather than to pure linguistic description or the inductive generation of theory.

At Nijmegen University, for instance, rationalist and empiricist approaches to grammar are combined within a paradigm based upon the development of primarily rationalist formal grammars and the subsequent testing of these grammars on real-life language contained in computer corpora (Aarts 1991). A formal grammar is first devised by reference both to the linguists' introspection and to existing accounts of the grammar of the language, in a similar manner to the research practices employed by rationalist grammarians such as Chomsky. However, in contrast to such purely rationalist grammatical research, this grammar is then loaded into a computer **parser** and is run over a corpus to test how far it accounts for the data within the corpus. (See Chapter 5 for a discussion of corpus based parsing technologies.) On the basis of the results of this corpus parsing experiment, the grammar is then modified to take account of those analyses which it missed or got wrong. This does not mean amending it to deal with every single instance in the corpus, but with the most important or frequent constructions. By proceeding in this way, it is possible to investigate the degree to which basically rationalist grammars can account for corpus data and how far they need to be amended to handle the data.

A more specific example of this kind of rationalist-to-empiricist approach to grammar is provided by the exchange of papers between the team of Taylor, Grover and Briscoe, and Geoffrey Sampson. Taylor, Grover and Briscoe (1989) had produced an automatic parser for English in the form of a generative grammar, not directly based on empirical data, which they wanted to test on corpus data. Independently, Sampson (1987) had manually analysed a set of noun phrases in the LOB corpus, concluding that a generative grammar could not be used successfully to parse natural English text, since the number of different constructions occuring in natural texts is so large as to make it impossible to account for them all in a set of grammatical rules. Nevertheless, Taylor, Grover and Briscoe ran their grammar over a superset of Sampson's data and obtained a success rate of 87.97 per cent of noun phrase types correctly parsed. Extrapolating this to the number of tokens of each type in the data, their success rate would have amounted to 96.88 per cent. If Sampson were right about the deficiencies of generative grammars, they argued, the remaining examples would be expected primarily to be single, syntactically odd types. However, the failures of the grammar could in fact be classified quite easily and tended to represent oversights in devising the set of grammar rules rather than syntactic oddities. Taylor, Grover and Briscoe were thus able to argue that, at least as far as noun phrases go, Sampson had considerably overstated the degree to which a generative grammar cannot account for the constructions to be found in natural texts.[2] From the perspective of methodology, this exchange is important in showing how a disagreement about grammatical theory can be tested and resolved empirically using a corpus and a corpus analysis tool.

One final note may be added to our brief consideration of corpora and grammar, and that is a case in which corpus-based approaches to grammar have actually dovetailed with grammatical theory. Michael Halliday's theory of systemic grammar is based upon the notion of language as a paradigmatic system, that is, as a set of choices for each instance from which a speaker must select one. Such a set of choices is inherently probabilistic, that is to say in each situation various choices are more or less likely to be selected by the speaker. Halliday (1991) uses this idea of a probabilistically ordered choice to interpret many aspects of linguistic variation and change in terms of the differing probabilities of linguistic systems. For example, it may be that written English prefers *which* to *that* as a relativiser. We might quantify this statement using a corpus and say that *which* is 39% probable as opposed to *that* which is 12% probable.[3] But it may be that, in contrast to writing, conversational speech shows a greater tendency towards the use of *that*, so that *which* is only 29% probable whereas *that* is 18% probable.[4] It is one of Halliday's suggestions that the notion of a **register**, such as that of conversational speech, is really equivalent to a set of these kinds of variations in the probabilities of the grammar. Halliday is enthusiastic about the role which corpora may play in testing and developing this theory further, in that they can provide hard data from which the frequency profiles of different register systems may be reconstructed. Here, then, in contrast to the frequent hostility between grammatical theory and corpus analysis, we see a theoretician actively advocating the use of corpus data to develop a theory.

5. CORPORA AND SEMANTICS

We have already seen how a corpus may be used to look at the occurrences of individual words in order to determine their meanings (*lexical semantics*), primarily in the context of lexicography. But corpora are also important more generally in semantics. Here, their main contribution has been that they have been influential in establishing an approach to semantics which is objective and which takes due account of indeterminacy and gradience.

The first important role of the corpus, as demonstrated by Mindt (1991), is that it can be used to provide objective criteria for assigning meanings to linguistic items. Mindt points out that most frequently in semantics the meanings of lexical items and linguistic constructions are described by reference to the linguist's own intuitions, that is, by what we have identified as a rationalist approach. However, he goes on to argue that in fact semantic distinctions are associated in texts with characteristic observable contexts – syntactic, morphological and prosodic – and thus that by considering the environments of the linguistic entities an empirical objective indicator for a particular semantic distinction can be arrived at. Mindt presents three short studies in semantics to back up this claim. By way of illustration, let us take just one of these – that of 'specification' and futurity. Mindt is interested here in whether what we know about the inherent futurity of verb constructions denoting future time can be shown to be supported by empirical evidence; in particular, how far does the sense of futurity appear to be dependent on co-occurring adverbial items which provide separate indications of time (what he terms 'specification') and how far does it appear to be independently present in the verb construction itself? Mindt looked at four temporal constructions – namely, *will*, *be going to*, the present progressive and the simple present – in two corpora – the Corpus of English Conversation and a corpus of twelve contemporary plays – and examined the frequency of specification with the four different constructions. He found in both corpora that the simple present had the highest frequency of specification, followed in order by the present progressive, *will*, and *be going to*. The frequency analysis thus established a hierarchy with the two present tense constructions at one end of the scale, often modified adverbially to intensify the sense of future time, and the two inherently future-oriented constructions at the other end, with a much lesser incidence of additional co-occurring words indicating futurity. Here, therefore,

Mindt was able to demonstrate that the empirical analysis of linguistic contexts *is* able to provide objective indicators for intuitive semantic distinctions: in this example, inherent futurity was shown to be inversely correlated with the frequency of specification.

The second major role of corpora in semantics has been in establishing more firmly the notions of fuzzy categories and gradience. In theoretical linguistics, categories have typically been envisaged as hard and fast ones, that is, an item either belongs in a category or it does not. However, psychological work on categorisation has suggested that cognitive categories typically are not hard and fast ones but instead have fuzzy boundaries so that it is not so much a question of whether or not a given item belongs in a particular category as of how often it falls into that category as opposed to another one. This has important implications for our understanding of how language operates: for instance, it suggests that probabilistically motivated choices of ways of putting things play a far greater role than a model of language based upon hard and fast categories would suggest. In looking empirically at natural language in corpora it becomes clear that this 'fuzzy' model accounts better for the data: there are often no clear-cut category boundaries but rather gradients of membership which are connected with *frequency* of inclusion rather than simple inclusion or exclusion. Corpora are invaluable in determining the existence and scale of such gradients. To demonstrate this, let us take a second case study from Mindt. In this instance, Mindt was interested in the subjects of verb constructions with future time reference, specifically the distinction between subjects that do or do not involve conscious human agency, which theory had previously identified as an important distinction. As a rough correlate of this distinction, Mindt counted the frequency of personal and non-personal subjects of the four future time constructions in the same two corpora referred to above. He found that personal subjects occurred most frequently with the present progressive, whereas the lowest number of personal subjects occurred with the simple future, refuting previous theoretical claims. *Will* and *be going to* had only a small preference (just 2–3%) for personal subjects, and the rank order was the same for both corpora. So this case study seemed to suggest that there is a semantic relationship correlating the type of agency with the verb form used for future time reference. But note that none of the constructions occurred solely with either conscious or non-conscious agency: rather, Mindt's analysis showed that the present progressive was simply *more likely* to have a personal subject than the other constructions and especially the simple future. In other words, the data formed a gradient of membership for the two fuzzy sets of verb constructions related to conscious agency and to non-conscious agency, on which some constructions are seen to belong more often than others in one of the two sets. What is important to recognise here is that the definition of this gradience of membership was only possible using corpus-based frequency data: a purely theoretical linguistic approach might conceivably not have recognised the fuzziness and indeterminacy present in such circumstances and instead might well have attempted, wrongly, to shoe-horn a given construction into just one clear-cut category.

6. CORPORA IN PRAGMATICS AND DISCOURSE ANALYSIS

The amount of corpus-based research in pragmatics and discourse analysis has to date been relatively small. This is perhaps at least in part due to the problem which Myers (1991) has observed, namely that pragmatics and discourse analysis rely on context – pragmatics has often been defined as 'meaning in context' – whereas corpora strip much of the context of utterances: they tend, on the whole, to take smaller samples of texts rather than entire texts and these samples are, moreover, removed from their social and textual contexts, although sometimes relevant social information is encoded with the corpus. Nevertheless, it is not always impossible to infer context from corpus texts and corpora have formed the basis for some important work in these areas.

Much of the work in these fields has been carried out using the London-Lund corpus, which is perhaps understandable given that until recently this was the only truly conversational corpus and that most work in pragmatics and related areas has in general concentrated on spoken language. The major contribution of such research to date has been to the understanding of how conversation works, especially with respect to lexical items and phrases with conversational functions. For example, in one study Stenström (1984a) has shown how the correlation of discourse items such as *well*, *sort of* and *you know* with pauses in speech may depend on whether or not the speaker expects a response from the addressee. In another study, Stenström (1987) looked at 'carry-on signals' such as *right*, *right o*, and *all right*. Here she was able to classify the use of these signals according to a typology of their various functions. For example, she found that *right* (which was the most common signal) was used in all functions but especially as a response and to evaluate a previous response and terminate the exchange. *All right* on the other hand was typically used to mark a boundary between two stages in the discourse, whereas *that's right* was used most often as an emphasiser and *it's alright* and *that's alright* served as responses to apologies. Furthermore, given the fact that 57 per cent of the lexical items studied were from telephone conversations which made up only 12 per cent of the subcorpus being studied, Stenström was also able to infer that the use of these carry-on signals in conversation was quite strongly linked to the channel used, i.e. telephone English.

Corpus-based studies such as those carried out by Stenström can provide quantitative typological accounts of conversational phenomena across broad samples of spontaneous natural discourse, something which was not feasible before computer corpora became available. The availability of new conversational corpora such as the spoken part of the BNC should provide a greater incentive both to extend and to replicate such studies, since there will simultaneously be more conversational data available than before and a wider social and geographical range of people recorded than is the case with the London-Lund corpus.

These quantitative approaches add to our understanding of linguistic behaviour because they can provide more specific accounts of what choices are available to the speaker in which contexts, and which of these choices are the most prototypical or unusual. But, apart from work such as that of Stenström, pragmatics has to date been poorly served in a quantitative corpus-based paradigm. However, there are models which could profitably be picked up on. In recent years, for example, Greg Myers has been analysing quite exhaustively a collection of molecular genetics articles, which, whilst it perhaps does not quite fit our definition of a 'corpus', is a useful paradigm example which could be extended. For example, he has in one study (1989) looked in detail (though largely qualitatively) at the various 'politeness phenomena' such as solidarity, hedging and indirectness. Although such aspects of language cannot easily be extracted from corpora by concordancing a few key words, careful quantitative accounts of linguistic behaviours such as politeness based on a wider and more representative corpus would be an important contribution to our understanding of pragmatics, which currently relies very much on qualitative data: as we see in several sections of this chapter, the quantitative analysis of corpora may sometimes have to lead to the revision of theories which are not supported by the data. Aijmer (1988) has in fact already carried out some work in this paradigm using the London-Lund corpus – in an analysis of requests she found that 33 per cent were expressed indirectly – but the approach deserves to be expanded.

7. CORPORA AND SOCIOLINGUISTICS

Sociolinguistics shares with historical linguistics, dialectology and stylistics the fact that it is an empirical field of research which has hitherto relied primarily upon the collection of research-specific data rather than upon more general corpora. But such data are often not intended for quantitative study and hence also are often not rigorously sampled. Sometimes the data are also elicited rather than naturalistic data. What is important about a corpus is that it can provide what these kinds of data do not provide – a representative sample of naturalistic data which can be quantified. Although corpora have not as yet been used to a great extent in sociolinguistics, there is evidence of an increasing interest in their exploitation in this field.

Most sociolinguistic projects with corpora to date have been relatively simple lexical studies in the area of language and gender. An example of this is the study by Kjellmer (1986), who used the Brown and LOB corpora to examine masculine bias in American and British English. He looked specifically at the occurrence of masculine and feminine pronouns and at the occurrence of the lexical items *man/men* and *woman/women*. Kjellmer found that the frequency of the female items was much less than the male in both corpora, but that female forms were more frequent in British English than in American English. He also found differences in male/female ratios by genre. In general, women featured more strongly in imaginative rather than informative prose, with romantic fiction, unsurprisingly, having the highest proportion of women. However, although these frequency distributions were unsurprising, Kjellmer found that his other hypothesis – that women would be less 'active', that is, would be more frequently the objects rather than the subjects of verbs – to be falsified: in fact women and men had similar subject/object ratios.

In a recent article, Holmes (1994) has looked more critically at the methodology of these kinds of studies. Taking three gender-related lexical issues – the frequency of *Ms* as compared with *Miss/Mrs*; the use of 'sexist' suffixes; and the use of generic *man* – Holmes makes two important method-ological points. First, she shows that it is important when counting and classi-fying occurrences to pay attention to the context and whether real alternatives are in fact available. For instance, whilst there is a non-gender marked alternative for *policeman* or *policewoman* (namely *police officer*), there is no such alternative for the *-ess* form in *Duchess of York*. The latter should there-fore be excluded from counts of 'sexist' suffixes when looking at this kind of gender bias in writing. Second, Holmes points out the difficulty of classifying a form when it is actively undergoing semantic change. As an example she takes the word *man*. She argues that whilst it has clearly a single male referent in a phrase such as *A 35 year old man was killed* and is clearly generic (referring to mankind) in phrases such as *Man has engaged in warfare for centuries*, it is diffi-cult to decide in phrases such as *We need the right man for the job* whether *man* is intended to refer solely to a male person or whether it is not gender specific and could reasonably be substituted by *person*. Because of the drift towards 'non-sexist' writing, it becomes harder to decide whether or not the usage is generic, because an alternative is available which was not previously available. These simple but important criticisms by Holmes should incite a more criti-cal approach to data classification in further sociolinguistic work using corpora, both within and without the area of gender studies.

Although, as stated, relatively little work on sociolinguistics has hitherto been carried out using the standard corpora, it seems likely that it will increase in quantity in the near future. Yates (1993), for example, has shown how quan-tifiable measures can be generated from the Hallidayan theory of language as social semiotic and has carried out studies using a body of computer-medi-ated communication (e.g. electronic mail) to examine the nature of this new genre in a sociolinguistic perspective, focusing on issues such as the presenta-tion of self, literacy practices and the presentation of knowledge. The greater expansion of sociolinguistic corpus work seems to be hampered really by only three practical problems: the operationalisation of sociolinguistic theory into measurable categories which can be applied to corpora; the absence of soci-olinguistic information encoded in current corpora; and the lack of sociolinguistically motivated sampling. Yates's work is an example of how the first problem may be addressed. The situation as regards the nature of the corpora is also changing. In historical corpora, sociolinguistic variables such as social class, sex of writer, and educational background are now being encoded. The Helsinki diachronic corpus already contains these variables, and the Lampeter Corpus of Early Modern English Tracts will also encode similar information. With modern language corpora, the Longman-Lancaster corpus already contains header fields for gender of writer, and furthermore the spoken part of the BNC has been collected using demographic market research techniques for age and social class as well as geographical location. These sociolinguistically annotated corpora should enable corpus-based work on social variation in language to begin in earnest.

8. CORPORA AND STYLISTICS

Researchers in stylistics are typically more interested in individual texts or the *oeuvres* of individual authors than in more general varieties of a language, and hence, although they may be interested in computer assisted textual analysis, they tend not to be large scale users of corpora as we have defined them. Nevertheless, some stylisticians are interested in investigating broader issues such as genre, and still others have found corpora to be important sources of data in their research.

The concept of style is based on the assumption that authors have a choice between different ways of putting things, for instance between using technical or non-technical vocabulary, between using long and short sentences, or between using co-ordination and subordination. The definition of what constitutes an author's individual style thus depends at least in part in examining the degree by which the author leans towards particular ways of putting things. To arrive at a picture of how far this constitutes a stylistic trend requires comparisons to be made not only internally within the author's own work but also with other authors or the norms of the language or variety as a whole. Furthermore, as Leech and Short (1981) point out in their monograph on style in fiction, stylistics often demands the use of quantification to back up such judgements which may otherwise appear to be subjective rather than objective.

Corpora, as standard representative samples of varieties or languages, form a particularly valuable basis for comparisons between an author, text, or collection of texts and a particular variety of a language. One example of the use of a corpus for this purpose is the Augustan Prose Sample collected by Milic. Milic's primary aim in collecting this corpus was to have a basis for a quantitative comparison of Jonathan Swift's prose style. The corpus contains 80,000 words, which were sampled from various genres of published texts. Texts were sampled so as to give as regular as possible a distribution of samples from throughout the period 1675–1725. Also, rather than concentrating on the best-known writers of the period, Milic chose texts which could be taken to represent a broad range of the sorts of things which educated people were reading at this time. The intention was therefore to arrive at a representative sample of the published English of this period so as to have a normative sample with which to compare Swift's style.

Another level of stylistic variation, which may often not explicitly be called 'stylistics', is the more general variation between genres and channels. Corpora have found a particular role in examining the stylistics of these more general constructs. One of the most common uses of corpora has been in looking at the differences between spoken language and written language. For instance, Altenberg (1984) has examined the differences in the ordering of cause–result constructions, and Tottie (1991) has examined the differences in negation strategies. Other work has looked at variation between particular genres, using subsamples of corpora as the database. Wilson (1992), for example, looking at the usage of *since*, used the learned, Belles-Lettres and fiction genre sections from the LOB and Kolhapur corpora in conjunction with a sample of modern English conversation and the Augustan Prose Sample, and found that causal *since* had evolved from being the main causal connective in late seventeenth century writing to being particularly characteristic of formal learned writing in the twentieth century. Recently, also, a project has begun at Lancaster University to build a speech presentation corpus. Speech presentation (i.e. how spoken language is represented in written texts) is an area of stylistics to which much attention has been given. The speech presentation corpus will contain a broad sample of direct and indirect speech from a variety of genres and allow researchers to look for systematic differences between, for example, fictional and non-fictional prose.

Allied to their use for comparing genres, corpora have been used to challenge empirically existing approaches to text typology. Variation studies, and also the sampling of texts for corpora, have typically been based on external criteria such as channel (e.g. speech and writing) or genre (e.g. romantic fiction, scientific writing). However, recent work has begun to approach textual variation from a language internal perspective. Biber (1988), for example, looking initially at the variation between speech and writing, carried out factor analyses of 67 linguistic features across text samples from 23 major genre categories taken mostly from the LOB and London-Lund corpora. From these analyses, Biber extracted 5 factors which, by reference to the highest loaded items on each, he interpreted as representing particular dimensions of linguistic variation. For instance, Biber's Factor 2 is taken to represent a distinction between narrative and non-narrative: past tense verbs, third person pronouns, and verbs with perfective aspect receive high positive loadings on this factor. In the factor analysis, each genre sample also received a factor score on each dimension so that, taken together, it is possible to see how genres differ from one another and on what dimensions. Having once arrived at this 5-factor framework, it is then possible to use it to score other texts. For example, Biber and his collaborators have already applied the framework to the historical development of English genres and to the examination of primary school reading materials. What is important about Biber's work from a methodological point of view is that it enables a broad, empirically motivated comparison of language variation to be made, rather than the narrow single-feature analyses which have often been used to add a little bit at a time to our understanding of variation. It is also a very clear example of how the quantitative empirical analysis of a finite sampled corpus may contribute new approaches to old issues.

Kay Wikberg has also in recent years looked critically at the genre classifications in corpora. One of the issues with which Wikberg has been concerned has been with the non-homogeneous nature of some corpus genre categories. Looking at category E of the LOB corpus ('skills and hobbies'), for example, Wikberg (1992) found that the distributions of certain high frequency words, together with other textual features, supported a division of this category into two subcategories of procedural discourse (that is, discourse which describes to the reader how to do something – for example a recipe or instruction manual) and non-procedural discourse. These findings have prompted Wikberg to suggest that corpus compilers should pay greater attention to text typology in constructing corpora and that users should pay more attention to the possibilities of intra-category variation in analysing the results of corpus-based investigations.

Work such as that of Biber and Wikberg has two important roles to play. First, it provides an incentive to stylistic analysis which is not only empirical and quantitative but which also takes greater account of the general stylistic similarities and differences of genres and channels rather than how they differ on individual features. Second, it should be influential in developing more representative corpora. Culturally-motivated, and hence possibly artificial, notions of how language is divided into genres can be replaced or supplemented by more objective language-internal perspectives on how and where linguistic variation occurs. Indeed, in this latter context it should be noted that Biber and Finegan have already been applying Biber's multidimensional model to the building of their ARCHER historical corpus.

9. CORPORA IN THE TEACHING OF LANGUAGES AND LINGUISTICS

Resources and practices in the teaching of languages and linguistics typically reflect the division in linguistics more generally between empirical and rationalist approaches. Many textbooks contain only invented examples and their descriptions are based apparently upon intuition or second-hand accounts; other books – such as the books produced by the Collins COBUILD project – are explicitly empirical and rely for their examples and descriptions upon corpora or other sources of real life language data.

Corpus examples are important in language learning as they expose students at an early stage in the learning process to the kinds of sentences and vocabulary which they will encounter in reading genuine texts in the language or in using the language in real communicative situations. The importance of such empirical data also applies as much in the teaching of linguistics as it does in the teaching of foreign languages. In our own teaching, we have found that students who have been taught using traditional syntax textbooks, which contain only simple example sentences such as *Steve puts his money in the bank* (from Horrocks 1987), often find themselves unable to analyse longer, more complex corpus sentences such as *The government has welcomed a report by an Australian royal commission on the effects of Britain's atomic bomb testing programme in the Australian desert in the fifties and early sixties* (from the Spoken English Corpus). It is this latter kind of sentence, however, which a prospective linguist would need to be able to analyse since such sentences reflect some of the sorts of language which he or she would encounter in analysing other texts.

However, corpora, much more so than other sources of empirical data, have another important role in language pedagogy which goes beyond simply providing more realistic examples of language usage. A number of scholars have used corpus data to look critically at existing language teaching materials. For example, Kennedy (1987a, 1987b) has looked at the ways of expressing quantification and frequency in ESL (English as a second language) textbooks; Holmes (1988) has looked at ways of expressing doubt and certainty in ESL textbooks; Mindt (1992) has looked at future time expressions in German textbooks of English; and Ljung (1990) has looked at the vocabulary in Swedish textbooks of English. The methodologies adopted by these scholars are broadly similar: they analyse the relevant constructions or vocabularies both in the sample textbooks and in standard corpora of English such as the LOB corpus and the London-Lund corpus, then they compare their findings between the two data sets. Most of these studies have found that there exist considerable differences between what textbooks are teaching and how native speakers actually use language as evidenced in the corpora. Some textbooks have been found to gloss over important aspects of usage or variations in usage, and sometimes textbooks may even foreground less frequent stylistic choices at the expense of more common ones. The more general conclusion which scholars such as Mindt and Kennedy have drawn from these exercises is that non-empirically based teaching materials can be positively misleading and that corpus studies should be used to inform the production of materials, so that the more common choices of usage are given more attention than those which are less common. This is the kind of approach which the COBUILD team at Birmingham have adopted in producing their materials.

One particular type of foreign language teaching is that which comes under the heading of 'languages for special purposes'. This refers to the domain specific teaching of a language for a particular area of application, for example, the teaching of medical English to medical students. Following similar logics to those espoused by Mindt and others, some researchers have built corpora of particular varieties of English with the aim of exploiting them in language teaching for specific purposes. One example of such a corpus is the Guangzhou Petroleum English Corpus, a corpus of approximately 411,000 words of English sampled from the petrochemical domain. A similar kind of corpus has been constructed at the Hong Kong University of Science and Technology, where a 1,000,000-word corpus of English has been built, sampled from the kinds of computer science textbooks which students of that subject are likely to use. Such corpora can be used to provide many kinds of domain-specific material for language learning, including quantitative accounts of vocabulary and usage which address the specific needs of students in a particular domain more directly than those taken from more general language corpora.

Corpora have been used not only in language teaching but also in the teaching of linguistics. Excellent examples of such use are the courses on varieties of English and corpus linguistics which John Kirk has run for several years at the Queen's University of Belfast (Kirk 1994). As the entire student assessment on these courses Kirk uses projects rather than traditional essays and exams. Kirk requires his students to base their projects on corpus data which they must analyse in the light of a model. The students are then required to draw their own conclusions about the data. Among the models which Kirk's students have chosen to apply to various samples of corpus data are Brown and Levinson's politeness theory, Grice's co-operative principle, and Biber's multidimensional approach to linguistic variation. The students must then submit their final project as a properly word processed research report. In taking this approach to assessment, therefore, Kirk is using corpora not only as a way of teaching students about variation in English but also to introduce them to the main features of a corpus-based approach to linguistic analysis.

One further application of corpora in language and linguistics teaching is their role in computer-assisted language learning. A computer system based upon a parsed corpus database is already being used in the teaching of English grammar at the University of Nijmegen (van Halteren 1994). Recent work at Lancaster University has also been looking at the role of corpus-based computer software for teaching undergraduates the rudiments of grammatical analysis (McEnery and Wilson 1993). This software – Cytor – reads in an annotated corpus (currently either part-of-speech tagged or parsed) a sentence at a time, hides the annotation, and asks the student to annotate the sentence him- or herself. The student can call up help in the form of a list of tag mnemonics with examples, or in the form of a frequency lexicon entry for a word giving the possible parts of speech with their frequencies. Students can also call up a concordance of similar examples. Students are given four chances to get an annotation right. The program keeps a record of the number of guesses made on each item, and how many were correctly annotated by the student. In the Lent Term of 1994, a preliminary experiment was carried out to determine how effective the corpus-based CALL system was at teaching the English parts of speech. A group of volunteer students taking the first-year English Language course were split randomly into two groups. One group was taught parts of speech in a traditional seminar environment, whilst others were taught using the CALL package. Students' perfomance was monitored · throughout the term and a final test administered. In general the computer-taught students performed better than the human-taught students throughout the term, and the difference between the two groups was particularly marked towards the end of the term. Indeed, the performance of CALL students in a final pen and paper annotation test was significantly higher than the group taught by traditional methods (McEnery, Baker and Wilson 1995).

The increasing availability of multilingual parallel corpora makes possible a further pedagogic application of corpora, namely as the basis for translation teaching. Whilst the assessment of translation is frequently a matter of style rather than of right and wrong, and therefore perhaps does not lend itself to purely computer-based tutoring, a multilingual corpus has the advantage of being able to provide side-by-side examples of style and idiom in more than one language and of being able to generate exercises in which students can compare their own translations with an existing professional translation or original. Such an approach is already being pioneered at the University of Bologna using corpora which, although they do not contain the same text in more than one language, do contain texts of a similar genre which can be searched for relevant examples (Zanettin 1994).

10. CORPORA IN HISTORICAL LINGUISTICS

Empirically based textual research is a *sine qua non* of historical linguistics. Historical linguistics can also be seen more specifically as a species of corpus linguistics, since the extant texts of a historical period or a 'dead' language form a closed corpus of data which may only be extended by the (re-)discovery of previously unknown manuscripts, books, or inscriptions. Indeed, sometimes it is possible to use most or all of the entire closed corpus of a language for research: this can be done, for example, for ancient Greek using the *Thesaurus Linguae Graecae* corpus, which contains most of extant ancient Greek literature. But in practice historical linguistics has not tended to conform strictly to a corpus linguistic paradigm. Given that the entire population of texts can be very large, historical linguistics has tended to take a more selective approach to empirical data, simply looking for evidence of particular phenomena and making at most rather rough estimates of frequency. Mostly there has been no real attempt to produce *representative* samples –

which is what corpora, as we have defined them, are – and to provide hard frequencies based on those: such frequency analyses have been largely confined to studies of individual literary texts or authors.

However, in recent years there has been a change in the way that some historical linguists have approached their data, which has resulted in an upsurge in strictly corpus-based historical linguistics and the building of corpora for this purpose. The Augustan Prose Sample, referred to above in section 8 on stylistics, is one example of a corpus which aims to represent a particular historical period and variety of the English language, but perhaps the most widely known English historical corpus is the diachronic Helsinki corpus.

The Helsinki corpus is a corpus of approximately 1.6 million words of English dating from the earliest Old English period (before AD 850) to the end of the Early Modern English period (defined by the compilers as being 1710). The corpus provides a continuous diachronic picture of the language between those dates: it is divided into three main periods – Old English, Middle English and Early Modern English – and each of these periods is divided into a number of 100-year subperiods (or 70-year subperiods in the case of Early Modern English and the second half of Middle English). The Helsinki corpus also aims to be representative not only in terms of chronological coverage, but also in terms of the range of genres, regional varieties and sociolinguistic variables such as gender, age, education and social class which are represented. For each text sample, the information on all these criteria is contained in COCOA format at the beginning of the sample to enable the researcher to select information from the corpus according to his or her specific needs. The Helsinki team have also produced 'satellite' corpora of early Scots and early American English to stand alongside the historical 'English' English corpus.

But the Helsinki team are not the only team involved in historical corpus building: indeed, this has almost become a growth industry. A few examples of other English historical corpora currently in development are the Zürich Corpus of English Newspapers (ZEN) (a corpus covering the period from 1660 up to the establishment of *The Times* newspaper), the Lampeter Corpus of Early Modern English Tracts (a sample of English pamphlets from between 1640 and 1740, all taken from the collection at the library of St David's University College, Lampeter), and the ARCHER corpus (a corpus of British and American English between the years 1650 and 1990).

The actual work which is carried out on historical corpora is qualitatively very similar to that which is carried out on modern language corpora, although in the case of corpora such as the Helsinki corpus, which provide diachronic coverage rather than a 'snapshot' of the language at a particular point in history, it is also possible to carry out work on the evolution of the language through time. As an example of this latter kind of work, one may take Peitsara's (1993) study of prepositional phrases denoting agency with passive constructions. She made use of four subperiods from the Helsinki corpus covering late Middle and Early Modern English (*c.* 1350–1640) and calculated the frequencies of the different prepositions introducing such agent phrases. The calculation showed that throughout the period the most common prepositions introducing agent phrases were *of* and *by*, but that from being almost equal in frequency at the very beginning of the period (a ratio of 10.6:9), *by* rapidly gained precedence so that by the fifteenth century it is three times more common than *of* and by 1640 around eight times as common. Peitsara also made use of the text type information, showing that whilst by the end of the period up to half of the individual texts contained agent phrases introduced by more than one preposition type, some texts showed an unusual tendency to use just one type. This was particularly marked in documents, statutes and official correspondence and it is suggested that this may be a result of bilingual influence from French. Individual authors of texts within categories are also shown to differ in their personal and stylistic preferences.

This kind of quantitative empirical study, by providing concrete data which it is now at last possible to obtain through the use of a computer corpus, can only help our understanding of the evolution of a language and its varieties: indeed, it has a particular importance in the context of Halliday's (1991) conception of language evolution as a motivated change in the probabilities of the grammar. But it is important, as Rissanen (1989) has pointed out, also to be aware of the limitations of historical corpus linguistics. Rissanen identifies three main problems. First, there is what he calls the 'philologist's dilemma', that is the danger that the use of a corpus and computer to extract specific data may supplant the in-depth knowledge of language history which is to be gained from the study of the original texts in their context. This is, however, not a danger inherent in corpus-based research *per se* but in an overreliance on corpora in training researchers. Second, there is the 'God's truth fallacy', which is the danger that a corpus may be used to provide representative conclusions about the entire language period without understanding the limitations of the corpus in terms of what it does and does not contain in terms of genres and so on: all corpus researchers need to keep in perspective what their corpora can reasonably be taken to represent. Finally, there is the 'mystery of vanishing reliability', by which Rissanen means that the more variables which are used in sampling and coding the corpus – periods, genres, sociological variables, and so on – the harder it is to represent each fully and to achieve statistical reliability. As he suggests, the most effective way of solving this problem is to build larger corpora which are proportionate to the distinctions which are encoded in them, but with current corpora it is simply necessary in designing research projects to be aware of the statistical limitations of the corpus. Rissanen's reservations are valid and important but should not be taken to diminish the value of corpus-based historical linguistics (he is, after all, one of the most well-known historical corpus linguists): rather, they should be considered as warnings of possible pitfalls which need to be taken on board by scholars, since they are surmountable with the use of appropriate care.

11. CORPORA IN DIALECTOLOGY AND VARIATION STUDIES

We have already seen the use of corpora to compare varieties in the sense of genres and channels. In this section we shall be concerned with geographical variation. Corpora have long been recognised as a valuable source for comparison between language varieties as well as for the description of those varieties themselves, since they are defined as constituting maximally representative samples of the respective language varieties. Indeed, certain corpora have even tried to follow as far as possible the same sampling procedures as other corpora in order to maximise the degree of comparability. Thus the LOB corpus contains broadly the same genres and sample sizes as the Brown corpus and is sampled from the same year, i.e. 1961. The Kolhapur Indian corpus is also broadly parallel to Brown and LOB, although in this case the sampling year was 1978 rather than 1961.

One of the earliest pieces of work with the LOB and Brown corpora was the production of a word frequency comparison of American and British written English, showing the several differences which exist between those two national varieties. In the years following this work, the corpora have been used as the basis for the comparison of more complex aspects of language such as the use of the subjunctive (Johansson and Norheim 1988). The increase in the number of corpora of national varieties of English has since led to further comparative studies between, for instance, Australian and New Zealand English (Bauer 1993). The forthcoming completion of the International Corpus of English (ICE), which in fact is a collection of many 1,000,000-word corpora of English from countries where English is a first or major language, will provide an even further range and motivation for comparative studies.

One of the roles for corpora in national variation studies has been as a testbed for two theories of language variation: Quirk *et al.*'s (1985) 'common core' hypothesis – namely that all varieties of English have central fundamental properties in common which differ quantitatively rather than qualitatively – and Braj Kachru's conception of national varieties as forming many unique 'Englishes' which differ in important ways from one another. To date, most work on lexis and grammar in the Kolhapur Indian corpus, studied in direct comparison with Brown and LOB, has appeared to provide support for the common core hypothesis (Leitner 1991). However, there is still considerable scope for the extension of such work and the availability of the ICE subcorpora should provide a wider range of data to test these hypotheses.

Compared to 'national variety', 'dialect' is a notoriously tricky term in linguistics, since dialects cannot readily be distinguished from languages on solely empirical grounds. However, the term 'dialect' is most commonly used of sub-national linguistic variation which is geographically motivated. Hence

Australian English might not be considered expressly to be a dialect of English, whereas Scottish English, given that Scotland is a part of the United Kingdom, might well be so regarded; a smaller subset of Scottish English – for example, the English spoken in the Lowlands – would almost certainly be termed a 'dialect'. Taking 'dialect' to be defined in this way, it is the case that rather few dialect corpora exist at the present time. However, two examples are the Helsinki corpus of English dialects and John Kirk's Northern Ireland Transcribed Corpus of Speech (NITCS). These corpora both consist of spontaneous conversations with a fieldworker: in Kirk's corpus, as the name suggests, from Northern Ireland, and in the Helsinki corpus from several English regions.

Dialectology is a firmly empirical field of linguistics but has tended to concentrate on elicitation experiments and less controlled sampling rather than using corpora. The disadvantage of this approach is that elicitation experiments tend to concentrate on vocabulary and pronunciation, whereas other aspects of dialects, such as syntax, have been relatively neglected. The collection of stretches of natural spontaneous conversation in a corpus means, however, that these aspects of the language are now more amenable to study. Moreover, because the corpus is sampled so as to be representative, quantitative as well as qualitative conclusions can be drawn from it about the target population as a whole and the corpus can also be compared with corpora of other varieties.

This ability to make comparisons using dialect data has opened up a new avenue of research for dialectologists, namely, the opportunity to examine the degree of similarity and difference of dialects as compared with 'standard' varieties of a language. A particularly good example of the latter type of research is the work carried out by John Kirk on the identity of Scots. Kirk has used corpora of Scots – both dramatic texts and natural conversations – alongside corpora of 'standard' British English such as LOB, London-Lund and *English* dramatic texts – to examine to what extent Scots deviates from 'standard' English on various elements. He has recently also begun to make a three-way comparison with Northern Irish English using his NITCS. In a recent study, Kirk (1993) examined the modal verb *will* in the NITCS, a corpus of Edinburgh speech, a corpus of Scots plays, the Lancaster/IBM Spoken English Corpus and a corpus of English plays. He classified the occurrences of root and epistemic *will* according to whether the following verb was stative or dynamic. The statistics were subjected to a VARBRUL analysis (see Chapter 3, section 4.6) to discover which variables were significant in accounting for variation in the data. Here Kirk found, in accordance with previous studies that he has carried out on other aspects of usage, that regionality is not a significant factor but that text type is a significant factor. Again, then, this appears to support the common core hypothesis for dialects as well as for national Englishes, but it has to be said that the systematic study of dialects at linguistic levels above the word has only recently begun in earnest: we may expect to see more of this type of work as more corpora along the lines of the NITCS are built.

12. CORPORA IN PSYCHOLINGUISTICS

Psycholinguistics is almost by definition a laboratory subject. In order to test hypotheses about how language is processed in the mind, it is necessary to measure correlates of mental processes such as the length of time it takes to position a syntactic boundary in reading, or how eye movements change during reading, or even to look at which parts of the brain itself function at different points in the language understanding process through the use of imaging equipment. However, corpora do have parts to play in psycholinguistics.

One important use for corpora is as a source of data from which materials for laboratory experiments may be developed. For instance, as Schreuder and Kerkman (1987) have pointed out, frequency – that is, the familiarity of words to speakers of a language – is an important consideration in a number of cognitive processes such as word recognition. The psycholinguist should not therefore go blindly into experiments in areas such as this with only intuitive notions of frequency to guide the selection and analysis of materials. Properly sampled corpora are able to provide psycholinguists with more concrete and reliable information about frequency, including, as more annotated corpora become available, the frequencies of different senses and parts of speech of ambiguous words. Basic word frequency data from the Brown and London-Lund corpora, accompanied by specific psycholinguistic data from other sources, are already being marketed directly at psycholinguists by Oxford University Press in the form of a lexical database, *The Oxford Psycholinguistic Database* (see Wilson 1992).

An example of a more direct role for a corpus in psycholinguistics is Garnham *et al.*'s (1981) study, which used the London-Lund spoken corpus to look at the occurrence of speech errors in natural conversational English. Before this study was carried out, nobody quite knew how frequent speech errors were in everyday language for the simple reason that such an analysis required adequate stretches of natural conversation and previous work on speech errors had been based upon the gradual *ad hoc* accumulation of data from many different sources. The spoken corpus, however, was able to provide exactly the kind of data which was required. Although, given that the London-Lund corpus cannot be obtained in the form of original sound recordings, it was not possible to state with certainty that every single speech error in the corpus had been accounted for, Garnham's study was able for the first time to classify and count the frequencies of different error types and hence provide some estimate of the general frequency of these in relation to speakers' overall output. This was a contribution to the study of language processing which could not have been achieved without a corpus of natural spoken language.

Another role for corpora lies in the analysis of language pathologies, where an accurate picture of the abnormal data must be constructed before it is possible adequately to hypothesise and test what may be wrong with the human language processing system, and in the analysis of language development. Although little such work has been done with rigorously sampled corpora to date, it is important to stress their *potential* for these analyses. Studies of the language of linguistically impaired people, and also analyses of the language of children who are developing their (normal) linguistic skills, lack the quantified representative descriptions which are available, or at least are becoming available, for normal adult language. There has certainly during the last decade been a move towards the empirical analysis of machine-readable data in these areas: at Reading University, for example, a corpus of impaired and normal language development has been collected; the Polytechnic of Wales (POW) corpus is a corpus of children's language; and the CHILDES database contains a large amount of normal and impaired child language data in several different languages. However, only a few of these data collections are properly sampled corpora in the sense of LOB or the BNC. Nevertheless, the interest in computer-aided analysis in these fields must mean that it will only be a matter of time before corpus collection in these areas becomes more statistically rigorous.

13. CORPORA AND CULTURAL STUDIES

It is perhaps now a commonplace in linguistics that texts contain the traces of the social conditions of their production. But it is only recently that the role of a corpus in telling us about culture has really begun to be explored. After the completion of the LOB corpus of British English, one of the earliest pieces of work to be carried out was a comparison of its vocabulary with that of the earlier 'parallel' American Brown corpus (Hofland and Johansson 1982). This revealed interesting differences which went beyond the purely linguistic ones such as spelling (e.g. *colour/color*) or morphology (e.g. *got/gotten*). Recently, Roger Fallon, in association with Geoffrey Leech, has picked up on the potential of corpora in the study of culture. Leech and Fallon (1992) used as their initial data the results of the earlier British and American frequency comparisons, along with the KWIC concordances to the two corpora to check up on the senses in which words were being used. They then grouped those differences which were found to be statistically significant into fifteen broad domain categories. The frequencies of concepts within these categories in the British and American corpora revealed findings which were suggestive not primarily of linguistic differences between the two countries but of cultural differences. For example, travel words proved to be more frequent in American English than in British English, perhaps suggestive of the larger size of the United States. Words in the domains of crime and the military were also more common in the American data and, in the crime category, 'violent' crime was more strongly represented in American English than in British English, perhaps suggestive of the American 'gun culture'. In general, the findings from the two corpora seemed to suggest a picture of American culture at the time of the two corpora (1961) that was more macho and dynamic than British culture. Although such work is still in its infancy and requires methodological refinement, it seems a interesting and promising line which, pedagogically, could also integrate more closely work in language learning with that in national cultural studies.

14. CORPORA AND SOCIAL PSYCHOLOGY

Although linguists have been the main users of corpora, we should observe that they have not been the sole users. Researchers in other fields which make use of language data have also in recent years taken an interest in the exploitation of corpus data. Perhaps the most important of these have been social psychologists.

Social psychologists are in a curious position. Unlike their colleagues in many other branches of psychology which rely on careful measurements carried out in laboratory conditions, they require access to *naturalistic* data which cannot be reproduced adequately in the laboratory owing to their spontaneous and context-governed nature. At the same time, however, they are also under pressure to quantify and test their theories rather than to rely solely upon qualitative data (although the latter do play a major part).

One area of research within social psychology is that of how and why people attempt to explain things. Explanations, or *attributions* as they are often called in social psychology, are important to the psychologist because they are revealing about the ways in which people regard their environment. To obtain data for studying explanations researchers have relied upon various sources of naturally produced texts such as newspapers, diaries, company reports, and so on. However, these have tended to be written texts: spoken data are reported to have been used less frequently, although most everyday human interaction takes place through the medium of speech.

Antaki and Naji (1987) hit upon the idea of using a spoken corpus – specifically the London-Lund corpus – as a source of data for explanations in everyday conversation. They took 200,000 words of conversation from the corpus and retrieved all instances of the commonest causal conjunction *because* (and its variant *cos*). An analysis of a pilot sample was used to arrive at a classification scheme for the data. The scheme was then used to classify all the explanations which had been retrieved from the corpus according to what was being explained – for example 'actions of speaker or speaker's group', 'general states of affairs', and so on. A frequency analysis of the explanation types in the corpus showed that explanations of general states of affairs were the most common type of explanation (33.8%), followed by actions of speaker and speaker's group (28.8%) and actions of others (17.7%). Previous theory in this field had suggested that the prototypical type of explanation is the explanation of a person's single action. However, Antaki and Naji's findings appear to refute this notion. Although the data do not include all the causal statements in the corpus (for example, those introduced by *since*) and the London-Lund corpus is made up of conversations taken from a largely restricted social group (primarily middle-class academics), work such as Antaki and Naji's shows clearly the potential of corpora to test and modify theory in subjects which require naturalistic quantifiable language data, and one may expect more social psychologists to make use of corpora in the future.

15. CHAPTER SUMMARY

Corpora have a number of features which make them important as sources of data for empirical linguistic research. We have seen a number of these exemplified in this chapter in several areas of language study in which corpora have been, and may be, used. In summary, however, the main important advantages of corpora are:

1. *Sampling and quantification* Because the corpus is sampled to be maximally representative of the population, findings on that sample may be generalised to the larger population. Hence quantification in corpus linguistics is more meaningful than quantification in other forms of empirical linguistics, because it can be assumed to tell us about a variety or a language, rather than just the sample which is being analysed.

2. *Ease of access* Using a corpus means that it is not necessary to go through a process of data collection: all the issues of sampling, collection and encoding have been dealt with by someone else. The majority of corpora are also readily available, often either free or at a low cost price to cover media and person time in handling distribution. But not only are the corpora themselves easy to obtain: once the corpus has been obtained, it is also easy to access the data within it. Because the corpus is in machine readable form, a concordance program can quickly extract frequency lists and indices of various words or other items within it.

3. *Enriched data* Many corpora are now available already enriched with additional interpretive linguistic information such as part-of-speech annotation, grammatical parsing, and prosodic transcription. Hence data retrieval from the corpus can be easier and more specific than with unannotated data.

4. *Naturalistic data* Not all corpus data are wholly unmonitored in the sense that the people producing the spoken or written texts included in the corpus are unaware until after the fact that they are being asked to participate in the building of a linguistic corpus. But, even with spoken data where surreptitious recording is no longer legally permitted, at least in the UK, the data are largely naturalistic, unmonitored and the product of real social contexts. Thus the corpus provides the most reliable source of data on language as it is actually used.

16. STUDY QUESTIONS

1. Carry out a literature search – perhaps using Altenberg's bibliography – on an area or topic in English linguistics which interests you. Try to look at as many of the studies you have found as you are able. Make a critical assessment of the differences that corpus analysis has made (if any) to our understanding of the area or topic you have chosen. How important has the use of corpus data been in that area?

2. As we have seen, open-ended monitor corpora have an important role in lexicography in that they enable researchers to keep abreast of new words and changes in the usage of existing words. Think about the kinds of issue which are important in some of the other areas of linguistics which we have looked at in this chapter. Do monitor corpora have any potential advantages over finite sampled corpora in other areas of language study?

3. In the discussions of sociolinguistics (section 7) and historical linguistics (section 10) we saw notes of caution by Holmes and Rissanen about the use of corpus data in specific circumstances. Thinking in a broader perspective, what dangers do you think are involved in corpus-based linguistics? How can these dangers be reduced?

4. What has the empirical analysis of corpora contributed to linguistic *theory*, and what does it have the potential to contribute?

17. FURTHER READING

There is a huge amount of research literature which has made use of corpus data. For English corpus research, there is an extremely valuable bibliography collated by Bengt Altenberg. This was published in Johansson and Stenström (1991) and is also available electronically from the ICAME file server (gopher: nora.hd.uib.no). More recent unpublished updates are also to be found on the ICAME server. Although not totally exhaustive, this bibliography contains the vast majority of published work using English language corpora.

For a more detailed overview of corpus-based projects than it has been possible to provide in this chapter, the student is recommended to look in the various specialist collections of papers. The festschrifts for Jan Svartvik (Aijmer and Altenberg 1991) and Jan Aarts (Oostdijk and de Haan 1994b) contain papers across a broad range of fields, whilst the books of proceedings from annual ICAME conferences (Aarts and Meijs 1984, 1986, 1990; Johansson and Stenström 1991; Leitner 1992; Johansson 1982; Meijs 1987; Kytö, Ihalainen and Rissanen 1988; Souter and Atwell 1993; Aarts, de Haan and Oostdijk 1993; Fries, Tottie and Schneider 1994) provide a diachronic as well as a broad perspective of corpus-based research. For corpus-based historical linguistics see two recent specialist collections of papers: Kytö, Rissanen and Wright (1994); and Rissanen, Kytö and Palander-Collin (1993). Papers, reviews and information are also to be found in the annual *ICAME Journal* (formerly *ICAME News*).

Foreign language corpus research is harder to track down, since it lacks the central organisation which English language research has. Students are advised to search keywords (e.g. *corpus/Korpus*) or citations of basic corpus linguistic texts in the standard linguistic bibliographies.

NOTES

1. It should be noted, however, that spoken corpus data are not always purely naturalistic. Naturalism is easier to achieve with pre-recorded material such as television and radio broadcasts. With spontaneous conversation, however, there are ethical and legal considerations which prevent the use of surreptitious recording without prior consent.
2. Taylor, Grover and Briscoe also show how Sampson's argument about generative grammars is tied to the way he has chosen to analyse his data. However, these details are too complex to consider here.
3. Frequencies, slightly simplified, from Schmied (1993).
4. Frequencies, slightly simplified, from Pannek (1988).

5

Corpora and computational linguistics

1. INTRODUCTION

Computational linguistics has undergone quite dramatic changes over the past decade. From being a discipline seeking to produce cognitively plausible systems by introspection, new, and alternative, goals have been added; such as the creation of working systems based on empirical data which sacrifice some or all cognitive plausibility for improved performance.

It must be emphasised from the start that this chapter is not a detailed introduction to corpus-based natural language processing (NLP). To fully appreciate the use of corpora in NLP, you would require a good grounding in information theory and statistics, which is well beyond the scope of this chapter. The chapter does not even attempt to comprehensively review all of the subareas of NLP in which corpora are deemed to be relevant. Even where a subarea of NLP is reviewed, the review does not pretend to be comprehensive. This chapter could never be a detailed comprehensive overview of the use of corpora in computational linguistics.

So what does this chapter seek to achieve? The aim of this chapter is to provide a *general* overview of the use of corpora in NLP, and to give the reader a *general* understanding of how they have been used and where. This chapter is either a brief excursion for the linguist who is not primarily interested in NLP, or a starting point for the linguist interested in corpus-based NLP. In the opinion of the authors it most certainly should not be the end of the road for either type of reader.

Several areas of computational linguistics are considered here, and the impact of corpora upon them assessed. These areas, split into sections of the chapter, are: part-of-speech analysis, automated lexicography, parsing and machine translation. Each section considers how the various techniques employed by specific systems exploit corpora to achieve some goal. But before starting to look at the use of corpora in NLP, it seems worthwhile to consider what, in general, corpora can provide for the computational linguist.

2. WHAT HAVE CORPORA GOT TO OFFER?

Throughout this chapter we will be making frequent reference to a basic distinction that is becoming apparent in computational linguistics and artificial intelligence, that of cognitively plausible and cognitively implausible systems. Cognitively plausible systems seek to take a model of cognition, thought to be relevant to how humans carry out some task which has intelligence ascribed to it, and to use it as a basis for making a machine carry out that same intelligent task. Such systems often make use of complex sets of rules to express implicit knowledge explicitly, in the form of a **knowledge base**. Systems which eschew cognitive plausibility simply seek to model an intelligent behaviour without making any claims about whether or not the system is operating in the same way as humans do. Such systems often make use of raw quantitative data to generate some statistical model of a behaviour to be mimicked, achieving the same behaviour as a human, but via a clearly different route. This distinction between cognitive plausibility/implausibility is very much a broad-brush one at present, and will be refined shortly. In its current form, however, it does allow a general statement to be made about the attraction of corpora for some computational linguists.

Corpora can, naturally, contribute equally to the development of cognitively plausible systems as well as to those systems less interested in claims of cognitive plausibility. But it is in the later case, especially where accurate quantitative data are required, that the corpus becomes, by degrees, essential. Quantitative approaches to the solution of problems in artificial intelligence have long had a difficult hurdle to leap, so clearly expressed by McCarthy: 'Where do all the numbers come from?' The answer for NLP is at least now clear – a corpus. As has already been stated in Chapter 1 of this book, humans are poor sources of quantitative data, whereas the corpus is an unparalleled repository of such information. So a good, indeed a balanced, picture of the impact of corpora on computational linguistics is this: corpora may be used to aid in the construction of systems which are interested in claims of cognitive plausibility – but where cognitive plausibility is sacrificed to brute force mathematical modelling, corpora are the *sine qua non* of such an approach. Corpora provide the necessary raw data for approaches to computational linguistics based upon abstract numerical modelling.

It must not be assumed, however, that any system employing statistical modelling is automatically one which eschews cognitive plausibility. We must now refine the broad, polarised description of corpus-based computational linguistics presented thus far. The sacrifice is almost inevitably a matter of degree rather than an absolute. There are actually very few systems in existence which sacrifice cognitive plausibility *entirely* in favour of, say, a statistical approach. It is far more common for corpus-based quantitative data to be employed as a subpart of a more traditional NLP system based on established methods in artificial intelligence. The task that this data is often most used for

is *disambiguation*.[1] In section 3.1 on part-of-speech taggers
point in much more detail. Suffice to say, for the moment
ourselves with the observation that corpus-based NLP syster.
utterly abandoned standard, pre-corpus, models in computatio
are very few and far between. This chapter actually presents
skewed view, in that quite a few systems of this sort are reviewed.   .eader
must bear in mind, however, that these systems have been singled out for
presentation here exactly because they are so rare and so radical. As a proportion of all of the systems in computational linguistics currently which use
some stochastic process, they are actually few in number. Most often the
corpus and data derived from it are used to enhance the effectiveness of fairly
traditional AI (artificial intelligence) systems. The main point is worth reiter-
ating: *any sacrifice of cognitive plausibility is most often one of degree, and rarely an
absolute.*

With this stated we can now begin to consider some specific examples of
the use of corpora in computational linguistics. In doing this, we present
systems which sacrifice cognitive plausibility in favour of effectiveness to various degrees. We also consider, however, how corpora have an impact upon
traditional rule-based computational linguistics.

3. PART-OF-SPEECH ANALYSIS

Assigning parts of speech[2] is a common first step in the automated analysis of
a text, and is also a task which the corpus linguist may want to undertake in
order to aid in the analysis of a text. It is fortunate, then, that part-of-speech
information is unique at present as being a useful form of annotation which
can be introduced into texts with a high degree of automation (Garside and
McEnery 1993; Cutting *et al.* 1992; Brill 1992).

The task of part-of-speech assignment consists of assigning a word to its
appropriate word class. In the systems developed to date,[3] the traditional basic
part-of-speech distinctions, such as adjective, verb, noun, adverb and so on,
have been supplemented with further relevant information, such as person
and number. The size of the categorisation system differs from system to
system, though methodologically the systems share some gross affinities, the
most notable of which are among the empirical, corpus-based (probabilistic)
systems.[4] We will examine in more detail shortly the basic methodology
behind such systems as those of Jelinek (1985), Church (1988), Black *et al.*
(1993), Déroualt and Merialdo (1986), El-Béze (1993) and Sanchez-Leon and
Nieto-Serrano (1995). For the moment, it is sufficient to say that all of these
systems share a broadly similar methodology, and that this methodology not
merely uses, but depends on the corpus.

This final point is an interesting one. The creation by hand of appropriately
annotated corpora can be seen as the raw 'fuel' for some quantitatively based
approaches to automated language processing. Again and again throughout

s chapter, we will be examining techniques which require annotated text corpora, sometimes of a very large size, in order to be able to go on to automatically generate annotated corpora. There is *no* chicken and egg relation here – before one develops large NLP systems to annotate corpora, it seems, at least on current evidence, that one requires a large text corpus, preferably annotated in the form you would like to be able to create, in the first place.[5] So the corpus, unlike the chicken or the egg, definitely comes first! A classic example of this is given in Garside *et al.* (1987) where the Brown corpus, created by the primitive TAGGIT program of Greene and Rubin (1971) and corrected by hand, was used as the raw data for an empirical part-of-speech tagger, CLAWS, which went on to out-perform the TAGGIT program using techniques predicated on the system having access to large bodies of reliable, empirically derived quantitative data, provided in the first instance by the Brown corpus. Other examples are returned to in later sections. But an important general principle to bear in mind in each section is that corpora are necessary for some modern approaches to natural language processing.

3.1. How are corpora used in part-of-speech tagging?

3.1.1. How a tagger works
Before we can begin to examine exactly how corpora are used in part-of-speech tagging, it seems useful to describe how part-of-speech taggers work. As noted in the previous section there are gross affinities between the various systems developed to date. On the basis of these affinities it is possible to posit a general process for the automated part-of-speech tagging of natural language texts (Figure 5.1).

It is possible now to say that the most important stage at which data derived from the corpus intervenes is at the stage of disambiguation. But before explaining how, let us briefly consider the other stages and consider whether the corpus may have a role to play elsewhere in this schema.

3.1.2. Lexicon
The system first tries to see if each word is present in a machine readable lexicon it has available. These lexicons are typically of the form <word> <part-of-speech 1, ... part-of-speech *n*>. If the word is present in the lexicon, then the system assigns to the word the full list of parts of speech it may be associated with. For example, let us say that the system finds the word *dog*. Checking its lexicon, it discovers that the word *dog* is present, and that *dog* may be a singular common noun or a verb. Consequently it notes that the word *dog* may have one of these two parts of speech. With this task achieved the lexicon moves on to considering the next word.

Annotated corpora can be of use to this stage of processing. They can, as noted later in this chapter in section 4 on lexicography, be used as a resource

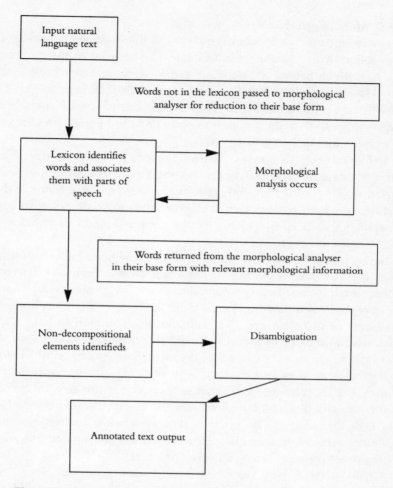

Figure 5.1 A schematic design for a part-of-speech tagger

for building lexicons such as these swiftly, automatically and reliably. Without corpora, these resources (often running to hundreds of thousands of entries) have to be constructed by hand. We have only to think back to the limitations of the pseudo-technique outlined in Chapter 1 to see what a limitation this may be.

Why do such lexicons often run to hundreds of thousands of words? The number of words in a natural language is very large. Some may even argue that there is philosophically no limit. So the larger the lexicon the better our chance of identifying a word and associating the appropriate parts of speech with it. But what happens when the word in question is not recognised as it inevitably must be at times? It is at this point that the morphological analyser comes into play.

3.1.3. Morphological analysis

Let us assume that the system has now found the word *dogs*. Checking its lexicon, it finds it has no entry for *dogs*. It sends the word to the morphological analyser, which detects an *-s* ending, and sends the message back to the lexicon 'Have found the word *dog* with an *s* ending'. The lexicon checks to see whether it has the word *dog* in its lexicon. It has, so it reads the tags accordingly – *dogs* can be a plural common noun or a third person singular verb. The morphological analysis is at an end.

Before moving on, however, there are several points to consider. First, note that the morphological analysis carried out is not a true morphological analysis, rather it is guesswork based on common word endings. Some of the word endings to which systems such as CLAWS are sensitive do not even constitute morphemes, such as *-ly*, which although it often denotes an adjective is not a true morpheme as such.

Second, note that the morphological unit may be called several times, as it tries to create different words by removing various endings. Let us assume a rather simple-minded morphological analyser and consider as an example the word *boxes*. Presented with this word by the lexicon, the morphological unit may well see that the word ends with a known common ending, *-s*, and send back the message 'Have found the word *boxe* with the ending *s*' for the lexicon only to say that it cannot find the word *boxe*. At this point the morphological analyser may be called upon to try again. Trying the next plausible ending, the morphological analyser sends back the message 'Have found the word *box* with the ending *es*'. At this the lexicon finds the word *box* and proceeds accordingly. The point is that even with smarter morphological analysers, there is often an interplay between the lexicon and morphology in the automated part-of-speech analysis of a text.

Finally, what if the lexicon, interacting with the morphological component, cannot identify the word at all? Usually the system would resort to contextually aided guesswork – what is the most likely part of speech for this word given the surrounding words? For the moment we will assume that the system assumes that the word may have any of the accepted parts of speech, and leave the assignment of a unique part of speech to the disambiguation phase.

3.1.4. Non-decompositional elements

What happens where a part-of-speech does not decompose to the word level, that is, where two or more words together combine to have one syntactic function, the so-called 'syntactic idiom'? Common in this category in English is the multiword preposition (see the section on idiom tags in Chapter 2, section 2.2.3 for examples). In such cases, part-of-speech analysis systems usually have a specialised lexicon to identify such non-decompositional sequences and to assign a special set of tags to the words involved in these complex sequences to denote a part-of-speech relation above the level of the word. Corpora may once again be a useful source of information on such sequences, and may be used as the basis for an empirically derived specialised lexicon to deal with such features.

3.1.5. Disambiguation

After a text has been analysed by the lexicon/morphological processor, and any non-decompositional features have been identified, the task of assigning unique part-of-speech codes to words is far from complete. As we saw in earlier examples, the lexicon and morphological component merely indicate the range of parts-of-speech that may be associated with a word. So, using a previous example, we may know that *dog* may be a noun or verb, but we have no idea of which it is in the current context, hence the need for disambiguation. It is possible to try a rule-based approach to disambiguation using rules created by drawing on a linguist's intuitive knowledge. Indeed it would be possible to base such a set of rules on a corpus, and it would certainly be possible to test such a system on a corpus. But this has not tended to be the use corpora have been put to for disambiguation in part-of-speech tagging. They have, much more frequently, been used to create a matrix of probabilities, showing how likely it is that one part-of-speech could follow another.

The basic idea behind probability matrix based disambiguation is very simple, and immediately demonstrable. Consider the following English sentence fragment: *The dog ate the*. Irrespective of what the actual form of the next word may be, what do you think the part-of-speech of the next word may be? Most readers would guess that a singular or plural common noun may be a distinct possibility, such as *The dog ate the **bone*** or *The dog ate the **bones***. Others may assume an adjective may occur, as in *The dog ate the **juicy** bone*. But not many would assume that a preposition, article or verb would occur next. Some may argue that this is because the readers have access to a grammar of the language which shows what is possible, and what is not possible.

But this would avoid an important point – why is it that native speakers of a language would feel that some answers are more *likely* than others? Halliday (1991) has argued human grammar is essentially a probabilistic grammar. This supports an observation that is very important about language, and which was noted by Claude Shannon (1949) earlier this century. When we utter words, they are not mutually independent[6] in terms of probability. Rather, uttering one word (or class of words) directly influences the likelihood of another word (or class of words) following it. Words are produced not as isolated random events, but as part of a coherent *structure*. This structure is provided by many features, included amongst which is grammar, and it is precisely structure which is required for a stochastic process such as a *transition matrix* to operate effectively. The existence of structure in language means that words are linked by dependent probabilities.[7] Part-of-speech taggers such as CLAWS try to use the fact that the structure of language means that words are not mutually independent of one another to disambiguate ambiguous part-of-speech assignments.

Let us return to our example. Given the sentence *The dog ate the bone*, our system might have been able to assign unique part-of-speech tags to all of the words bar *dog*. Here the system would be unsure whether *dog*, in this context, was a noun or a verb. At this point it would consult a probability matrix to decide whether it was more likely that a noun or a verb would be preceded by a definite article and be followed by a verb. On this basis, the system would decide that it was more likely that the word *dog* was a noun rather than a verb. It is in the construction of this matrix of probabilities that the corpus could be most useful. Human beings are relatively poor at assigning a priori probabilities to part-of-speech sequences, or any other language sequences for that matter. However, if we have access to a large, part-of-speech annotated corpus, these probabilities may be reliably and automatically determined. As noted previously, this is exactly the approach described by Garside, Leech and Sampson (1987). Their CLAWS system used a system of probabilistic disambiguation based on probabilities derived from the previously constructed Brown corpus.

To return briefly to a point made previously in the section on morphological analysis, it is also by the use of such a matrix that words unknown to a system are assigned a tag by it. They are assigned the tag that is *most likely* given the known surrounding context. Stochastic processes of this sort allow for probabilistic decision making – possibly better described as informed guesswork!

3.1.6. Is disambiguation of parts-of-speech an example of radical statistical NLP?
The answer to this is both yes and no. The system outlined uses some statistics, transition probabilities derived from large corpora, to determine the relative likelihood of *n* sequences. But note that if the disambiguation procedure was carried out by rules derived from an expert, then the system would indeed have the aspect of a rather traditional piece of AI software, based on various knowledge bases and rule bases. The quantitative data derived from the corpus is merely used during the phase of disambiguation. Such a use of corpus induced probabilities is not the radical paradigm shift that some have suggested. Indeed, as shown, the basic framework of the system is almost indistinguishable from systems which might use no probabilities. So although probabilistic disambiguation is an example of the use of corpus-based quantitative data in NLP, it is true to say that disambiguation remains the predominant use of quantitative data in NLP. As will be demonstrated shortly, probabilistic parsing systems, probabilistic machine translation systems and lexicography based on quantitative data all too often only exploit quantitative corpus data for some process of disambiguation.

As stated, there are exceptions to this general rule, but they are so few as to merely accentuate the strength of this generalisation. But as each section will try to present one or two, it is time to consider what radical use of corpora have been made in part-of-speech assignment systems.

In part-of-speech tagging, one notable exception to the run of the mill probabilistic disambiguation systems comes to mind. Brill and Marcus (1992) used a corpus not merely as a source of data for a disambiguation matrix, but as the source of their **tagset**.[8] Usually the set of part-of-speech distinctions recognised in a corpus is pre-set by a linguist, who uses intuition/expert knowledge to draw up a credible set of part-of-speech distinctions. Brill and Marcus used a clustering algorithm[9] to determine how many empirically distinguishable part-of-speech functions there were in a corpus. In other words, Brill and Marcus used quantitative data derived from a corpus as not merely the basis of, but also the justification for, their tagset. Admittedly, human experts imposed an interpretation on the data produced by their analysis, but this is an interesting and rare example of corpus-based quantitative data used for something other than straightforward disambiguation[10] in part-of-speech assignment.

3.1.7. So what?

Although we are casting doubt in this chapter on whether computational linguistics is moving towards some model of language which would be based more on statistics and information theory than on linguistics, it is true to say that, in spite of what may perhaps be described as the conservative use of corpus-based quantitative data for language modelling to date, the results have been impressive. Comparing the success of Greene and Rubin's TAGGIT program with that of CLAWS allows us to see that a probabilistic approach to tagging may be seen as the sole source of an improvement of some 19 per cent in tagging accuracy.

The architecture outlined for automated part-of-speech analysis can exploit corpora in several ways, and the corpus can be the source of many useful resources, such as the lexicon. But it is no exaggeration to say that the corpus is a key resource in the development of the probability matrix that seems to be of such use to modern automated part-of-speech assignment. Although modern techniques have somewhat alleviated the need for large starting corpora, and taggers such as those developed by Cutting et al. (1992) can even train on unannotated sections of text, it is exposure to raw data in a corpus and some training, either from humans or from learning algorithms, that is important to this particular technology. Cutting et al. cite a success rate which is comparable to that achieved by the leading English language part-of-speech tagger, CLAWS (Garside 1987). The Cutting tagger employs similar probabilistic techniques to CLAWS. However, as noted, it also claims to do something which CLAWS does not, namely, construct its lexicon and trained probabilistic model directly from an automatically analysed corpus, rather than from a manually corrected corpus and a manually constructed lexicon. This suggests that the tagger is adaptable for use on any language without the need for initial resource construction by human researchers. A language-independent tagger requiring the minimal amount of manual preparatory work would clearly be a desideratum for multilingual NLP, and the suitability of the Cutting tagger for this work is currently being assessed in several projects in Europe.

Automated part-of-speech taggers are amongst the very best NLP applications in use today, in terms of reliability and hence usefulness. Before leaving our discussion of them, let us consider the benefits that accurate automated part-of-speech tagging bring.

3.2 Error rate and processing

Part-of-speech information, as mentioned previously, can now be introduced into corpora with a high degree of automation. Table 5.1 shows typical error rates for automated part-of-speech taggers. With such a high degree of accuracy attainable without human correction, some corpus building projects are now providing corpora which are wholly automatically annotated with parts of speech. The advantage of this is that processing time and expense can be greatly reduced because human intervention, which is slow and expensive, is no longer required. The corollary of this, however, is that any corpus produced by such a method will have a degree of error associated with it, as Table 5.1 clearly shows.

The British National Corpus (Leech, Garside and Bryant 1994) is one such project that has built a corpus using this technique. Leech *et al.* built a monolingual part-of-speech annotated corpus of 100,000,000 words over a three year time span. The corpus has a 2–3 per cent degree of part-of-speech classification error associated with it. Another corpus developed with automated part-of-speech analysis was the ITU corpus.[11] Here a parallel aligned English–French corpus was developed with a 2–3 per cent error rate associated with the part-of-speech tagging of each language.

So it is clear to see that part-of-speech taggers, based on quantitative data derived from corpora, exist and are being employed gainfully in corpus creation projects world-wide. Based upon modest resources initially, these taggers have become a marvellous source of linguistic information, and are capable of near automated creation of part-of-speech annotated corpora.

Reference	Error rate (%)
De Rose 1991	4
Cutting *et. al.* 1992	4
Greene and Rubin 1971	23
Garside 1987	4
Brill 1992	5

Table 5.1 Automatic part-of-speech tagging error rates by system

4. AUTOMATED LEXICOGRAPHY

In this section we will look at the corpus-based construction of:

1. lexicons for part-of-speech taggers;

2. monolingual lexicons

3. multilingual lexicons

4. term banks.

Following a brief overview of these topics a concluding paragraph considers the impact of corpora on lexicography to date and in the future.

It is worthwhile considering a question before we continue, though: why bother to look in a corpus for lexical information that is available to a trained lexicographer via intuition? Needless to say, the entire discussion undertaken in Chapter 1 addresses this point, and readers may well care to bear in mind this detailed rationale for corpus-based linguistics when considering the reasons why resources developed from corpora are becoming increasingly common. To explain the need for corpus-based lexicography in a nut shell, all corpus-based approaches to lexicography seek to exploit the corpus as a source of information on language that is representative of language, or of a particular genre of language, as a whole, in a way that is economical and reliable.

4.1. Automating lexicon production for part-of-speech tagging

Automated lexicon construction is a goal which seems increasingly realistic thanks to corpus-based NLP systems. Garside and McEnery (1993) show how comprehensive English lexicons for use by part-of-speech taggers can be generated automatically from annotated corpora. The development of such lexicons is not only of use to systems such as CLAWS (Garside 1987): such linguistic resources are prerequisites for boot-strapping language models such as the Cutting tagger (Cutting *et al.* 1992). Also, taggers such as the DeRose tagger (DeRose 1991) need the precise word–tag pair frequencies that the Garside and McEnery (1993) technique produces. Hence the generation of these large part-of-speech tagged lexicons can be seen as an important step towards improving the quality of taggers in any language where appropriate corpora exist.

4.2. Automating monolingual lexicon production

Setting aside the practical need for large lexicons if we are to achieve efficient automated part-of-speech annotation, the existence of annotated and un-annotated corpora make the work of the lexicographer somewhat easier, and potentially more effective. The application of statistical techniques to monolingual corpora can be an important step in the process of deriving both quantitative and qualitative information for the lexicographer (see Chapter 4, section 3). A wealth of frequency based information is available almost instantly at the word level, and if the corpus is annotated with part-of-speech information, a similar wealth of material is available at the syntactic level also.

Qualitatively speaking, the use of measures such as co-occurrence statistics (mutual information, for example, as discussed in Chapter 3, section 4.4) allows us to derive certain semantic relations from the corpus. Lafon (1984) has done work such as this on French, Church and Hanks (1989) on English and Calzolari and Bindi (1990) on Italian. Although the precise method is slightly different in each of these cases, the basic idea remains the same – postulate semantic affinities between words by measuring the frequency with which words co-occur in close proximity to one another. If words co-occur in a manner which is so frequent that it cannot be ascribed purely and simply to random collocation, then we may assume that there is some special relationship between those words. Note that we are in the realm of dependent probabilities again!

Let us consider the work of Church *et al.* (1991) briefly considered in Chapter 3. They use mutual information to determine a score which expresses the degree to which two words co-occur. Mutual information is essentially an association ratio; how often does a word co-occur with this word as a proportion of the number of times it occurs in the corpus? If the association is one-to-one,[12] that is, the words always co-occur, then we may assume that there is some special relationship between the words. Church and Hank's measure assigned a score to each word pairing possible in a corpus (i.e. all possible pairs of tokens from the corpus), assigning values below 0 to collocations viewed as random, and values above 0 to collocations viewed as non-random. The further the score below 0, the more likely that a collocation was random. The higher the score above 0, the more likely it was that the collocation was non-random. Their finding was most interesting. Using an association score, two classes of relation were revealed:

1. between pairs of words bringing together, compounds, subparts of set expressions/proper nouns and so on;

2. between pairs of words with strong semantic associations.

These findings are crucial, and are echoed in both the work of Lafon, and Calzolari and Bindi. As such, the point seems fairly language independent in a European context, and allows for the identification of qualitative data in a corpus using quantitative techniques.

4.3. Automating multilingual lexicon production and the construction of termbanks

It is interesting to note that the availability of parallel aligned corpora is making the promise of automated lexicography true in a multilingual as well as a monolingual domain. Using quantitatively based measures it is possible to extract correspondences between languages not only at the word level, but also above the level of the word. Multiword units may be retrieved from a parallel aligned corpus, making multilingual dictionary building an easier task. The corpus can also be scanned for frequent collocations.

With a specialised corpus it is possible to construct terminology databases. Such databases are extremely important in machine translation, since within specialised domains there exists (ideally) a one-to-one unambiguous mapping between a concept and its linguistic representation (the term) which makes translation within that domain an easier task (Pearson and Kenny 1991).

Multilingual term banks are capable of being derived from parallel aligned corpora. As noted by Daille (1995), dynamic and non-dynamic **finite state machines** (FSMs)[13] can be developed to provide automated terminology extraction, including the extraction of multiword equivalences, where a parallel aligned corpus is available.

5. CORPORA AND LEXICOGRAPHY

The impact of corpora upon lexicography has been a beneficial one, it would seem (as already noted in Chapter 4). This perceived benefit is one which can easily be seen if we only care to observe the large number of dictionary publishers investing in corpus technology. Browsing along the shelves of any bookshop will add to this impression, as new corpus-based dictionaries will not be hard to find. Corpora have had an important and lasting effect upon work on monolingual lexicography. Major works such as the COBUILD dictionary have been constructed using corpora, and corpora are now being cited by publishers as though they were the very touchstone of credibility for work in modern lexicography. Yet the impact of corpora on multilingual dictionary production has yet to be seen so demonstrably. This is due in part, of course, to the dearth of parallel corpora in comparison to the number of monolingual corpora and to the special needs these corpora present in terms of retrieval. But as these points are slowly being addressed, it does not take somebody with great powers of prophecy to predict that the changes that have been wrought upon monolingual lexicography will be wrought on multilingual lexicography as soon as parallel corpora become generally available and multilingual retrieval tools more widespread.

6. PARSING

As shown in Chapter 4 (section 4.4), the field of automated parsing is an active one (see the reference to the Nijmegen work) and a lively one (see the references to the Briscoe–Sampson debate). In some senses, some of the prerequisites for a powerful automated parsing system already exist. To substantiate this claim, consider what such a system should be able to do. It should, minimally, be able to:

1. identify the words of a sentence;

2. assign appropriate syntactic descriptions to those words;

3. group those words into higher-order units (typically phrases and clauses) which identify the main syntactic constituents of a sentence;

4. name those constituents accordingly.[14]

It should also be able to do this with a high degree of accuracy, producing plausible parses for any given input sentence, a goal often described as **robustness**.

Considering the advances made in automated part-of-speech recognition, it is quite easy to see that some of these goals have been as good as achieved. The elusive goal, however, remains the identification of structural units above the word level and below or at the sentence level.[15] Indeed, such is the difficulty of this goal that if you are reading this book twenty years from its publication date, the authors would not be in the least surprised if no robust parser for general English has yet been created. The current state of the art is somewhat unimpressive for everyday English. Black *et al.* (1993) provide a brief overview of parsing system testing. The review makes somewhat depressing reading for the ambitious linguist hoping to annotate automatically a corpus with syntactic information above the word level. Satisfactory parses in automated broad-coverage parsing competitions rarely seem to break the 60% barrier, and more commonly languish in the region of 30–40% accuracy. To compare this to the state of the art in part-of-speech tagging, recall that the tagger of Greene and Rubin (TAGGIT) achieved an accuracy rate of 77% in the 1970s. Considering such comparisons, we are tempted to conclude, appropriately we think, that the parsing problem is much more complex than the part-of-speech assignment problem. As a consequence the tools currently available are certainly much more crude than part-of-speech taggers and as a practical tool probably useless for the corpus linguist at present.

So why discuss it in a book such as this? Well, as with other areas of computational linguistics, corpora have been utilised to address the parsing problem, and again seem to provide the promise of superior performance. To assess the impact of corpora in the field, it is useful to describe the different approaches that may be taken to the problem by splitting the field into four broad approaches. These are summarised in Table 5.2.

The two axes which differentiate these approaches – Human vs. No human rule creation, and Quantitative motivation vs. Non-quantitative motivation are easily explained. In systems which use human rule creation, there exists within the system a body of rules, such as phrase structure grammar rules, written in some formal notation. These embody certain syntactic principles and describe what the composition of certain constituents may be. Systems using no human rule creation lack this hand-crafted set of rules. To move to the second distinction, quantitatively motivated systems attempt to use raw quantitative data from a corpus to perform all or a subpart of the task of parsing. Non-quantitatively motivated systems may use a corpus, but quantitative data derived from the corpus is of no necessary interest to such systems. With

	Human Rule Creation	No Human Rule Creation
Quantitatively motivated	Black *et al.* 1993	Magerman 1994, Bod 1993
Non-quantitative motivation	Most traditional AI and computational linguistics	Brill 1992

Table 5.2 A summary of different approaches to corpus-based parsing

this brief explanation of the distinction, it is possible to see why it is useful to quarter the field of parsing system development. In essence, the systems which are quantitatively motivated do not merely exploit corpora as a matter of choice. The corpora are absolutely *necessary* for their operation. Corpora, as noted time and again in this book, are an excellent source of quantitative data, so it is no surprise to see them underpinning a quantitative approach to parsing. Of the non-quantitative approach, we shall see shortly that corpora do have a role to play there also. But it is in the domain of the quantitatively oriented approach to parsing that they reign supreme!

6.1. Traditional grammars

Parsing systems in computational linguistics have most often made use of some linguistic formalism to express syntactic relations. These may be motivated very strongly by theoretical concerns, such as the implementation of parsers based on principles of Government and Binding theory, or may take aspects of syntactic theory, such as phrase structure rules, to encode syntactic relations. Indeed, some AI languages such as PROLOG, have mechanisms which allow the expression of certain aspects of syntactic theory very elegantly. For instance, in PROLOG, the definite clause grammar formalism allows phrase structure grammars to be written in a notation that linguists find familiar and which the machine is able to interpret appropriately.

The variety of systems of this type in existence is so bewilderingly large that it cannot be covered in any real sense here. Suffice to say, these systems are constructed almost exclusively from human created rule sets – large bodies of rules hand-crafted by linguists or system designers, that seek to encode enough human knowledge to construct a credible parser.[16] It will come as no surprise to the reader when it is stated that, except in limited domains, the goal of a robust general English parser by this route seems as distant as when researchers began working towards this goal some three decades ago.

Even if the goal seemed attainable via this route, there is a hideously large problem facing system designers using this route, the so-called 'knowledge acquisition bottle-neck'. This is a common problem in AI – how do we sit down and write a huge set of rules which describe how to perform some task accurately and consistently? The problem seems at best unpalatable, and at worst impossible. We will return to a brief discussion of this topic in section 7 on machine translation later in this chapter. For the moment note that another limitation of this approach is the scale of the task of enumerating a set of rules which would encapsulate a credible grammar of a natural language.

But what of the use of corpora in such systems? Corpora are having an impact in this area, most commonly as training sets for parsers developed by reference to intuition. Some researchers are also trying tentatively to include some corpus-based stochastic modelling within linguistic models of syntactic competence in order to improve the efficiency of parsing systems based on these. An example of this is the work of Fordham and Croker (1994). These researchers sought to use a corpus to parameter set and control aspects of a government and binding parser. Such work appears to be in its infancy, but indicates that a synthesis of probabilistic and cognitively plausible approaches to parsing is an idea that has penetrated the area of computational natural language parsing. As we shall see in section 6.3, some researchers have taken this synthesis further. An important distinction to note however, is that Fordham and Crokers' work is a direct amendment of current linguistic theory, while the work of Black *et al.* (1993) described later is decidedly pre-theoretical. As a consequence, the linguist and especially the psycholinguist may find more attraction in the goal of employing and justifying some stochastic elements in current theories of language, rather than relinquishing the goal of theoretically motivated cognitive plausibility to move to a more pre-theoretic, or even linguistically atheoretic account of language.

6.2. Radical statistical grammars
If traditional AI systems stand at one end of a continuum representing approaches to parsing, then what are described here as radical statistical grammars stand at the opposite extreme. These systems are what were called *linguistically atheoretical accounts* of language in the previous section. They are called that here because they eschew all expert linguistic knowledge expressed as hand-crafted rules – the grammar derived by these systems are most certainly not any which a linguist would recognise, or that anyone would claim had the remotest claim to cognitive plausibility.

Radical statistical grammars seek to use abstract statistical modelling techniques to describe and ascertain the internal structure of language. At no point is any metaknowledge used beyond the annotated corpus, such as a linguist's or system designer's intuitions about the rules of language. The system merely observes large treebanks and on the basis of these observations decides which structures, in terms of word clusterings, are probable in language and which are not. In many ways it is best described as a statistical derivation of syntactic structure.

Magerman's system is an interesting example of this. Magerman (1994) looks at a sentence in a radical way – he assumes that any 'tree' which can fit the sentence is a possible parse of the sentence. There is no pre-selection of trees – Magerman simply generates all right-branching trees that fit a given sentence. He then clips through this forest of parses and uses his corpus-based probabilities in order to determine what is the most likely parse. Magerman's system uses little or no human input – the only implicit input is that language can be analysed as a right-branching tree and annotated corpora are used as a source of quantitative data. Otherwise linguistic input to Magerman's model is nil. Bod (1993) produces similarly radical work, again organising language independent of any hand-crafted linguistic rules.

The work of Magerman and Bod is genuinely radical. It is common to find works which, as this book has noted, merely augment traditional AI systems with some stochastic information and claim that a radical paradigm shift has taken place. An example of this is Charniak (1993), who develops a probabilistic dependency grammar and argues that this constitutes a major paradigm shift. A careful examination of Charniak's work reveals that the major paradigm shift is constituted by the incorporation of statistical elements into a traditional parsing system, not surprisingly at the stage of disambiguation. When we compare this to the radical paradigm shift Magerman or Bod promise, we see that while Charniak's work is, in some ways, novel, it is by no means as powerful a radical paradigm shift as that proposed in the work of Magerman and Bod.

The main point of importance for the corpus linguist is this: if the radical statistical paradigm shift in computational linguistics is to take place, corpora are *required* to enable it. Both Magerman and Bod rely on annotated corpora for training their statistical parsers. Without corpora the a priori probabilities required for a linguistically atheoretical approach to parsing would be difficult to acquire. With this stated, it is now possible to move on and consider the pre-theoretical hybrid approach to parsing mentioned in the previous section.

6.3. A hybrid approach – human rules and corpus statistics

This approach was pioneered by Black *et al.* (1993) at IBM. Here the system uses corpus statistics to choose between a variety of conflicting parses available for a sentence produced by a large hand-crafted grammar. The parses are of a pre-theoretical nature; although they are useful surface parses of a given sentence, the parsing formalisms are not motivated by a particular linguistic theory, and do not produce parses which would conform to all of the needs of, say, Extended Standard theory, or Dependency Grammar theory. But they could provide a useful first step to most forms of theoretically motivated linguistic analysis.

Even so, Black *et al.*'s system had to deal with a classic problem for parsing system designers which has been touched on already in this chapter: ambiguity. One of the recurrent problems for the builders of parsing systems, is that while there seems little or no difficulty in ascribing structures to sentences, there is a certain overproductivity entailed in the operation – in short any given sentence may have many potential parses. Which one do you choose and why? Take the sentence *The dog heard the man in the shed*, for example. Whether we believe the man or the dog to be in the shed is one crucial factor in deciding how this sentence is to be represented. This example is based upon a classic problem – prepositional phrase attachment; in essence, in the absence of further evidence, the attachment seems a fairly arbitrary decision in contexts such as this. But where we have a corpus that is appropriately annotated (a treebank), it may be possible to indicate which rules of attachment are *most likely* to be active in such a syntactic context, by examining the frequency with which these rules were invoked in the corpus in similar contexts. That is precisely what Black *et al.* sought to do. The human created rules were conditioned with empirically derived probabilities extracted from a treebank. For any given situation covered by the human created grammar, it would be possible not only to interrogate the rule base to produce a series of parses that were potentially plausible analyses of the sentence, but also to rate the plausibility of those parses by manipulating probabilities associated with the rules invoked to produce them.

Black trained his grammar on a training corpus, using a learning algorithm called the 'inside outside algorithm'[17] to condition his rule base with probabilities. Black did this on a corpus of computer manuals texts in the first instance, creating a parser for that genre. He then used a test corpus to assess the accuracy of his system. The test corpus was also a treebank, and accuracy was gauged with respect to the decisions made by human analysts.

He found that roughly 1.35 parses per word was the norm for the grammar that he developed. In other words, for a 10-word sentence, the system would have to choose between 13.5 potentially plausible parses on average. Not surprisingly then, the success of Black's system decays as the average length of sentence exposed to the system increases. But even so, the system attained some respectable accuracy scores, with results running from 96% to 94% for computer manual sentences averaging 12 and 15 words respectively. Black's work is interesting as it shows how raw quantitative data and traditional linguists' grammars can be combined to achieve a useful goal – accurate parses of sentences in restricted domains. It also shows again quite clearly the need for appropriately annotated corpora in computational linguistics.

6.4. Non-quantitative corpus-based grammars
Brill (1992) produced an interesting parsing system, though it was a pre-theoretical system once again. It was one which required no hand-crafted grammar rules, but which also avoided the use of statistical learning and decision making. This final class of grammar parallels the work of Magerman and Bod in some respects, in that it is again based solely upon an annotated corpus – no hand-crafted rules are used by the system at all. The grammar is induced

directly from the corpus and no human interven[tion]
needed beyond that encoded in the corpus anno[tation]
what it does with the corpus – it does not use th[e quan-]
titative data. Rather it uses the corpus annota[tion]
which allow it to generate parses for a given se[ntence.]

When the system has derived the grammar [it]
can proceed to analyse new sentences. At this [differ-]
ence between the systems of Brill and Mager[man ...]
system does not use probabilities to decide between conflicting [parses,]
it uses a heuristic called 'rules of bracket permutation'. This allows the syste[m]
to assign a set of default brackets to a sentence, and then to shift the brackets
until the system is happy with the result. In other words, the system assumes a
parse for a sentence in the first instance, and then literally plays around with
the brackets to see whether it can get a parse that better matches the nature of
the sentence, a decision made based upon the system's experience with the
annotated corpus. The system adds, deletes and moves brackets until it judges
that it has found the optimal parse for the sentence.

The minutiae of how Brill's system works are not of great interest to us
here. The main point of interest is that Brill's system not merely has the option
to exploit corpora – rather the entire approach is predicated upon access to
suitable corpora. More specifically, it is predicated upon access to suitably
annotated corpora. Corpora seem once again to be permitting a form of
research in computational linguistics that would otherwise be inconceivable.

So what, in summary, can we say about the impact of corpora upon parsing
systems? If the four-part distinction between parsing systems outlined is credible, then we are forced to the conclusion that most paradigms of research into
computational parsing require corpora, especially annotated corpora, and
without them only traditional broad-coverage parsers of English would be
under construction. Although traditional systems could make use of corpora,
as training data for example, or as a crutch to support the linguistic intuition
of the system designer/linguist, the approach does not *require* corpora. It is
hardly surprising, therefore, to discover that in this field corpora have had relatively little impact. However, beyond the traditional systems, the other three
approaches to parsing have been *enabled* by the creation of suitably annotated
and reliable corpora. There would only be traditional parsers without corpora.
The importance of this observation needs underlining. If we take Black's
(1993: v) observation regarding traditional parsers to be true:

> The programs that do exist … are actually not very good even at estab-
> lishing the event pool for everyday sentences, let alone choosing the
> intended event [the 'intended parse'].

then, if corpora had never been developed for anything else, people may have
had to create them anyway if progress towards the construction of a broad

er of English was to be made. Traditional parsing systems have
show no promise for a long time. Not only were they limited in
accuracy, but they also faced another classic AI problem – scaling up.
it is relatively easy to build an AI system that acts credibly within some
ly constrained subdomain. The problem comes when you try to build any
stem up to operate in the world at large, not in some falsely circumscribed
subdomain. Just as with other AI problems, traditional parsers face a problem
of scale. They may work well in a world in which only 100 grammar rules and
1,000 words are allowed. But wishing to expand the system to deal with an
infinitely generative set of rules and an ever-expanding lexicon creates a
hurdle that all systems seem to fall at. Corpus-based broad-coverage parsing
systems are in the ascendant purely and simply because they seem easier to
create and they produce better results than traditional systems. Corpora have
facilitated positive developments in an area of computational linguistics that
has been unpromising for some time.

7. MACHINE TRANSLATION

Machine translation (MT) systems and research programmes are increasingly
making use of corpora, especially parallel aligned corpora. The appeal of
corpora to machine translation can be appreciated fairly quickly, if we refer
back to the problem of scaling up AI systems as discussed in the last section. If
enormous amounts of world knowledge and formally expressed rules are
needed to achieve effective automated parsing of language, imagine how
much more world knowledge and how many more formal rules are necessary
for translating between languages. The size of the problem has been described
as being prohibitively large. The systems developed for MT need to routinely
build massive resources, yet the technology and techniques for this process do
not yet exist. In the field of MT studies several avenues of escape from this
problem of scale have become apparent over the past decade or so.

The first, and possibly, we may argue, the most painful avenue, is to labori-
ously construct, by hand, the resources needed for these full scale systems.
Some initiatives are underway in this area, including the Cyc project of Lenat
and Guha (1990). This project aims to build a world knowledge encyclopae-
dia which machines would be able to use. Yet to give an idea of exactly how
painful this process may be, Lenat has been working for nigh on a decade and
has yet to put his results in the public domain. Even when the results are
publicly available, it is inevitable, as pointed out by Minsky (1994), that the
result will be a first approximation to the eventual solution by this route. A
satisfactory machine exploitable world knowledge base may be a long, long
way into the future.

Needless to say, some see ways of accelerating this process, and it is at this
point that corpora make their entrance into the field of MT studies. Some have
sought to extract relevant information from text corpora to speed the process

of compiling effective resources for MT systems. Smadja (1991) used text corpora in an attempt to automate the process of knowledge acquisition for MT systems, while McEnery *et al.* (1995) used a bilingual English–French corpus and similarity metrics to extract a series of language-specific cognates for this language pair. Such systems develop resources for existing MT systems by exploiting corpora as sources of, say in the case of McEnery *et al.*; bilingual lexical knowledge. But some researchers have gone further in their application of text corpora to the MT problem, and in doing so have developed new paradigms of machine translation. Of these paradigms, two in particular seem predicated upon the use of corpora, especially of the parallel aligned variety. These approaches are statistical translation and example-based machine translation (EBMT).

7.1. Statistical translation

Statistical translation is very much one of those rare examples of what here has been termed genuinely radical quantitatively based computational linguistics. It is quite unlike, say, probabilistic tagging. The approach does not amend an existing model, patching it up with statistics where necessary. Statistical MT entails the total rejection of existing paradigms of MT, based upon fairly traditional AI, in favour of an approach to MT which totally eschews any goal of cognitive plausibility. As a consequence, we see notions of transfer, interlanguages and rule-based grammars, the common staples of most MT, replaced by an approach to translation based upon complex calculations using co-occurence data and distribution probabilities derived from corpora.[18] There is a telling anecdote from the time that the early work on this approach was undertaken on this at IBM T. J. Watson Research Center. The story is this: the manager in charge of this research noticed that every time he sacked a linguist the system's productivity went up. Although possibly apocryphal, this story exposes the essential idea behind the system and of most radical non-cognitively plausible models in computational linguistics; are models of cognition relevant to human beings the best models on which to base computer models? We shall not seek to discuss this question here. It is simply interesting to note that corpora are fundamental to non-cognitively plausible approaches to computational linguistics as they actively seek to model performance.

With this stated, let us briefly consider one such system. The first approach to MT taken within this paradigm was that of Brown *et al.* (1990, 1993). This work attempted to build upon the success of probabilistic methods in other areas of language processing and apply them to the problem of machine translation. Brown *et al.* implemented a fully probabilistic machine translation system trained on an aligned French–English corpus. This system chose the most probable translation sentence in the target language given a sentence in the source language using two probability models: a translation model based on lexical alignments and word position probabilities, and a language model based on trigram probabilities (i.e. sequences of three words).

Brown *et al.* achieved success rates that seemed impressive, but a key criticism of their work stands; their work dealt only with English and French. Would this method work on languages which differed more, syntactically and lexically? For the moment one can only speculate as to what the answer to this question would be. Future work depends upon the creation of corpora aligning language pairs other than English and French. Such work is underway, and it could be that some time soon there will be an answer to this criticism. For the moment we must keep an open mind. But the fact that we must wait, admirably underscores the point that this approach to MT requires parallel aligned corpora. Corpora are not an option here. They are a necessity.

7.2. (Example-based machine translation) EBMT

The first approach to EBMT was initially proposed by Nagao (1984), and elaborated at the subsentence level by Sadler (1989). Nagao had a basic, yet elegant idea. If we have two corpora, aligned at the sentence level, say in language *A* and language *B*, then if we are asked to translate sentence *x* from language *A*, into some sequence in language *B*, we can consult our corpus to see if we already have sentence *x* in language *A*. If we do indeed have this sentence in our corpus, then we may find its translation, via alignment, in language *B*. We have the translation of *x* without having done anything beyond examining our parallel aligned corpus.

The basic EBMT idea has proved very powerful in computational linguistics.[19] The prospect of relatively painless translation systems has caused a growing amount of work along these lines. Yet the limitations of the basic EBMT idea are obvious. As noted in Chapter 1 the prospect of the corpus being the sole explicandum of language via enumeration is one which is not credible. It therefore stands that any given parallel aligned corpus, no matter how large it is, can only cover a subset of all of the possible required translations between two unconstrained natural languages at the sentence level.[20] Sadler (1989) built upon the basic idea of EBMT and suggested a more elaborate method of exploiting parallel corpora for MT systems. This approach entailed a very large bilingual database being constructed, with each language in the database being parsed using dependency grammar annotations. Resulting units were to be aligned between languages. Translation would be carried out by isolating possible units in the source text, retrieving these units and their 'translation' in the database, and combining the retrieved translation units. The work is still somewhat untested, though the work carried out by Tsujii *et al.* (1991) on machine translation by example is similar in spirit to this work and also requires parallel aligned corpora for its operation.

The important point to note here is that again a hybrid model seems to be developing. EBMT does not reject the intuition of the linguist. Similarly it does not eschew the wealth of information available to us from these fabulous modern Rosetta stones, parallel aligned corpora. EBMT seeks a middle path between the cognitively plausible approach of the rule-based systems and the abstraction of statistical MT. It seeks to avoid the high cost of knowledge-base building and the disappointingly poor results of traditional rule-based systems by using the corpus as a means of both supporting the translation process by direct example-based translation where possible, and as a source of relevant linguistic information where direct example-based translation is not possible. On the other hand it also seeks to avoid the abstract non-linguistic processing of pure statistical MT, in favour of a more cognitively plausible approach to the problem. The important point is that without parallel aligned corpora this approach to MT would simply not be possible. Corpora have once again provided the raw resources for a new and promising approach to a difficult problem in computational linguistics.

To return to the general discussion of MT, it is obvious that corpora have had quite an impact on the field of MT. Even where traditional rule-based MT is being undertaken, it may be the case that the system designers may exploit corpora to clear the knowledge acquisition bottle-neck for their system in certain key areas (e.g. the lexicon). But where EBMT or statistical MT are taking place, the corpus is of paramount importance and is, indeed, a necessity. EBMT and statistical MT, like so many other areas of computational linguistics, have been enabled by the creation of certain kinds of corpora. Without parallel aligned corpora, there would be no EBMT and there would be no statistical MT.

8. CONCLUSION

In general then, what have corpora got to offer to computational linguistics? From what has been reviewed in this chapter it is apparent that corpora have a great deal to offer computational linguistics. Apart from being excellent sources of quantitative data, corpora are also excellent sources of linguistic knowledge, in such systems as EBMT.

Indeed, corpora are essential to some applications in computational linguistics, such as so-called 'probabilistic' part-of-speech annotation systems. Their use in such systems is, however, revealing of the general trend of the use of corpora in computational linguistics. Although in general these systems are highly effective in terms of reliability, they are also generally of the 'disambiguation' variety. As noted in this chapter, 'radical' applications of corpus data in computational linguistics are relatively rare. Some variety of disambiguation seems to be the most commonplace use of corpora in computational linguistics, with few exceptions.

The impact of corpora on computational linguistics is increasingly profound. At the time of writing, there seems no reason to suppose that this trend will not be amplified on an on-going basis. The use of corpora in computational linguistics, especially within hybrid systems where corpus data are used in some process of disambiguation, is burgeoning.

9. STUDY QUESTIONS

1. Using the lexicon listed below, suffix list and tagset given below, try to estimate what analyses a part-of-speech analysis system would assign to the sentence *The dog ate the bone*. Disregard case information (*A* as opposed to *a*) when searching through the lexicon, which is all lower case.

SIMPLIFIED PART-OF-SPEECH TAGSET

A	Article (*the, a, an* etc.) or Possessive Pronoun (*my, your* etc)
C	Conjunction (*and, or, but, if, because*)
D	Determiner (*any, some, this, that, which, whose*)
E	Existential *there*
F	Formulae or Foreign Words
G	Genitive *'s*
I	Preposition (*of, on, under*)
J	Adjective (*fat, young, old*)
M	Number or Fraction (*two, 10's, 40–50, tens, fifth, quarter*)
N	Noun (*cat, cats, book, north*)
P	Pronoun (*he, him, everyone, none*)
R	Adverb (*else, namely, very, how, more, alongside, where, longer*)
T	Infinitive marker (*to*)
U	Interjection (*oh, yes, um*)
V	Verb (*is, was, had, will, throw*)
X	Negator (e.g. *not*)
Z	Letter or letters of the alphabet (*a, bs, c* or *as*)
O	Other (e.g. punctuation)

LEXICON

ARTICLES (A)

the a an

PREPOSITIONS AND CONJUNCTIONS (I OR C)

abaft aboard about above across afore after against albeit along alongside although amid amidst among amongst and anent anti around as aslant astraddle astride at atop bar because before behind below beneath beside besides between betwixt beyond but by circa contra despite down during ere ergo except for forasmuch from how howbeit however if in inasmuch inside insomuch into less lest like minus modulo near neath nor notwithstanding o'er of off on once onto opposite or out outside over pace past pending per plus pro qua re round sans save since so than that therefore though through throughout till to toward towards under underneath unless unlike until unto up upon versus via vis-à-vis when whence whenever whensoever where whereas whereat whereby wherefrom wherein whereinto whereof whereon wheresoever wherethrough whereto whereunto whereupon wherever wherewith wherewithal whether while whilst whither whithersoever why with within without worth yet

DETERMINERS (D)

a all an another any both double each either enough every few half last least less little many more most much neither next no none other several some the twice here that there these this those

NUMBER OR FRACTION (M)

zero one two three four five six seven eight nine ten eleven twelve thirteen fourteen fifteen sixteen seventeen eighteen nineteen twenty thirty forty fifty sixty seventy eighty ninety hundred thousand million billion trillion quadrillion quintillion sextillion septillion octillion nonillion decillion zillion

ORDINALS (M)

(irregular only) first second third fifth eighth ninth twelfth (M)

PRONOUNS (P)

anybody anyone anything 'em everybody everyone everything he he'd he'll he's her hers herself him himself his hisself i i'd i'll i'm i've it it's its itself me mine my myself nobody nothing oneself ours ourselves she she'd she'll she's somebody someone something their theirs them themselves they they'd they'll they're they've 'tis 'twas us we we'd we'll we're we've what what're whatever whatsoever where'd where're which whichever whichsoever who who'd who'll who's who've whoever whom whomever whomso whomsoever whose whoso whosoever yer you you'd you'll you're you've your yours yourself yourselves

ADVERBIALS (R)

anyhow anymore anyplace anyway anyways anywhere e'en e'er else elsewhere erstwhile even ever evermore everyplace everyway everywhere hence henceforth henceforward here hereabout hereabouts hereafter hereby herein hereinabove hereinafter hereinbelow hereof hereon hereto heretofore hereunder hereunto hereupon herewith hither hitherto ne'er never nohow nonetheless noplace not now nowadays noway noways nowhere nowise someday somehow someplace sometime sometimes somewhat somewhere then thence thenceforth thenceforward thenceforwards there thereabout thereabouts thereafter thereat thereby therefor therefore therefrom therein thereinafter thereinto thereof thereon thereto theretofore thereunder thereunto thereupon therewith therewithal thither thitherto thitherward thitherwards thrice thus thusly too

AUXILIARIES (V)

ain't aint am are aren't be been being did didn't do does doesn't don't had hadn't has hasn't have haven't having is isn't was wasn't were weren't can can't cannot could couldn't may mayn't might mightn't must mustn't needn't ought oughtn't shall shan't should shouldn't used usedn't will won't would wouldn't

SUFFIX-MATCHING RULES FOR A SIMPLE PROBABILISTIC TAGGER

Suffix	Rules
–s	Remove –s, then search lexicon
–ed	V J@
–ing(s)	–ing V N J@ ; –ings N
–er(s)	–er N V J ; –ers N V
–ly	R J@
–(a)tion	N
–ment	N
–est	J
–(e)n	J N
–ant	J N
–ive	No rule possible
–(e)th	N M
–ful	J N%
–less	J
–ness	N
–al	J N%
–ance	N
–y	J N
–ity	N
–able	J

DEFAULT

If nothing else works, the word in question may be VERB , NOUN or ADJECTIVE (V, N, J).

2. How would you disambiguate the analysis of the sentence from question (1), using your linguistic knowledge?

3. Using the table and equation below, show how we could disambiguate the part-of-speech analysis of the sentence given in question (1).

SIMPLIFIED TRANSITION MATRIX.

This matrix stores a transition probability, going from one part-of-speech (entries along the side) to another part-of-speech (entries along the top).

	A	C	D	E	F	G	I	J	M	N	P	R	T	U	V	X	Z	O
A	0	0	1	0	0	0	0	29	4	64	0	2	0	0	0	0	0	1
C	14	2	5	2	0	0	9	7	1	19	14	9	1	0	13	1	0	3
D	5	1	3	0	0	0	8	6	2	42	6	3	0	0	16	0	0	7
E	2	0	1	0	0	0	0	0	0	0	0	2	0	0	93	0	0	0
F	0	2	0	0	49	0	2	0	1	7	0	1	0	0	6	0	0	30
G	1	1	1	0	1	0	0	7	1	84	0	1	0	0	0	0	0	2
I	46	0	10	0	0	0	0	6	4	22	4	1	0	0	4	0	0	1
J	0	5	0	0	0	0	5	3	0	72	0	1	4	0	0	0	0	9
M	0	2	1	0	1	0	4	3	2	57	1	2	0	0	2	0	0	26
N	1	6	1	0	0	1	27	0	1	8	1	3	1	0	17	0	0	31
P	1	2	1	0	0	0	4	1	0	1	1	7	2	0	71	0	0	9
R	9	4	3	0	0	0	14	11	1	3	6	11	1	0	21	0	0	16
T	0	0	0	0	0	0	0	0	0	0	0	0	0	99	0	0	0	0
U	1	1	1	0	0	1	1	0	0	1	1	2	0	3	0	0	0	89
V	17	2	3	0	0	0	11	5	1	4	5	16	5	0	18	3	0	10
X	7	1	2	0	0	0	5	4	0	1	6	8	4	0	56	0	0	6
Z	0	4	1	0	2	0	19	2	0	4	0	1	0	0	10	0	0	55
O	9	10	4	0	1	0	5	4	1	10	13	6	0	1	7	0	0	29

EQUATION

For each of the possible tag sequences spanning an ambiguity, a value is generated by calculating the product of the values for successive tag transitions taken from the transition. Imagine we were disambiguating the sequences N followed by a word which is either N or V, followed by a word which is either N or V:

$$N - N - V \ = \ 8 + 17 = 25$$
$$N - N - N \ = \ 8 + 8 \ = 16$$
$$N - V - V \ = 17 + 18 = 35$$
$$N - V - N \ = 17 + 4 \ = 21$$

The probability of a sequence of tags is then determined by dividing the value obtained for the sequence by the number of sequences, e.g., for the this example the most likely answer is the third:

$$= \frac{35}{2} = 17.5\%.$$

If a tag has a rarity marker (@ for 10 per cent rare, % for 100 per cent rare, then divide the percentage from the matrix by either 10 (@) or 100 (%) before inserting it into the equation.

4. Use the resources provided to analyse sentences taken at random from this book. How easy is it to analyse these sentences using the materials provided? Do any shortcomings of the materials provided become apparent?

10. FURTHER READING

A great deal of the work described in this chapter has been published in conferences and journals. As such, picking out easily available key readings is difficult. One text which recommends itself is Black, Garside and Leech 1993, as it covers in detail the shortcomings of various parsing systems, while covering probabilistic part-of-speech tagging, issues in corpus construction and one variety of probabilistic parsing. Another useful book is Zernik 1991, as this contains a variety of papers covering corpus-based approaches to lexicography. Finally, Karlsson *et al.* 1995 is worth reading as it reviews probabilistic part-of-speech taggers, as well as introducing constraint grammars, which have not been covered here.

NOTES

1. Disambiguation: choosing the preferred analysis from a variety of possible analyses. This may occur at many levels, from deciding the meaning, in context, of a polysemous word, through to choosing one possible translation from many.
2. See Chapter 2, section 2.2.3 for a brief overview of part-of-speech annotation. In this chapter we cover this form of annotation in more detail.
3. See Chapter 2 for coverage of this topic from another angle.
4. There is an increasing interest and awareness in the use of constraint grammars for tagging (Voutilainen, Heikkila and Anttila 1992), but at the present the probabilistic, corpus-based, approach is dominant.
5. Actually, it is possible to develop a probabilistic part-of-speech tagger training the system on un-tagged text, using the Baum-Welch algorithm. However, as noted by Sánchez-León and Nieto-Serrano (1995), training on a hand-annotated corpus produces better results.
6. Mutually independent events do not influence the probability of following events, and are not influenced by previous events of the same variety. Tossing a coin is a good example of this. No matter how many heads or tails you happen to produce by tossing a coin, the probability of a head or tail being tossed on each occasion that the act is done is still 50/50.
7. Mutually dependent events are influenced by previous events, and in their turn influence future events. A good example of a system in which dependent probabilities exist is a simple bag of coloured marbles. Imagine we have such a bag, containing five blue and five red marbles. When we reach in to grab the first marble, we have a 50/50 chance of pulling out either a red or blue marble. Assume we happen to pick out a blue marble, and we do not return it to the bag. This event has influenced the probability of the following event. When we reach in for our next marble, there will no longer be a 50/50 chance of picking a red or blue marble. There will now be a 4 in 9 chance of extracting a blue marble, and a 5 in 9 chance of pulling out a red marble. It is now more likely that we will extract a red marble.
8. Tagset: the basic part-of-speech distinctions to be made by a system.
9. In this case based on the distributional similarity of words.
10. See section 6.2 on radical statistical grammars below for further exceptions.
11. Developed as part of the Eurotra programme of the Commission of the European Communities (CEC). The corpus is built from the publications of the International Telecommunications Union (ITU).
12. Note that in using the mutual information measure, one must take account of the frequency of occurrence of items involved in a collocation. Without this, we would be in the position of assuming that two words, which occurred once only but when they did they co-occurred, were as significant as two different words which occurred 1,000 times each and always co-occurred. Cubing elements in the measure can have the effect of disfavouring examples with few occurrences (see Daille 1995).
13. It is usually desired that such systems should be able to analyse plausibly any naturally occurring sentence in a given language; you should be able to input a sentence from a book you are reading, from a letter you are writing or even off the top of your head and get a credible response. But often

parsers are restricted to particular genres in the hope of limiting the scale of the problem faced by system designers.

14. It may be that in the literature you will see sentences described as S-units. This is a more neutral term, reflecting the difficulty of unambiguously defining what is and what is not a sentence.

15. For readers interested in seeing a detailed example of this see Markantonatou and Sadler 1994.

16. Needless to say, the probabilistic element is used for ambiguity resolution.

17. Needless to say, these were parallel aligned corpora. It also goes without saying that as a rule of thumb, the larger they are the better. Though recent research has shown that one can overtrain a statistical model, and actually force the performance of a statistical model to degrade by exposing it to a larger sample (Merialdo 1994).

18. So powerful in fact, that some have sought to apply the methodology to other problems in the field, such as text generation and source language analysis (Jones 1992).

19. Though it is only fair to point out that EBMT as originally envisaged is acknowledged to be most valid in strictly limited domains, where the system is dealing with a restricted subset of language.

6
A case study: sublanguages

In this chapter, we use a variety of corpora to examine the nature of so-called **sublanguages**.[1] In doing so, various tools for corpus manipulation will be introduced and, where appropriate, the corpus annotations used in the study will be described. The aim of this chapter is to demonstrate how corpora may be used to investigate a hypothesis, not necessarily to present new and shocking findings to the world. Although the chapter presents some interesting insights into the nature of restricted languages, the reader should concentrate at least as much on the process of the investigation as its outcome.

It must also be emphasised that a case study like this can only illustrate the potential of corpora in examining language. There is no way in which a case study of this size can ever portray in detail all of the emerging potential uses of corpora in the study of language. The case study presented here limits itself to one language – English – three corpora and limited mathematical analyses. These limitations are enforced in part by the aim of this book – remember that the key goal of this chapter is to present what use corpora can be put to where appropriate tools for their manipulation are available and where the analysis occurs within an academic context where mathematical sophistication may not be expected. We aim not to obscure the basic methodology presented here through reference to a wide variety of genres or language types. That is not to say that the reader, having considered the findings of this chapter, may not wish to carry out the same experiment on a wider sample of texts. This, however, is the reader's decision. Our aim is to illustrate how corpora may be *used* to examine a linguistic hypothesis, other goals, such as generalisability of the findings, have been subordinated to this key goal.

With this note of caution sounded, we may now consider what this chapter presents. Our aim here is to examine a specific hypothesis – that sublanguages are different from unconstrained natural language in several important ways. The chapter will begin with a definition of the term sublanguage (section 1). Following on from this, the corpora to be used in this study will be presented (section 2) and the tools used in annotating and manipulating the corpora described (section 3). Having presented the corpora, we will pause for a moment to consider how generalisable and valid the results that we may draw from this study may be (section 4). This will provide us with a sound foundation for making any claims on the basis of our study. With this groundwork in place, we will then proceed to an investigation of the corpora in question, and examine a series of claims made under the general banner of the sublanguage hypothesis (sections 5, 6, 7 & 8). With our study complete, we can then make a series of claims of our own (section 9), based on the findings of our study, and tempered by any limitations following from section 4 we may place upon our results.[2]

1. FORMULATION OF OUR HYPOTHESIS: SUBLANGUAGES

The case study in this chapter is seeking to explore a sublanguage. So first, what is a sublanguage? It has been hypothesised that certain genres of writing actually represent a constrained subset of a natural language: these are sublanguages – a version of a natural language which does not display all of the creativity of that natural language. One key feature that has been hypothesised for a sublanguage is that it will show a high degree of **closure** at various levels of description. Closure for a particular feature of a variety of language means that that it is tending towards being finite, for example, it is possible to develop a simple list of sentence type rules for the language. Any reader who has followed the arguments concerning the non-finite nature of natural language presented in Chapter 1 should see quite clearly how this sets a sublanguage apart from unconstrained natural language. A key criticism of early corpus linguistics was that it seemed to make this 'closure' assumption about natural language. While this is demonstrably untrue for unconstrained varieties of a natural language, it has been hypothesised that this is not so for sublanguages.

So the type of investigation that this case study will undertake should become apparent at this point. We will be looking for various forms of closure in one corpus, which we will hypothesise represents a sublanguage, and comparing it against two other corpora that we hypothesise are not sublanguage corpora. To prove the sublanguage hypothesis we should see higher closure consistently in the sublanguage corpus, and a tendency away from closure in the unconstrained language corpora.

Second, why should we bother to do this? Is this simply some unsatisfying intellectual exercise developed by the authors to demonstrate, in a rather academic way, how corpora can be manipulated? To answer the questions in reverse order, this is not just an academic exercise, and the result of proving the sublanguage hypothesis is potentially useful. For example, proof of the existence of sublanguages would be of particular help to at least two groups: computational linguists and translators. In the first case, if a computational linguist can deal with a stable, finite subset of language, the task of producing a working natural language processing system is greatly simplified, as noted by McEnery (1992). With small finite lexicons and grammars the task of language understanding may begin to seem manageable in some particular domain associated with the sublanguage. In the second case, if texts requiring translation are in fact sublanguage texts, then the translation task is simplified. Not only are mechanical aids for such a task feasible, but dictionaries and termbanks associated with the sublanguage may also become exhaustive and authoritative.

At this point we should understand what a sublanguage is and be satisfied that seeking to prove the sublanguage hypothesis is a sufficiently interesting task to warrant time being spent on it! But now we come to the obvious third question: why bother trying to prove the sublanguage hypothesis using corpora?

The answer to this must already be at least partly apparent: if a corpus is a finite body of language, and the sublanguage tends towards being finite, it follows that it would be possible, in this case and this case alone, to develop a corpus that was a sole explicandum of a particular variety of language. In short, a corpus should be an exceptionally good tool for identifying and describing a sublanguage, because they both have one important feature in common – a finite nature. Given a large enough corpus of a sublanguage we should see our description of that language beginning to complete itself, whereas for a corresponding corpus of unconstrained language we should see a continuing growth and diversity in such features as sentence types. In short, corpora should give us a very sharp contrast in terms of closure between any supposed sublanguage and any unconstrained language.

Notice that the promise of the study outlined earlier for computational linguists and translators is apparent here: we should be able to see a large scale description of the sublanguage emerging as our study progresses. If the sublanguage hypothesis is correct and if we are looking at a sublanguage corpus, we should be able to see such items as comprehensive lexicons and grammar rules developing for the sublanguage as this study progresses.

It is worth considering for a moment what the study here represents. In it a variety of computing tools will be used to manipulate some millions of words of data in various ways. The study itself took around two weeks to process. This is the *first lesson* of this case study: *without the computer this would not have been practicable*. Millions of words were processed for this study in a variety of ways in a relatively short period of time. Before the advent of the computer, as noted in Chapter 1, such a study would have been to all intents and purposes impossible.

2. CHOOSING THE CORPORA: THE IBM, APHB AND HANSARD CORPORA

We now know what we are interested in studying and have an idea of a set of features to look for, all based on forms of linguistic closure at various levels of description. But before considering what linguistic features we may care to examine, it seems appropriate to introduce the text corpora which will be used for this study.

In processing this study we have used three separate corpora: one suspected sublanguage and two unconstrained language corpora.

The suspected sublanguage is that of a set of IBM manuals. IBM manuals are concerned with a very limited set of subjects, and the authors of such documents are quite tightly restricted to using certain items of vocabulary and set expressions. Hence on the surface they look like an ideal candidate for examining the nature of sublanguages. At Lancaster University there is a 1,000,000-word corpus of IBM manuals texts, developed in collaboration with IBM T. J. Watson Research Center, New York, and it was this corpus that was used for the current study.

Two corpora of unconstrained language were available at Lancaster, again all developed in conjunction with IBM T. J. Watson Research Center. It should be noted that at this point in the study we are assuming that the two corpora which are about to be described are unconstrained. We cannot, at this juncture, assert that they are certainly unconstrained. Although there is strong intuitive evidence to suggest that this must be the case, we shall reserve final judgement until we have examined all three corpora.

The first unconstrained language corpus is the Canadian Hansard corpus. This corpus is composed of just over a million words of transcribed proceedings from the Canadian parliament in the mid-1970s. Although it is thus a corpus of spoken data, the conventions used in transcribing the corpus are such that the text is heavily normalised: pauses, interruptions and false starts, all common in spoken corpora, are absent from this corpus. The Canadian Hansard thus has far more in common with written text corpora than spoken corpora. In terms of constraints placed upon the language, the corpus shows no obvious closure. For example, the topic can shift quite freely, and the lexis, we can assume, is consequently quite unconstrained.

The second unconstrained language corpus that this study uses is the APHB (American Printing House for the Blind) corpus. This is a corpus of fictional texts, and is some 300,000 words in size. There are many a priori reasons for assuming that this should not exhibit the traits of a sublanguage corpus. The corpus is composed of writings by a variety of authors, none of whom colluded to ensure that the corpus had a rigidly defined style and lexis. The stories in the corpus were written for a variety of audiences: samples of horror writing and romantic fiction are included within the corpus. If there are styles peculiar to various forms of fictional writing, then the APHB corpus can only be described as a corpus with a stylistically heterogeneous set of texts. Hardly a good example of a potential sublanguage!

So we have three corpora available. One, the IBM manuals corpus, where there exists a priori evidence to suggest that it may well be a sublanguage, and

Corpus	Size	Accuracy of Annotation	
		Part-of-Speech	**Parsing**
IBM	1,000,000	100%[a]	100%
Hansard	1,000,000	100%	100%
APHB	200,000	100%	100%

Note [a]A figure of 100% means that the corpus annotation has been checked by human grammarians and is assumed to be correct. It must be conceded, however, that human error will mean that a residual, finite degree of error will remain in the corpus. See Baker (1995) for an interesting study of how reliable the correction of corpus annotation can be.

Table 6.1 The annotation of the corpora used in this study

two, the Hansard and APHB corpora, where there exists persuasive intuitive evidence that they are not sublanguages. This contrast, between the potential sublanguage corpus and the potential non-sublanguage corpora, explains the selection of these corpora for the study. But there is one other important factor which commended these corpora over other corpora which are available in the public domain: annotation.

Annotated corpora will prove of particular use to this study, for while it would be possible to study some levels of closure using an unannotated corpus, most notably lexical closure, other levels of closure would have been more difficult; indeed, some would have been impossible given an unannotated corpus. By using corpora which have been annotated to record various forms of linguistic description, we can move our observation from the level of word form to more interesting levels of linguistic description. Again, advances in natural language processing, as well as the development of intensive human-aided editing, allow us here to undertake a study by means which would have been nothing more than a psuedo-technique only fifty years ago.

So annotation exists in all of these corpora – some introduced automatically using state-of-the-art annotation tools, others input by semi-automated means using human-friendly corpus annotation software.[3] Table 6.1 describes, for each corpus, three things: the size of the corpus, what variety of annotation is available in that corpus, and how much of that annotation is reliable.

With this range of annotation available, it should now be apparent that when we test for closure in these three corpora we can do so in a variety of ways. As well as lexical closure based upon word forms, we can also test for morphosyntactic closure, using the part-of-speech codes, and grammatical closure using the parsing information.

But before beginning the study, it is useful to pause and consider what software tools were essential to the processing of this study.

3. PROCESSING THE CORPORA: CORPUS ANNOTATION AND MANIPULATION

The corpora used in this study had been processed in a variety of automatic and semi-automatic ways. This processing will be reviewed briefly in this section. For the reader interested in the full range of possible annotations at present, Chapter 2 describes a much wider range of annotations than this section.

3.1. Part-of-speech tagging

The texts had all been annotated with part-of-speech information using the CLAWS system (see Chapter 5, section 3 for a description of this system). This left the texts annotated to around 97 per cent accuracy. Human grammarians had then worked using specialised editing software to remove the errors in the annotation.[4]

Part-of-speech systems similar to CLAWS are now freely available for non-commercial use (see Appendix C for details of a part-of-speech tagger available from the Xerox corporation). These systems currently tend to run on powerful workstations and are written in a variety of programming languages. However, their wide availability and high reliability make them a good tool in the analysis of corpora.

3.2. Parsing

The parsing of the texts had been done by a combination of human and machine annotation. Using a program called EPICS, human grammarians parsed the corpora for the study. EPICS allows humans to parse texts quite rapidly. It has a variety of useful features which allow for speedy annotation.[5]

Specialised editors such as EPICS are not generally available in the public domain at present, and neither are the corpora which have been produced by them. There are certain exceptions such as the Penn Treebank (see Appendix B), but on the whole parsed corpora are hard to find, and time-consuming to produce, even with editing tools such as epics.

3.3. Tools for corpus analysis

Having the annotation present in a corpus is one thing – *using* that annotation is quite another. In the public domain the program that is typically used to manipulate a corpus is a concordancer (as outlined in Chapter 1). In addition to this, however, it is possible to develop specialised tools to manipulate annotated corpora in various ways. These programs tend to be strictly 'in-house' programs, built to meet a specific need in a research centre as a need arises. In the processing of this study, two specific 'in-house' programs were developed to help with the measurement of closure. One, the On-line Text Developer produces frequency lists of word–part-of-speech pairs.[6] The second, the Phrase-Structure Rule Browser, allows a treebanked corpus to be browsed and the syntactic patterns within it to be extracted.

3.4. What can I do?

This section has shown, in no uncertain terms, that the study undertaken here is being done using corpus resources and tools not generally available to the public in the mid-1990s. This is quite deliberate. As corpora percolate into the public domain, it is certain that corpora such as these will be available to all. The use of these corpora and tools allows us to demonstrate what will be possible in the future. For those users who would like to experiment with some of this annotation, sections of corpus are available from the World-Wide-Web site associated with this book, as is a concordancer incorporating the Phrase Structure Rule Browser.

4. LIMITING CLAIMS: WHAT ARE WE LOOKING AT?

Having described the corpora that are being used in this study, and having considered how they have been annotated and how they may be manipulated, one further step remains before we can begin our study. We must consider carefully what we are looking at when we are using these corpora and judge whether the goals we have set for this study are realistic.

We have characterised the three corpora to be used in this study as two unrestricted language corpora, and one sublanguage corpus. But how homogeneous are the texts in this study? Is it possible to use a simple definition, such as 'unrestricted language' or 'sublanguage' to categorise these texts? There are a series of issues which influence this decision which we should consider before continuing.

First, the texts themselves have an ever-changing purpose. May it not be possible also that the style of the text may change as its purpose does? For example, in the APHB corpus, there are sections of text with different narrative functions, for example, introduction, conclusion, description or dialogue. Consequently we may be convinced that the texts themselves have different styles represented within them, for example the style of the introduction, the style of the conclusion, and so on. It may well be, for example, that closure is higher in some part of a corpus text than another. The validity of our observations will be crucially dependent upon whether we are making claims about the general character of the texts involved or making specific claims about elements of each text. Fortunately, in this exercise we want a general characterisation of the text, hence taking whole corpus texts, and possibly even random fragments of texts, serves our purpose well. This may not always be the case, however, and in carrying out any other study one would have to be aware of how the organisation of a text by its author may be of importance: if you are interested in the representation of direct speech in fictional texts, then you want to base your observations on the parts of the corpus relevant to that goal.

The second issue we will address is one of size: when is a corpus big enough to allow results to be significant? This seemingly simple question is actually quite thorny. If the observations to be made are upon features with a relatively high frequency of occurrence, then relatively small samples of text can yield interesting results – Biber and Finegan (1991) for instance use corpus samples of around 1,000 words for such features (as discussed in Chapter 3, section 4). But the lower the frequency of the feature you wish to observe, the larger the corpus you need. For the purpose of the current study, the corpora are certainly large enough to monitor the various forms of closure we wish to observe. But if, for instance, our goal was to observe, say, the relative frequency of the verbs *spy* and *snoop*, we may need a much larger corpus. In the 2.25 million words of English gathered for this study, the verbs *spy* and *snoop* did not occur at all! This is hardly a surprise as, in general, words with an open-class[7] part-of-speech will tend to occur with a low frequency. So for the purpose of that study, the corpora collected may be quite inadequate.[8] For the study in hand, however, corpus size is not a concern.

A final issue we may address is whether the prior categorisation of corpus texts, which our study may rely upon, is in itself valid. Corpora tend to be balanced for genre (see Chapter 2, section 1), and we may wish to proceed using these genre distinctions as a series of anchor points for our study. However, the genre distinction itself is one which is largely reflects purpose, not necessarily style, (see the section 'Corpora and Stylistics' in Chapter 4 for a fuller discussion). We have already seen that style may vary within a text, depending on the function of a section of writing. Similarly, texts within a corpus may not be stylistically homogeneous. The texts usually have a wide range of writers. Within certain genres, where there may be some control over the writers' style (such as in a corpus of newspaper reports, or in a technical manual), we may expect the style of individual authors not to vary widely. But what if our corpus contains a 'fiction' category, which contains writers as diverse as D. H. Lawrence and George Orwell? Should we really expect them to have an homogeneous style? Of course not. So, when composing our study, we should also have regard to how valid any prior corpus organisation may be from the point of view of a linguist interested in the form of the language contained in the corpus. We should not assume that any corpus categorisations are linguistically motivated. For the purpose of the current study, the two largest corpora – the Hansard and the IBM manuals – may both be assumed to be fairly homogeneous stylistically, because of editorial decisions made in their production. The smaller corpus – the APHB – is not as homogeneous stylistically, and this should certainly be one factor we take into account when explaining any difference in behaviour between this corpus and the other unrestricted language corpus, the Hansard corpus.

We have now considered three important methodological issues. We have decided that

1. as we are seeking a gross characterisation of the corpora concerned we need not worry about heterogeneity of purpose in sections of the corpus text;

2. the corpora we have are large enough for the purposes of this study;

3. stylistic heterogeneity may only be a factor which influences the smallest corpus we will be using.

With the corpora used in the study described, the source of their annotation explained, the tools used to manipulate them briefly reviewed and relevant methodological issues addressed, we are now ready to start our study.

5. BEGINNING WORK: THE STUDY

The three corpora were taken and run through two programs. The corpora were first run through a program that gave a token list for each corpus, with each token associated with all of the parts of speech with which it occurred. This produced two important sets of data. First, a type/token ratio for each corpus. Second, a set of lexicons, showing what parts of speech were associated with what words in the corpus.

The corpora were then run through the phrase structure rule browser. This yielded an important set of data: a list of sentence types present in the corpus.

Using these data we will be able to examine closure at the lexical, morpho-syntactic and constituent level. Our method will be to compare the outputs from the programs with respect to the unrestricted language and the sublanguage corpora. Our hope is that the sublanguage corpus will behave quite differently from the unrestricted language corpora, showing a greater tendency towards closure. In the following sections we will see whether this is so.

6. THE FIRST STUDY OF CLOSURE: LEXICAL CLOSURE

The table below summarises the output of the lexicon extraction program, showing the size of the lexicons produced from each corpus and giving a type token ratio for each.

On the basis of this evidence, it does seem that the IBM manuals reach a higher degree of closure than the Hansard or APHB corpus. The IBM manuals seems to be composed of very few word forms, which are repeated often, whereas a corresponding section of the Hansard corpus has a demonstrably freer lexical usage associated with it. This is reflected clearly in the type-token ratio. For the IBM corpus, we can see that, on average, any given word form in the corpus will be repeated nearly 140 times throughout the corpus, while in the Hansard corpus, each word is repeated on average 53 times. Now, obviously, we must treat all averages with caution. But as the type/token ratio

Corpus	Size (tokens)	Types	Type/Token Ratio
IBM	1,000,000	7,594	1:139.69
Hansard	1,000,000	18,817	1:53.14
APHB	200,000	11,638	1:17.18

Table 6.2 The type/token ratios of the three corpora

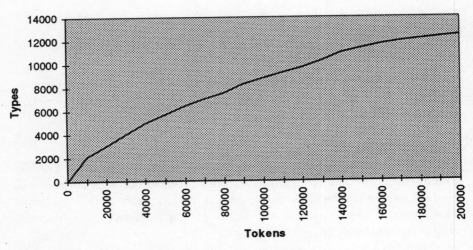

Figure 6.1 Lexicon growth in the APHB corpus

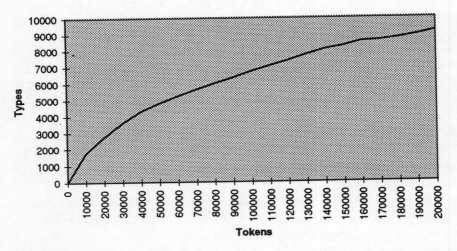

Figure 6.2 Lexicon growth in the Hansard corpus

and the relative sizes of the lexicons seem to be pointing in the same direction – towards the IBM manuals having a more restricted lexicon – then we should investigate further.

The APHB corpus has a yet lower type/token ratio, but as this corpus is significantly smaller than the Hansard or IBM corpora, we have some reason for caution in comparing this figure to the other two. To give an example of why we might be cautious: what if, in a further 800,000 word sample of APHB we did not spot one new word form? The type/token ratio of the corpus would rise to 1:85.9! Although this is an extreme case, it does at least allow us to see the

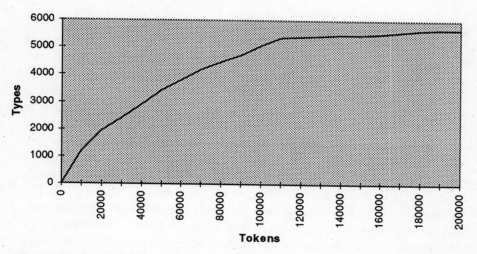

Figure 6.3 Lexicon growth in the IBM corpus

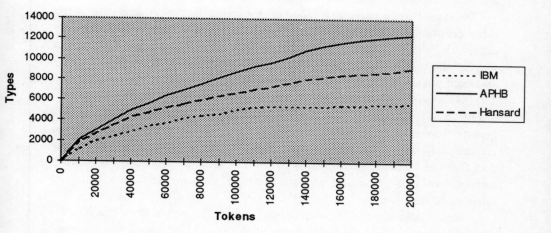

Figure 6.4 Lexicon growth in all three corpora

potential perils of comparing samples of differing sizes. When we compare the
first 200,000 words of the Hansard and IBM corpora, however, we gain further
reliable evidence that the type/token ratio of the IBM corpus is rather high: the
first 200,000 words of the IBM manuals give rise to a type/token ratio of 1:35
and the Hansard corpus gives rise to a type/token ratio of 1:22. It is clear that
in terms of lexicon growth, new word forms are encountered most frequently
in the APHB corpus, followed closely by the Hansard corpus. The IBM manuals
corpus only seems to use new word forms on average relatively infrequently.
This is our first clue that the IBM manuals corpus may indeed be somewhat

different to the Hansard and APHB corpora, as our intuition suggested.

But the average presented by the type/token ratio can partly cloud the issue of closure. It does not show us whether the lexicon of the IBM manuals is prematurely finite, merely that the corpus is prone to lexical repetition, which may or may not be an indication of a finite lexicon. If we return to the question of closure, a clearer indication of closure might be given by plotting the **growth** of the three lexicons as graphs. If the IBM manuals are using a limited lexicon, then we might expect to see that, as we look through the corpus, we observe new words with decreasing frequency. If, on the other hand, the unrestricted language corpora or the IBM manuals are not limited, then we should see a fairly steady trickle of new words being added as we scan through the corpus. The type/token ratio does not show this – it merely indicates how often, on average, a new word form appears in the text. Figures 6.1, 6.2, 6.3 and 6.4 below plot the number of types spotted in the corpus against the number of tokens processed by the lexicon building program. The figures use the first 200,000 words of each corpus for two reasons: first, to make the graph more presentable and second to ensure that the sample size for all three corpora is the same.

The story that emerged first when we looked at the type/token ratio in the three corpora is now much clearer – the IBM corpus does indeed act very differently from the Hansard and APHB corpora. Looking at Figure 6.4, we can see that the lexicon used by the language of the IBM manuals nearly enumerates itself within the first 110,000 words of the corpus. After viewing the first 110,000 words, lexicon growth in the IBM manuals hardly occurs at all. The unrestricted language corpora, on the other hand, show continuous, steady growth throughout the sample studied. They do not seem to be approaching closure at all within the sample studied. So in lexical terms, it would appear that the IBM manuals, on the basis of the evidence presented, do tend very strongly towards premature closure, whereas the unconstrained language corpora do not.

If our corpora were unannotated, this is where we would leave this investigation. Having studied the word forms in the available corpora, and comparing the results of our study to the claims of the sublanguage hypothesis, we could conclude that the IBM manuals seem to be a variety of sublanguage, and that the sublanguage hypothesis has some empirical grounding. However, as our corpora are annotated, we have the chance to go on and study closure at other levels, and test the sublanguage hypothesis further. That is the goal of the following sections.

7. THE SECOND STUDY OF CLOSURE: PART-OF-SPEECH CLOSURE

In the previous section we saw how the lexicon of the IBM manuals corpus seems decidedly finite. However, is it necessarily the case that the syntactic functions of those words are similarly finite? Most words of the English

Corpus	Size	Types in the corpus	Average number of parts-of-speech tags per type
IBM	1,000,000	7,594	1.61
Hansard	1,000,000	18,817	1.26
APHB	200,000	11,638	1.19

Table 6.3 Type/part-of-speech tag ratio

language can have a variety of syntactic functions, for example, *spy* can be a verb (*I came to the window to* **spy** *on my neighbour*) or a noun (*The* **spy** *was caught in East Berlin*). Now while the IBM manuals have an enumerable lexicon, is it the case that the functions associated with those words are similarly finite? If we look at the evidence, we can see some interesting evidence to suggest that, while the IBM manuals have a more carefully controlled lexicon, the words in that lexicon seem to have a wider variety of syntactic functions than entries in the unconstrained language lexicons. Table 6.3 lists, for each corpus, the number of words in the corpus, and the average numbers of parts–of–speech associated with each word in the corpus.

Surprisingly, the IBM manuals corpus has lexicon entries which are associated, on average, with more parts of speech than the unrestricted language corpora. But could it simply be the case that the unrestricted language corpora have lexicon entries composed of a large number of words which are only used once, and consequently that the average is brought down for them by this large number of *hapex legomena*, appearing only once and consequently with only one part of speech? In order to test this, the average number of parts of speech per entry was recomputed excluding entries which were only associated with one part of speech to give a more representative sample. Table 6.4 gives, for each corpus, how many word forms in the corpus were associated with more than one part of speech, and the average number of parts of speech for each of these entries.

It is interesting that the picture does not change, but rather becomes somewhat clearer. Not only is it the case that any given lexicon entry in the IBM manuals corpus is likely to be, on average, associated with more parts of speech than in either of the two unconstrained language corpora, it is also the case

Corpus	Types	Multiply-tagged types	Word-part-of-speech tag average
IBM	7,594	2,117 (27.9%)	3.19
Hansard	18,817	3,403 (18.01%)	2.45
APHB	11,638	2,002 (17.2%)	2.34

Table 6.4 Word/part-of-speech tag average

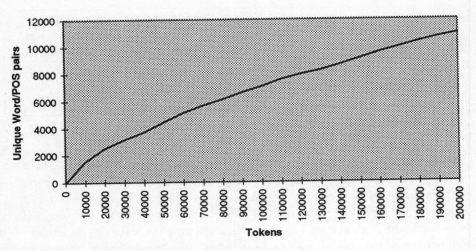

Figure 6.5 Word/part-of-speech growth in the APHB corpus

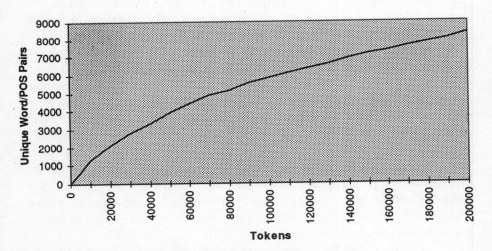

Figure 6.6 Word/part-of-speech growth in the Hansard corpus

that it is more likely that any given lexicon entry generated from the IBM corpus will have multiple parts of speech associated with it. Although the IBM manuals lexicon appears limited, it also appears that the limited lexicon is used inventively, with any given word being more likely to be used with a variety of parts of speech.

But what would be of most interest is a series of graphs showing how often a new usage for a word was added. As noted previously, the average represented by the type of ratio given above does not guarantee that closure has or has not been achieved. If there is closure of syntactic word category as of lexis in the

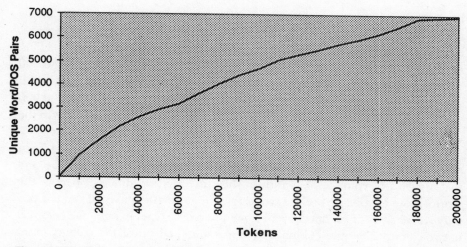

Figure 6.7 Word/part-of-speech growth in the IBM corpus

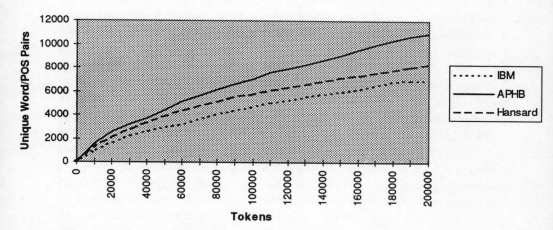

Figure 6.8 Word/part-of-speech growth in the three corpora

sublanguage, then we should see that the growth of unique word–tag pairs levels off for the sublanguage, yet does not for the unconstrained language corpora. Figures 6.5 to 6.8 are a series of graphs which chart the growth of those word/part-of-speech tag pairs for the first 200,000 words of each corpus.

Having looked at these graphs we see a different story from the simple ratios revealed. Although the IBM corpus takes longer to level off in this case than it did when lexical growth was being examined, it none the less levels off after about 180,000 words have been processed. The other corpora do not level off, but continue to develop. In this graph we see the answer to our conundrum. The IBM manuals have a lexicon which practically enumerates itself after some 100,000 words have been observed. It continues to find different syntactic uses of those words fairly steadily, however, for a further 80,000 words or so. The other corpora, on the other hand, are adding both new words and new functions for their words already observed throughout the 200,000 words studied. The higher ratio of parts of speech to words is due solely to the limited nature of the lexicon of the IBM manuals.

Let us use an analogy to illustrate. Imagine that you, person *a*, have been given the job of seeing over a 1-hour period what colours a car may be, and that a friend of yours has been given the same job in a different part of the world. Now in your part of the world there may be 100 makes of car, but you only see 50 types of car during your hour. You see 40 types in only one colour, 5 in two colours, 3 in three colours, 1 in four colours and 1 in all five colours. From your observation, you may guess that, on average, there are 68/50 car–colour combinations. Your friend, person *b*, however, lives in a part of the world with only twenty types of car. She sees nearly as many cars as you during her hour, but she sees a smaller range of cars in a wider range of colours. She sees 12 types in three colours, 4 types in four colours, and 4 types in five colours. From her observation, she may guess that, on average, there are 72/20 car–colour combinations. When you both check with manufacturers, you discover that there are always five possible colours for a car in any part of the world. Person *b* came closest to this answer because person *b* had a smaller range of cars to look at, but just as wide a range of colours, so she is likely to see a higher number of car colours on average (given that all other things are equal).

How does this relate to the work here? We simply switch the cars into words and the colours into part-of-speech tags to see the point. In the IBM corpus we have a smaller number of words (the cars observed by person *b*) exhibiting just as wide a variety of parts of speech (colours) as words in another corpus where there are a wider variety of words (the cars observed by person *a*). So the higher part-of-speech count per word is explicable not in terms of a wider range of meaning associated with words as of right in the IBM corpus, but rather as a function of the lexical closure of the IBM corpus.

We can now see that the IBM manuals achieve closure not just at the lexical level, but also at this level of morphosyntax. Not only do all of the words enumerate themselves, but the parts of speech associated with those words enumerate themselves also.

8. THE THIRD STUDY OF CLOSURE: PARSING CLOSURE

Let us now move from the lexical/morphosyntactic level of analysis to consider whether the constituent structure of the three corpora can provide any further evidence of closure.

The examination which we will undertake is on the number of sentence types in each corpus. In Chapter 1, we noted that Chomsky had stated that the concept of a sentence type was empirically indistinguishable from zero. In other words, language is so endlessly productive that the chance of one sentence mirroring another perfectly is so low that it may as well be viewed as having a probability of zero. We can use this observation to test our corpora further: if the ibm manuals are subject to closure at the level of constituent structure, the consequent reduction of the variety of sentences generated by the grammar associated with this sublanguage may well lead to the probability of a sentence type moving away from zero. To test this we will need a working definition of sentence type. As we have three syntactically parsed corpora, our concept of a sentence type will be at the level of annotation. Each sentence will be judged not on the basis of the word forms it contains, but rather in terms of its 'parse tree'. So two sentences such as *The dog bit the cat* and *The man hid the cash* will be said to be of the same type, as in terms of constituent structure they are identical:

[S [N The dog N] [V bit [N the cat N] V] S]
[S [N The man N] [V hid [N the cash N] V] S]

With this definition in place we can consider what evidence the corpora yield. This is summarised in Table 6.5.

It would appear that the unconstrained language corpora broadly confirm Chomsky's suspicion about sentence types. Only 6.28% of the Hansard sentences are repetitions of a previously observed sentence type.[9] A mere 2.17% if the APHB corpus is composed of repeated sentence types. The IBM manuals on the other hand seem to have a much more constrained set of sentence types: 39.8% of the corpus is composed of sentences constituting repeated sentence types. It would appear that some persuasive evidence exists to suggest that sentence type within the IBM manuals corpus may be constrained.

To discover the degree of constraint, it seems sensible once again to plot the

Corpus	Number of words in valid sentences[a]	Average length of sentence	Number of sentences analysed	Number of sentence types	Ratio of sentence types to sentences
IBM	422,548	10.88	46,455	27,967	1:1.66
Hansard	825,910	23.79	34,750	32,569	1:1.07
APHB	162,000	21.34	7,590	7,425	1:1.02

[a] The term 'valid' here refers to whether or not a human grammarian decided that the corpus sentence was grammatical.
[b] Note that a possibly more sensitve measure than sentence length is the t-unit length (Hunt, 1965). A t-unit is an independent unit of analysis, usually taken to be a clause (Quirk *et al.*, 1985). We will use sentence length here for simplicity.

Table 6.5 Ratio of sentence types to sentences

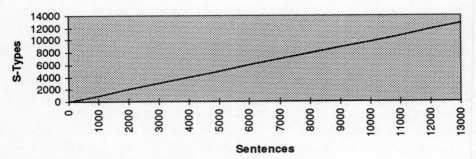

Figure 6.9 Sentence-type growth in the APHB corpus

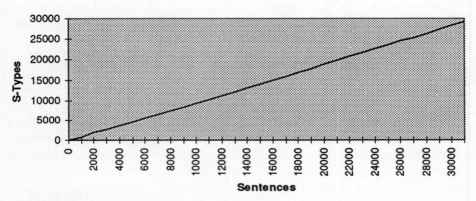

Figure 6.10 Sentence-type growth in the Hansard corpus

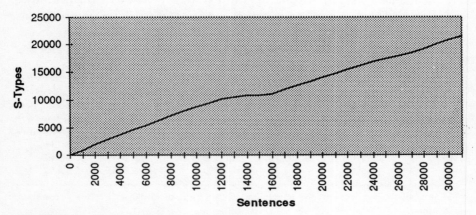

Figure 6.11 Sentence-type growth in the IBM corpus

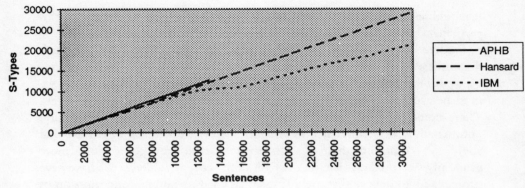

Figure 6.12 Sentence-type growth in the three corpora

growth of sentence-types within the three corpora. If Chomsky's statement about sentence-types is true, we should see roughly one new sentence-type per sentence examined. If the sublanguage hypothesis is correct, the IBM corpus should not follow this pattern. Figures 6.9 to 6.12 show the rate of sentence-type growth for the three corpora.

Looking at these graphs we can see that the IBM corpus is markedly different from the APHB and Hansard corpora. The two unconstrained language corpora do seem to exhibit the general pattern 'each new sentence means a new sentence type'. This is not true of the IBM corpus. While the corpus does not achieve closure, which would be indicated by a 'flattening-off' of the curve showing sentence-type growth, the curve is dramatically slower in terms of growth compared to the unconstrained language corpora. While the unconstrained language Hansard and APHB corpora add a new sentence-type for each 1.06 and 1.02 sentences processed respectively, the IBM corpus adds a new sentence-type for each 1.45 sentences processed. Repetition of sentence-types is clearly more marked in the IBM corpus than in the Hansard corpus and is far from being of the 'one sentence equals one new sentence type variety'. This particular example is interesting. It may be that the corpus concerned is not large enough to demonstrate sentence-type closure for the IBM manuals, hence we cannot say for sure that there is a tendency towards closure at the sentence-type level for the IBM corpora. We can say, however, that the IBM corpus seems to be the least prone to a repetition of sentence-types, which again distinguishes it quite clearly apart from those unconstrained language corpora.

9. DRAWING CONCLUSIONS: FINDINGS
On the basis of the findings presented, it would seem fair for us to conclude that the language of the IBM manuals represents a register which displays a high degree of closure, by comparison to two other corpora, across the board.

It would appear that the sublanguage hypothesis is largely supported by this particular corpus. Yet we have seen at least one surprise – that any given type in the IBM corpus will, on average, be associated with more parts of speech than in less restricted genres. So as well as proving the sublanguage hypothesis, we have also found an interesting side effect produced by closure. Also we must be cautious – we examined closure on many levels – but not all levels. There could yet lurk within the corpora, at levels of linguistic description untouched by this study, such as semantic description, a lack of closure that could yet confound these results. So to couch our conclusions more prudently, we could say that, on the basis of the corpus evidence used, we have strong cause to believe that the IBM manuals corpus exhibits constraints on its productivity at the lexical, part-of-speech function and sentence-type level.

What are the practical benefits, if any, brought about by this conclusion? Well, as noted, one discipline which could benefit from working with known sublanguages is computational linguistics. With a finite lexicon and a restraint on sentence creativity, the task of analysing and generating language in this particular register would be greatly simplified. Similarly lexicographers trying to develop specialised dictionaries for registers of this sort would know that, in principle, a substantially complete dictionary of that particular language type would be possible.

Perhaps the most important point of all, is that by comparing a sublanguage to an unconstrained language, the nature of natural language is shown quite vividly. The boundless creativity of human languages is there for all to see in Figure 6.12 – nearly one sentence-type per sentence examined. This in itself should urge caution in the formation of any linguistic hypothesis, and prudence in the application of corpus data to the testing of that hypothesis. The findings of this chapter should also show, however, that useful facts can be derived from a corpus in spite of the boundless creativity of the speakers of a natural language.

10. STUDY QUESTIONS

1.   Using the experience gained in this chapter, how would you set about studying the difference between spoken and written English? What methodological issues would you have to address when undertaking such a study?

2.   How might you collect a corpus to study the language of introductory sections in scientific prose?

11. FURTHER READING

Sekine (1994) published an excellent paper on using corpora to define the nature of sublanguages. This paper uses various measures not used in this chapter and is well worth pursuing.

In terms of readings of a more general variety, Biber and Finegan 1991 is an accesible potted description of their work on studying language variation using corpora. Bauer 1993 is an good example of the use of corpora to show variation between to varieties of the same language, while Kirk 1993 is a study of use to those wishing to study dialectal variation using corpora.

NOTES

1. See section 1 for a definition of the term sublanguage.
2. For readers interested in seeing samples of the corpora used in this chapter, and also sample outputs from the programs used to process this study, these are available on the World-Wide-Web at http://www.ling.lancs.ac.uk/staff/tony/tony.htm – please feel free to browse the resources.
3. See Chapter 2 for a description of the process of corpus annotation and the form of annotated corpora.
4. See Garside and McEnery 1993 for a description of the software used in this so-called 'corpus cleanup' process.
5. Garside and McEnery (1993) describe the EPICS program in detail.
6. Garside and McEnery (1993) again describe this program in some detail.
7. The open classes of words, such as nouns, verbs, adjectives are notable as a set for being composed of a large number of members which are capable of increasing frequently in number over time.
8. As a matter of interest, in the 100,000,000-word BNC, the word *spy* occurs 709 times, and the word *snoop* occurs only 22 times.
9. Calculated by the formula $r = 100 - ((100/a) \star b)$, where a is the number of valid sentences analysed, b is the number of sentence types observed and r is the percentage of corpus sentences based upon the repetition of a sentence type.

Where to 7 now?

In this, the final chapter of this book, we would like to indulge in a little crystal ball gazing, and speculate as to what the future of corpus linguistics will be. But before we do that, now seems a good point at which to reflect on the point of development that has been reached by corpus linguistics.

1. THE PAST AND THE PRESENT

As this book has clearly demonstrated, the history of the use of corpus data in language studies has been somewhat tumultuous. From being the *sine qua non* of linguistic research until the early 1950s, we saw that, for a variety of reasons, corpora tumbled from their place of pre-eminence in linguistics to a position of near total discredit. The criticisms which caused this were in part valid, and it has only been by sifting the valid from the invalid criticisms that corpora have re-emerged as a powerful tool for anybody interested in studying language. Gone is the concept of the corpus as the sole explicandum of language use. Present instead is the concept of a balanced corpus being used to aid the investigation of a particular language.

The large scale readoption of corpora has been mirrored by an increase in the construction of corpora, the publication of corpus-based studies, and a wide-spread recognition of the validity of the corpus as a tool in the analysis of language. This book has shown, if nothing else, that the number of uses to which corpora are being put, and the results forthcoming from those applications, are wide and numerous. Corpora are proving their worth by the results gained from their use. Authoritative grammars, language processing tools, better dictionaries, and new methods for constructing thesauri are, among a variety of other benefits, all tangible results of the use of corpora which have been presented in this book. Though the philosophical worth of corpora has been doubted in the past, their utility in the present is undeniable. Used in harmony with intuition and computer-based processing, a corpus is a formidable ally for anybody interested in the study of language.

2. THE FUTURE

With such a robust defence of the use of corpora made, it might appear that this chapter is adopting a slightly too self-congratulatory air. Corpora, though they are useful in their present form, will undoubtedly adapt to meet the needs of future users. These adaptations will, we believe, reflect four major pressures – size, international concerns, scope and computing. Each of these pressures will be described in the following sections, and their potential impact upon corpus linguistics described.

Before this, however, one important point must be made. One undoubted feature of the future development of corpus linguistics must, in the view of the authors, be an increasing rapprochement between the 'rationalist' linguists on the one hand and the 'empirical' linguists on the other. This rapprochement is apparent at the time of writing anyway – increasingly the two types of linguist are becoming less distinct. As time goes on, it must be assumed that this sharp, and false, distinction between one type of language study and another, will be replaced by a synthesis of both approaches.

Returning to pressures peculiar to corpus linguistics as a methodology, let us think about what forces will shape the corpora of the future.

2.1 Pressures Related to Size

There has been an ever-increasing pressure in corpus linguistics to increase the size of corpora. From the early 1,000,000-word corpora such as LOB and Brown, we have moved on in a relatively short period of time to 100,000,000-word (BNC) and 200,000,000-word (Bank of English) corpora.

The move towards larger corpora does not simply reflect a fashionable trend in corpus linguistics. As noted in Chapter 6, certain observations require, by their very nature, large samples of language in order for them to be made successfully.

Further to that, certain techniques in computational lexicography, such as mutual information statistics, require relatively large samples of language to work with in order to be effective. There is little point in trying to assess what words frequently collocate with, say, *powerful* or *strong* using a 1,000-word mini-corpus. There will not be enough, if any, examples in such a sample in all likelihood. There is similarly most likely little point in doing this with a 1-million-word corpus for the same reasons. In order for such techniques to be effective when examining relationships between words which have a relatively low frequency of occurrence a very large sample is needed in order to provide sufficient examples for such a technique to work.

The move towards increasing corpus size will probably be ongoing. In part, it has been facilitated by three important changes during the 1980s.

First, more electronic text has become available. Corpus building projects in the 1970s and 1980s were often limited by the availability of electronic text in the age of manual typesetting. Now that electronic texts are more common, more text is available which can be easily incorporated into a computerised corpus.

Second, a great many issues of corpus representation and processing have been addressed by early pioneering work, such as the SEU and LOB. The knowledge of how to build a corpus is now better developed and more widespread than it has ever been.

Finally, computing machinery has developed in leaps and bounds over the past fifteen to twenty years. Not only has the power of the machinery increased – putting high-speed machines on desktops, but the memory and disk capacity of the machines has spiralled while their cost has fallen. Storing a 100-million-word corpus is now relatively cheap – a few thousand pounds for a six gigabyte hard disk will do the trick. In the mid-1970s, or even mid-1980s, such storage capacity would have been unthinkable – hence corpora of such a size would have been unthinkable. In short, corpora will be able to continue to grow as the cost of storing them falls, and the machine's ability to search through ever larger corpora at ever greater speeds increases.

One point must be made before proceeding, however. Corpora must not become huge just because they can. Small, specialised, corpora may be perfectly good for some applications – big is not always beautiful. Why bother to wade through 200 million words when, as Biber and Finegan (1991) point out, 1,000 words will be sufficient for certain types of analysis?

2.2. Pressures Related to International Concerns

As more corpora are developed, and ever larger corpora appear to be à la mode, the cost entailed in corpus development and the need to make corpus resources as widely usable as possible have become very live issues. This can be seen in the increasing pressure at a national and international level for initiatives which identify the corpora that need to be developed and the form in which those corpora should be stored/annotated. Building a 100-million-word corpus of a particular language, or three 1-million-word parallel aligned corpora can be costly. Those putting their money into the development of corpora, such as national research bodies, for example, EPSRC (Engineering and Physical Sciences Research Council) in the UK, and international research sponsors, for example, the CEC in Europe, want to ensure that their money is well spent. They want to develop the 'right' corpora and they want those corpora to be used widely. How are they trying to do this?

Let's take the CEC as a specific example. They have begun to develop a policy on corpus development, and have funded projects, for example, PAROLE, to try to discover what corpora should be developed in Europe to bring the benefits of corpus linguistics to as wide an audience as possible. They have also funded an ongoing body of advisory reports on corpus storage and annotation in the form of EAGLES.[1] Their aim is precisely that outlined – to generate the 'right' corpora for Europe encoded in a way which makes their exploitation, distribution and reuse as easy as possible. Whether or not they will achieve this goal only time will tell. But the important thing to notice is that the CEC will be sponsoring corpus production under the constraints of the policy for corpus building that they lay down – they will directly influence what corpora are developed and how they look.

To move away from this example for a moment, we can see that the goals of the CEC are not unique. International standards for corpus encoding have also been attempted – such as the TEI.[2] In the United States the Linguistic Data Consortium is attempting to become both a clearing house for corpus data, and an instigator of corpus building initiatives which they see a need for within the context in which they operate. The move towards funding bodies in consultation with academia and industry, rather than academia alone, deciding what large scale corpora are developed in the future is perceptible at present.

2.3. Pressures Related to the Scope of Corpora

Part of what was being said in the previous section, is that funding bodies are trying to find out where the need for certain types of corpora exist, and then they are trying to assess whether they should address that need. However, independent of the decisions of these bodies, it is almost certain that small scale corpus collection initiatives will be undertaken over the next few decades related to a need of certain researchers and teachers to develop certain types of corpora not currently available (or planned by bodies such as the CEC). In short, there is, and will be for the foreseeable future, a pressure for the types of corpora available to expand as people want to study different things using corpora.

Let's review an example of this covered in this book, the Lampeter corpus mentioned in Chapter 4, section 10. Schmied has developed this corpus specifically in response to a theoretical need in text linguistics to study whole texts rather than excerpts of text. A theory of linguistics is driving a need here for a new type of corpus – it isn't that Schmied likes wasting his time building corpora and thus ignores existing corpora. No existing corpora fulfill his theoretical needs. In order to undertake corpus based research within this particular theory of linguistics he therefore *needs* to develop a new corpus – he has no choice.

Another example of an area of linguistics into which the computer-based corpus methodology is penetrating is stylistics. A recent example of a new type of corpus here is the speech presentation corpus of Short, Semino and Culpeper (1996). Here they wanted a new type of annotated corpus – a corpus of fictional texts where different varieties of speech presentation (direct speech, indirect speech, free indirect speech, etc.) was marked so that they could undertake a quantitative study of this feature. No such corpus existed – so they *needed* to create one.

Finally, consider the researcher who decides to exploit the work undertaken on parallel aligned corpora in a study of English and Urdu. There is no parallel corpus of English and Urdu. The researcher would *need* to create one.

The needs placed upon corpora by linguistics, natural language processing and language teaching are only partly predictable, in the authorsí view. Hence, no matter how thorough the reviews by bodies such as the CEC, it seems certain that people will need corpora in the future that can barely be imagined in the present.

2.4. Pressures Related to Computing

Mention of corpora that can barely be imagined at the moment brings us neatly to the question of computing. Developments in computing technology has, as we have already seen, allowed the development of ever larger corpora. But what other developments will computing allow? What technical innovations are afoot in the world of computing that may make the form of corpus storage and retrieval change?

2.4.1. New developments

Computing is a field that is developing fast. New technologies are becoming available which, though yet untapped by corpus linguists, have clear relevance for them. Take for example the ability to represent, manipulate, annotate and edit video data that is now possible on multimedia video workstation PCs. When we consider this type of technology, we can see that questions of whether or not audio-tapes of interactions used in a transcribed spoken corpus sound rather archaic.

Rather than asking for primitive audio recordings, those who use corpora could, and should, be demanding corpora which integrate audio-visual representations of interactions with a corpus in which the language represented in the video can be studied. Imagine the ability to switch between a section of transcribed text and a segment of video showing the interaction? Imagine the ability to introduce annotation to the video so that, when somebody was viewing your corpus video on their PC screen they could switch out to one of many levels of annotation – transcription, a grammatical analysis of the text, on-line notes describing the social background of the speakers, a conversation analysis of the sequence and an ethnographic description of the context within which the discourse takes place. The possibilities are mind-boggling – the ability at last to use the same platform to store, analyse and describe the data.

There is an amazing amount of potential for the exploitation of multimedia technology to improve the representation, manipulation and retrieval of corpus data. It cannot be too long before somebody takes this challenge up and develops a truly multimedia corpus.

2.4.2 New problems

Putting to one side for the moment future changes in corpus storage and representation that advances in computing technology may allow, what changes are being forced on the computational side of corpus linguistics by current changes in the form of corpora? Two notable cases spring to mind. First the pressure put on retrieval software forced to deal with presenting a user with thousands of answers; and second, pressure on software developers to generate software that uses the various corpus encoding schemes being pioneered as standards.

Returning to the first point, it is useful to note that while bigger corpora are useful for some tasks, they bring in their wake the prospect of 'bigger answers' to certain questions. We use the term 'bigger answers' here to refer to one of two things, either a useful increase of data on a feature previously observed, or a simple increase of data on a feature that gives no further information on it. The answers presented in either case can, for the user, be unwieldy. It is fine to use a software package to search through the BNC, and to look for the word *spy*, for example. It is slightly less appealing to realise that there are 709 occurrences of the word in the corpus for the user to look through and to categorise. Wouldn't it be wonderful if, in advance, the computer could pre-organise the results of a search to say something like 'I have found x examples of *spy* as a head noun in a noun phrase, y examples of *spy* as a premodifying noun in a noun phrase and z examples of *spy* as a verb'. Our task in searching through the data would in part be aided by the machineís ability to interpret it.

Sutton and McEnery (1992) argued some time ago for 'smart' concordance software which, in some sense, understood the annotation in a corpus and could use it. This would, obviously, be one way to improve the output from a concordancer.

A second means, such as that practised by Collier (1994), is to develop a series of procedures which, given an unannotated corpus, can try to group together corpus lines which have similar lexical repetitions.

The least acceptable form of ordering, and sadly the one that is most common at the moment, is simply to truncate the output – just give, say, the first 200 examples found and throw the rest away.[3]

It is obvious that as corpora increase in size, so the issue of retrieval from a corpus will become an increasingly central one within corpus linguistics.

Moving back to the second case cited of pressure brought to bear on computing by the change of form of corpora, the adoption of encoding standards has exerted pressure on software developers to generate software for corpus exploitation and construction which conforms with these standards. Looking at an SGML encoded text in the raw is not a pleasant task.[4] The encoding standard has created an instant market for SGML-aware word processors, concordance programs and natural language processing tools.

Needless to say, software is slowly evolving to meet those demands. For example, the CLAWS part-of-speech tagging system was updated to deal with SGML for the British National Corpus Project (Leech, Garside and Bryant 1994) and the concordancer developed to work with the British National Corpus, SARA, can interpret the SGML encoding of the corpus for the user. To say, however, that the market for SGML aware software has been saturated is far from the truth. It is almost certain that as initiatives like the TEI and EAGLES take hold on corpus representation, so corpus related software will develop to cater for the developing standards.

3. CONCLUSION

It is obvious that this book cannot, in any real sense, conclude definitively. Although we have reviewed the past and the present of corpus linguistics, we can only partly review its future. Corpus linguistics is constantly developing. That is the important message of this chapter. Yet as those changes are realised, the effect will surely be better resources for any researcher, student, natural language processing engineer, lexicographer – but most of all linguists!

NOTES

1. See Chapter 2, section 2.1 for more information on EAGLES.
2. See Chapter 2, section 2.1 for more information on TEI.
3. A strategy akin to this is adopted by the SARA concordance program developed to search the BNC. This program will retrieve a maximum of 2,000 examples for any given query. Infuriatingly, though, it actually reports on how many cases it really found!
4. The sceptical should see Chapter 2, section 2.1 for a refresher on SGML.

Glossary

alignment the practice of defining explicit links between texts in a parallel corpus

anaphora pronouns, noun phrases, etc. which refer back to something already mentioned in a text; sometimes the term is used more loosely – and, technically, incorrectly – to refer in general to items which co-refer, even when they do not occur in the text itself (*exophora*) or when they refer forwards rather than backwards in the text (*cataphora*).

annotation (i) the practice of adding explicit additional information to machine-readable text; (ii) the physical representation of such information

Baum–Welch algorithm a way of finding the path through the states of a hidden-Markov model which maximizes the probability score output from the model. The algorithm arranges the calculations undertaken so that they are done efficiently using a programming technique called 'dynamic programming'

CALL computer-aided (or assisted) language learning

COCOA reference a balanced set of angled brackets (<>) containing two things: a code standing for a particular type of information (e.g. A=AUTHOR), and a string or set of strings, which are the instantiations of that information (e.g. CHARLES DICKENS). Thus a COCOA reference indicating that Charles Dickens is the author of the text might look like this: <A CHARLES DICKENS>

concordance a comprehensive listing of a given item in a corpus (most often a word or phrase), also showing its immediate context

context-free phrase structure grammar a phrase structure grammar is a grammar made up of rules which define from which elements phrase types (such as noun phrases and verb phrases) are built up and how sentences are built from these phrase types; a context-free grammar is one in which these rules apply in all cases, regardless of context

corpus (i) (loosely) any body of text; (ii) (most commonly) a body of machine-readable text; (iii) (more strictly) a finite collection of machine-readable text, sampled to be maximally representative of a language or variety

dependency grammar a type of formal grammar which shows the dependencies between different items in a sentence, e.g. which items are governed by which items; e.g. in the sentence *Drop it*, the verb governs the pronoun *it*

DTD (Document Type Description) in the TEI, a formal representation which tells the user or a computer program what elements a text contains and how these elements are combined. It also contains a set of entity declarations, for example, representations of non-standard characters

EAGLES (Expert Advisory Groups on Language Engineering Standards) an EU-sponsored project to define standards for the computational treatment (e.g. annotation) of EU languages

element in TEI terminology, a unit of text

empiricism an approach to a subject (in our case linguistics) which is based upon the analysis of external data (such as texts and corpora); contrast *rationalism*

entity reference in the TEI, a shorthand way of encoding information in a text

full parsing a form of grammatical analysis which represents all of the grammatical relationship within a sentence

header a part of an electronic document preceding the text proper and containing information about the document such as author, title, source and so on

immediate constituent in a phrase structure grammar, an immediate consituent is one which belongs directly within a phrase

knowledge base a source of rules used by an artificial intelligence program to carry out some task. Note that these rules are usually written in a formal, logical notation

KWAL key word and line, a form of concordance which can allow several lines of context either side of the key word

KWIC key word in context, a form of concordance in which a word is given within *x* words of context and is normally centred down the middle of the page

lemma the headword form that one would look for if looking up a word in a dictionary, e.g. the word-form *loves* belongs to the lemma LOVE

lexicon essentially synonymous with 'dictionary' – a collection of words and information about them; this term is used more commonly than 'dictionary' for machine readable dictionary databases

modal verb a verb which represents concepts such as possibility, necessity, etc. English examples include *can, should, may*

monitor corpus a growing, non-finite collection of texts, of primary use in lexicography

multivariate statistics those statistical methods which deal with the relationships between many different variables

mutual information a statistical measure of the degree of relatedness of two elements

parallel corpus a corpus which contains the same texts in more than one language

parse to assign syntactic structure (often of a phrase structure type) to text

rationalism an approach to a subject (in our case linguistics) which is based upon introspection rather than external data analysis; contrast *empiricism*.

representative of a sample, one that approximates the closest to the population from which it is drawn

semantic field a mental category representing a portion of the universe as we perceive it; in linguistic terms, a semantic field can be said to consist of a set of words that are related in terms of their senses or the domain of activity with which they are associated. For example, the words *football*, *hurdles*, *javelin* and *Olympics* could all be said to be members of a notional semantic field of 'sport'.

significance/significant reaching a degree of statistical certainty at which it is unlikely that a result is due purely to chance

skeleton parsing a form of grammatical analysis which represents only a basic subset of the grammatical relationships within a sentence

sublanguage a constrained variety of a language. Although a sublanguage may be naturally occurring, its key feature is that it lacks the productivity generally associated with language

tag (i) a code attached to words in a text representing some feature or set of features relating to those words; (ii) in the TEI, the physical markup of an element such as a paragraph

tagset a collection of tags in the form of a scheme for annotating corpora

TEI (Text Encoding Initiative) an international project to define standards for the format of machine readable texts

thesaurus a lexicographic work which arranges words in meaning-related groups rather than alphabetically; the term is also sometimes used to refer to any dictionary-style work; however, this latter definition is only rarely encountered in work on modern languages

transition matrix a repository of transitional probabilities. This is an n-dimensional matrix, depending on the length of transition under question. So, for example, with a digram transition, we require a two-dimensional matrix

treebank a corpus which has been annotated with phrase structure information

variable rule analysis a form of statistical analysis which tests the effects of combinations of different factors and attempts to show which combination accounts best for the data being analysed

WSD (Writing System Declaration) in the TEI, a formal specification defining the character set used in encoding an electronic text

Z-score a statistical measure of the degree of relatedness of two elements

Appendix A:
Corpora mentioned in the text

This appendix contains brief details of corpora mentioned in the text of this book. More detailed information, and information on a number of other corpora, can be found in the surveys carried out by Taylor, Leech and Fligelstone (1991) and Edwards (1993).

We include here details of e-mail, Gopher and World-Wide-Web information sources as well as ordinary postal addresses. For specific information on how to access these electronic information sources, please contact the computer services department of your university, college or institution.

TEXT COLLECTIONS:

APHB
The American Printing House for the Blind corpus is a treebanked corpus of fiction text produced for IBM USA at Lancaster University. Not available for research purposes.

THE BANK OF ENGLISH
The Collins COBUILD monitor corpus built at the University of Birmingham. It is quoted as containing 'hundreds of millions' of words and is still expanding. The data have been part-of-speech tagged and parsed using the Helsinki English constraint grammar.
Availability The corpus can be consulted by arrangement. For further details contact The Bank of English, Westmere, 50 Edgbaston Park Road, Birmingham, B15 2RX.

THE CHILDES DATABANK
A collection of machine-readable samples of child language and language pathologies. The samples are mainly American and British English, but other languages are also represented.
Availability The corpus is available to other researchers. For further details Contact CHILDES Project, Department of Psychology, Carnegie Mellon University, Pittsburgh, PA 15213, USA. (E-mail: brian@andrew.cmu.edu). This project also has a World-Wide-Web page (ftp://poppy.psy.cmu.edu/www/childes.html) and an e-mail mailing list.

CURIA

An ongoing project sponsored by the Royal Irish Academy to make available machine-readable texts in the several languages used in Ireland during its history – Irish (both old and modern), Hiberno-Latin and Hiberno-English.
Availability The corpus will be made available. For further information contact Patricia Kelly at the Royal Irish Academy, Dawson Street, Dublin, Ireland (e-mail: CURIAPK@CCVAX.UCD.IE). There is an e-mail discussion list relating to this project which provides periodic updates on the work. (The discussion list is, however, currently suspended – April 1996.)

THESAURUS LINGUAE GRAECAE (TLG)
A machine-readable collection of most of ancient Greek literature.
Availability The corpus is available on CD-ROM. For details Contact TLG Project, University of California at Irvine, Irvine, CA 92717-5550, USA. This project also has its own Gopher page (tlg.cwis.uci.edu).

DIALECT CORPORA
HELSINKI CORPUS OF ENGLISH DIALECTS
A corpus of approx. 245,000 words of spoken dialect English from several regions of England. Speakers are elderly and rural in conversation with a fieldworker.
Contact the Department of English, University of Helsinki, Porthania 311, 00100 Helsinki, Finland.

NITCS (NORTHERN IRELAND TRANSCRIBED CORPUS OF SPEECH)
A corpus of approx. 400,000 of spoken English from 42 localities in Northern Ireland. Speakers are taken from three age groups – children, middle-aged and elderly – and the data represent conversations with fieldworkers.
Availability Contact the Oxford Text Archive, Oxford University Computing Service, 13 Banbury Road, Oxford, OX2 6NN. (E-mail: archive@vax.ox.ac.uk).

HISTORICAL CORPORA
ARCHER (A REPRESENTATIVE CORPUS OF HISTORICAL ENGLISH REGISTERS)
A corpus of both British and American English divided into 50-year periods between 1650 and 1990. The corpus contains both spoken and written language. It is being part-of-speech tagged.
Contact Doug Biber, Department of English, Northern Arizona University, Flagstaff, AZ 86011-6032, USA (E-mail: biber @nauvax.ucc.nau.edu).

AUGUSTAN PROSE SAMPLE
A corpus of approx. 80,000 words of British English reading material from between *c.* 1675 and 1705.
Availability Contact the Oxford Text Archive, Oxford University Computing Service, 13 Banbury Road, Oxford, OX2 6NN (E-mail: archive@vax.ox.ac.uk).

HELSINKI CORPUS OF EARLY AMERICAN ENGLISH

A corpus of approx. 500,000 words of late 17th and early 18th century North American English.

Contact Department of English, University of Helsinki, Porthania 311, 00100 Helsinki, Finland.

HELSINKI CORPUS OF OLDER SCOTS

A corpus of approx. 600,000 words of Scots from between 1450 and 1700.

Contact Department of English, University of Helsinki, Porthania 311, 00100 Helsinki, Finland.

HELSINKI DIACHRONIC CORPUS

A corpus of approx. 1,500,000 words of English from between AD 800 and 1710. The corpus covers a wide range of genres and sociolinguistic variables and is divided into 3 periods and 11 subperiods.

Availability Contact the International Computer Archive of Modern English (ICAME), Norwegian Computing Centre for the Humanities, Harald Hårfagresgt. 31, N-5007 Bergen, Norway (E-mail: icame@hd.uib.no).

THE LAMPETER CORPUS OF EARLY MODERN ENGLISH TRACTS

A corpus of approx. 500,000 words of pamphlet literature dating from between 1640 and 1740. This corpus contains whole texts rather than smaller samples from texts. It is likely to increase in size in the near future.

Contact Prof. Dr. Josef Schmied, Englische Sprachwissenschaft, TU Chemnitz-Zwickau, D-09107 Chemnitz, Germany (E-mail: Josef.Schmied@phil.tu-chemnitz.de).

THE ZURICH CORPUS OF ENGLISH NEWSPAPERS (ZEN)

A corpus of English newspapers from 1660 to the beginning of *The Times*.

Contact Prof. Dr. Udo Fries, Englisches Seminar, Universität Zurich, Plattenstr. 47, CH-8032 Zurich, Switzerland (E-mail: ufries@es.unizh.ch).

MONOLINGUAL CORPORA

MIXED CHANNEL

THE BIRMINGHAM CORPUS

A corpus of approx. 20,000,000 words. Approximately 90% of the corpus is written material and 10% is spoken material. The corpus consists mainly of British English, although some other varieties are also represented.

Contact The Bank of English, Westmere, 50 Edgbaston Park Road, Birmingham, B15 2RX

THE BRITISH NATIONAL CORPUS (BNC)

A corpus of approx. 100,000,000 words of written and spoken British English, including everyday conversation. The entire corpus is tagged for part-of-speech and a 1,000,000-word subset is tagged with a finer tagset and skeleton parsed. The corpus is available on CD-ROM.

Contact The British National Corpus, Oxford University Computing Service, 13 Banbury Road, Oxford, OX2 6NN.

THE INTERNATIONAL CORPUS OF ENGLISH (ICE)
A collection of 1,000,000 word corpora – one written and one spoken – from each country or region in which English is a first or major language (e.g. East Africa, Australia, New Zealand, as well as the UK and USA). The corpus will be tagged for part of speech. Contact Survey of English Usage, University College London, Gower Street, London WC1E 6BT.

THE NIJMEGEN CORPUS
A corpus of approx. 130,000 words. The corpus is mainly taken from written sources but includes some sports commentary.
Contact Department of English, University of Nijmegen, Erasmusplein 1, NL-6525 HT Nijmegen, The Netherlands.

THE PENN TREEBANK
A part-of-speech tagged and parsed corpus consisting primarily of articles from the *Wall Street Journal* but also including some samples of spoken language.
Availability Extracts are available on the ACL/DCI CD-ROM (contact Mark Liberman, Department of Linguistics, University of Pennsylvania, Philadelphia, PA 19104, USA (E-mail: myl@unagi.cis.upenn.edu). For further information regarding the whole corpus Contact Penn Treebank, Department of Computer and Information Science, University of Pennsylvania, Philadelphia, PA 19104, USA.

THE SURVEY OF ENGLISH USAGE (SEU)
An approx. 1,000,000 word corpus of British English collected in the 1960s. Approximately half is written and half spoken. The spoken half constitutes the London-Lund corpus.
Availability Spoken: see under London-Lund Corpus.
written : contact Survey of English Usage, University College London, Gower Street, London WC1E 6BT.

THE OXFORD PSYCHOLINGUISTIC DATABASE
A database of information on approx. 99,000 English words, including frequency data and semantic psycholinguistic and phonetic features. For the Macintosh.
Availability Contact The Oxford Psycholinguistic Database, Oxford Electronic Publishing, OUP, Walton Street, Oxford OX2 6DP (Fax: 01865-56646).

SPOKEN
A CORPUS OF ENGLISH CONVERSATION
The London-Lund corpus, minus the additional examples of more formal spoken English added in the 1970s.
Availability In book form: Svartvik and Quirk (1980).

THE LONDON–LUND CORPUS
Approx. 500,000 words of spoken British English collected in the 1960s and early 1970s. Mainly conversational with some additional genres such as legal proceedings and commentary added later. The corpus is prosodically annotated.
Availability Contact International Computer Archive of Modern English (ICAME), Norwegian Computing Centre for the Humanities, Harald Hårfagresgt. 31, N-5007 Bergen, Norway (E-mail: icame@hd.uib.no)

THE POLYTECHNIC OF WALES CORPUS (POW)
A corpus of approx. 61,000 words of children's spoken English. The corpus is parsed using a systemic functional grammar.
Availability Contact International Computer Archive of Modern English (ICAME), Norwegian Computing Centre for the Humanities, Harald Hårfagresgt. 31, N-5007 Bergen, Norway (E-mail: icame@hd.uib.no).

THE LANCASTER/IBM SPOKEN ENGLISH CORPUS (SEC AND MARSEC)
A corpus of approx. 53,000 of formal spoken English, primarily taken from radio broadcasts. The corpus is annotated prosodically, part-of-speech tagged, and skeleton parsed. MARSEC is a version of the SEC which exists in the form of a relational database and also includes some additional information, such as phonetic transcription.
Availability Contact International Computer Archive of Modern English (ICAME), Norwegian Computing Centre for the Humanities, Harald Hårfagresgt. 31, N-5007 Bergen, Norway (E-mail: icame@hd.uib.no).

WRITTEN
THE BROWN CORPUS
A corpus of approx. 1,000,000 of written American English text dating from 1961.
Availability Contact International Computer Archive of Modern English (ICAME), Norwegian Computing Centre for the Humanities, Harald Hårfagresgt. 31, N-5007 Bergen, Norway (E-mail: icame@hd.uib.no).

THE FREIBURG CORPUS
A corpus of approx. 1,000,000 words of written British English dating from 1991. The aim of this corpus is to parallel as closely as possible the contents of the LOB corpus, primarily as a basis for the study of language change in the 30 years separating the two corpora.
Contact Prof. Dr. Christian Mair, Englisches Seminar I, Institut für Englische Sprache und Literatur, Albert-Ludwigs-Universität, D-7800 Freiburg i. Br., Germany.

THE GUANGZHOU PETROLEUM ENGLISH CORPUS
A corpus of 411,612 words of written English from the petrochemicals domain.
Contact Zhu Qi-Bo, Guangzhou Training College of the Chinese Petroleum University, Guangzhou, China.

THE HKUST COMPUTER SCIENCE CORPUS
A corpus of approx. 1,000,000 words of written English sampled from undergraduate course textbooks in computer science.
Contact Gregory James, Language Centre, Hong Kong University of Science and Technology, Clear Water Bay, Hong Kong (E-mail: lcgjames@usthk. bitnet).

THE KOLHAPUR CORPUS OF INDIAN ENGLISH
A corpus of approx. 1,000,000 words of written Indian English texts dating from 1978. The corpus parallels closely the genres and proportions of the LOB and Brown corpora.
Availability Contact International Computer Archive of Modern English (ICAME), Norwegian Computing Centre for the Humanities, Harald Hårfagresgt. 31, N-5007 Bergen, Norway (E-mail: icame@hd.uib.no).

THE LANCASTER PARSED CORPUS
A subsample of approx. 133,000 words taken from the LOB corpus. The corpus is tagged for part-of-speech and parsed with a scheme intermediate between the full parsing of the Lancaster-Leeds treebank and the skeleton parsing of e.g. the Lancaster/ IBM Spoken English Corpus.
Availability Contact International Computer Archive of Modern English (ICAME), Norwegian Computing Centre for the Humanities, Harald Hårfagresgt. 31, N-5007 Bergen, Norway (E-mail: icame@hd.uib.no).

THE LANCASTER–LEEDS TREEBANK
A subsample of approx. 45,000 words taken from the LOB corpus. The corpus is tagged for part-of-speech and fully parsed.
Contact Prof. Geoffrey Leech, Department of Linguistics and Modern English Language, Lancaster University, Lancaster LA1 4YT. (e-mail: G.Leech@lancs.ac.uk).

THE LANCASTER–OSLO/BERGEN) CORPUS (LOB)
A corpus of approx. 1,000,000 words of written British English texts which were published in the year 1961. The genre categories are parallel to those of the Brown corpus. The entire corpus has been part-of-speech tagged, and various subsamples have also been parsed (see: Lancaster Parsed Corpus; Lancaster-Leeds Treebank).
Availability Contact International Computer Archive of Modern English (ICAME), Norwegian Computing Centre for the Humanities, Harald Hårfagresgt. 31, N-5007 Bergen, Norway (E-mail: icame@hd.uib.no).

THE LONGMAN–LANCASTER CORPUS
A corpus of approx. 30,000,000 words from a broad range of subject fields. Texts date from the early part of the century up to the 1980s. As well as British and American English, the corpus contains smaller samples of other national varieties (e.g. West African).
Contact Della Summers, Longman Dictionaries, Longman House, Burnt Mill, Harlow, Essex, CM20 2JE.

THE MACQUARIE CORPUS

A corpus of approx. 1,000,000 words of written Australian English from 1986 and after. Contact Pam Peters, School of English and Linguistics, Macquarie University, 2109 NSW, Australia.

THE SUSANNE CORPUS

An approx. 128,000 word subsample of the Brown corpus. The corpus is part-of-speech tagged, parsed, and lemmatised.
Availability Contact Oxford Text Archive, Oxford University Computing Service, 13 Banbury Road, Oxford, OX2 6NN (E-mail: archive@vax.ox.ac.uk).

THE SCOTTISH DRAMATICAL TEXTS CORPUS

A corpus of approx. 101,000 words of drama in traditional and Glaswegian Scots.
Availability Contact John Kirk, School of English, The Queen's University of Belfast, Belfast, BT7 1NN.

THE TOSCA CORPUS

A corpus of approx. 1,500,000 words of written English from dates between 1976 and 1986. The corpus is part-of-speech tagged and parsed.
Contact Department of English, University of Nijmegen, Erasmusplein 1, NL-6525 HT Nijmegen, The Netherlands.

MULTILINGUAL CORPORA

THE AARHUS CORPUS OF CONTRACT LAW

Three 1,000,000 word subcorpora of Danish, English and French respectively. Texts are taken from the area of contract law. This is not a parallel corpus.
Availability Contact Karen Lauridsen, The Aarhus School of Business, Fuglesangs Allé 4, DK-8210 Aarhus V, Denmark.

THE CANADIAN HANSARD CORPUS

A corpus of proceedings from the Canadian parliament. The corpus is a parallel French–English corpus of approx. 750,000 words of each language. The English version of the corpus has been part-of-speech tagged and parsed at Lancaster University.
Availability The raw text corpus will be made available on CD-ROM by the ACL Data Collection Initiative (contact: Mark Liberman, Department of Linguistics, University of Pennsylvania, Philadelphia, PA 19104, USA (E-mail: myl@unagi.cis.upenn.edu). The parsed and tagged version is not available for distribution.

THE CRATER CORPUS (ITU CORPUS)

A trilingual parallel corpus of French, English and Spanish from the telecommunications domain. This corpus is currently in development. When complete it will be available in part-of-speech tagged, lemmatised and aligned form.
Availability Contact Tony McEnery, Department of Linguistics and Modern English Language, Lancaster University, Lancaster LA1 4YT
(E-mail: mcenery@comp. lancs.ac.uk).

Appendix B:
Some software for
corpus research

Here we provide brief details of some of the more important software for corpus-based research. More detailed information, and information on other software, can be obtained from Hughes and Lee (1994) and Lancashire (1991).

CONCORDANCERS ETC.

FOR IBM-COMPATIBLE PCS

LEXA

Sophisticated PC-based corpus analysis system. Lexa produces lexical databases and concordances. The program is able handle texts marked with COCOA references. Lexa goes beyond the basic frequency and concordance features of most corpus analysis programs and also enables simple (i.e. pattern-matched) tagging and lemmatisation routines to be run.

Availability Contact International Computer Archive of Modern English (ICAME), Norwegian Computing Centre for the Humanities, Harald Hårfagresgt. 31, N-5007 Bergen, Norway (E-mail: icame@hd.uib.no).

LONGMAN MINI CONCORDANCER

Produces KWIC concordances, frequency lists and basic statistics (e.g. type/token ratio). This program is easy to use and works on plain ASCII text but it cannot handle corpora much larger than approx. 50,000 words. It is also possible to call up concordances of specific collocations using the program.

Availability Contact Longman Group UK, Longman House, Burnt Mill, Harlow, Essex, CM20 2JE.

MICRO CONCORD

KWIC concordancer for the PC, especially suited to pedagogic applications.

Availability Contact ontact: Janet Caldwell, Oxford University Press, Walton Street, Oxford, OX2 6DP.

OXFORD CONCORDANCE PROGRAM (OCP) AND MICRO-OCP

Powerful but somewhat user-unfriendly program. Versions are available for mainframes (OCP) and IBM-compatible PCs (Micro-OCP). The PC version is slightly more user-friendly, as it is partially menu-driven. There is no apparent size limit on texts used with these programs apart from that imposed by the memory of the user's computer. OCP produces KWIC concordances, word frequency listings, indexes, and basic textual statistics (e.g. type/token ratio). The program is quite rich in options for handling references, output layout, etc. It is also possible to specify searches for collocations.

Availability Contact Micro: Janet Caldwell, Oxford University Press, Walton Street, Oxford, OX2 6DP; mainframe: Oxford University Computing Service, 13 Banbury Road, Oxford, OX2 6NN.

SARA

A sophisticated PC-based concordancer designed specifically to handle texts which use TEI/SGML markup.

Contact Lou Burnard, Oxford University Computing Services, 13 Banbury Road, Oxford OX2 6NN.

TACT

Freeware package. TACT is sometimes called 'the poor man's Wordcruncher' (q.v.) as its functionality is quite similar to that of Wordcruncher. The program's basic outputs are KWAL and KWIC concordances and frequency lists. It also enables the user to produce graphs of the distribution of words through a text or corpus, and includes an option for identifying statistically significant collocations using the Z-score. Further features are a basic collocation list generator and the ability to group words for searching according to user-defined categories (e.g. semantic fields). Tact requires the user to convert the raw text into a TACT database using a program called MAKBAS: this requires a certain amount of skill if full advantage is to be taken of referencing etc.

Availability Contact Centre for Computing in the Humanities, Room 14297A, Robarts Library, University of Toronto, Toronto, Ontario, M5S 1A5, Canada (E-mail: cch@epas.utoronto.ca); also available by anonymous FTP from the latter (epas.utoronto.ca) and from ICAME (nora.hd.uib.no).

WORDCRUNCHER

Easy to use package which can produce frequency listings, KWAL and KWIC concordances, and concordances of user-selected collocations. It can also produce word distribution statistics. Like TACT, Wordcruncher requires texts to be in a specially indexed format. The LOB, Brown, London-Lund, Kolhapur and Helsinki Diachronic corpora are available on CD-ROM from ICAME in a ready-indexed form for use with Wordcruncher (the address of ICAME is given under entries for those corpora in Appendix A).

Availability Contact Johnston and Company, PO Box 446, American Fork, UT 84003, USA.

FOR THE APPLE MAC
CONC

A text analysis program which produces KWIC concordances and indices.
Availability Contact International Academic Bookstore, Summer Institute of Linguistics, 7500 W. Camp Wisdom Road, Dallas, TX 75236, USA
(E-mail: ACADEMIC. BOOKS@SIL.ORG).

CONCORDER

A KWIC concordancer
Contact David Rand, Les Publications CRM, Université de Montréal, CP 6128-A, Montréal, Québec, H3C 3J7, Canada (E-mail: RAND@ERE.UMONTREAL.CA). Free Text Browser

FREE TEXT BROWSER

Freeware program. Another Concordancer for the Mac.
Availability Contact International Computer Archive of Modern English (ICAME), Norwegian Computing Centre for the Humanities, Harald Hårfagresgt. 31, N-5007 Bergen, Norway (E-mail: icame@hd.uib.no).

SOURCE CODE FOR COMPILING (ESSENTIALLY SYSTEM-INDEPENDENT)
CLAN

Set of programs intended to be used with the CHILDES data sets. Includes programs to produce basic KWAL, KWIC, and co-occurrence concordances. Availability: by anonymous FTP from ICAME (nora.hd.uib.no).

HUM

A freeware package of C programs which includes, amongst other things, a concordancer, frequency program, and word length charting program. The concordancer produces an exhaustive concordance of a text rather than a concordance of a selected word or words.
Availability By anonymous FTP from ICAME (nora.hd.uib.no).

PART-OF-SPEECH TAGGERS
CLAWS

A part-of-speech tagger for English which makes use of a probabilistic model trained on large amounts of manually corrected analysed text.
Contact Prof. Geoffrey Leech, Department of Linguistics and Modern English Language, Lancaster University, Lancaster LA1 4YT (E-mail: G.Leech@lancs.ac.uk).

XEROX TAGGER

A part-of-speech tagger, developed at the Xerox Parc laboratories, which is based upon a largely self-training Markov Model. The basic tagging program is language-independent and is being used at the Universidad Autónoma de Madrid to tag the Spanish part of the CRATER corpus.
Availability By anonymous FTP from parcftp.xerox.com in the directory pub/tagger.

STATISTICAL SOFTWARE

VARBRUL

A statistical package for the production of cross-tabulations and regression analyses, very similar to loglinear analysis (see Chapter 3). Versions are available for most computer platforms.

Availability Contact Centre de Recherches Mathématiques, Université de Montréal, CP 6128-A, Montréal, Québec, H3C 3J7, Canada.

Appendix C:
Suggested solutions to exercises

CHAPTER 1

1. It is highly unlikely that you will find the sentence repeated in its exact form anywhere except in quotation. This in itself is a powerful example of the highly productive nature of natural language grammars. Look at the section on sentence types in Chapter 6. You will see that even if we change our definition of matching sentence to one that matches at the level of constituent structure, it is unlikely that we will find a repetition of any given sentence in unconstrained natural language.

2. It is, of course, easy to start infinite sentences. Reflexive rules in natural language grammars, such as clause subordination rules, ensure that infinitely many and infinitely long sentences are technically possible. Such rules alone guarantee the infinite nature of natural language.

3. The word *sorting* is used three times in this chapter. This took us about five seconds to discover using a concordance package. Using the human eye, it would have taken us a great deal longer, and the result may have been inaccurate.

4. The ten most frequent words (with their frequencies, ignoring case) in the chapter are:

540	the
438	of
231	a
226	to
184	in
168	corpus
159	and
152	is
137	that
110	this

While it is likely that you will have guessed some of the words on this list, it is less likely that you guessed all of them. Even less likely is that you guessed the relative and precise frequencies accurately.

CHAPTER 3

1.   The mountain dialect shows a stronger preference than the coastal dialect for the use of a relativizer to introduce the relative clause. The chi-square value has a p value of 0.0477. This means that $p < 0.05$ and therefore the difference is statistically significant, i.e. it is most probably due to a real difference in the two dialects rather than chance.

3.   DO, HAVE and TAKE have the same proportion in both corpora.

4.   a) the chi-square test (or a similar test such as the t-test) is used to test for simple significance between two or more sets of frequencies
        b) correspondence analysis will give you a pictorial representation of the texts and the words on the same set of axes so that you can see how similar or different individual texts are and in roughly what aspects of their vocabularies. Factor analysis would provide very similar results. Cluster analysis *could* be used to group the texts according to similarity, but it would be harder to see what areas of the vocabulary are influencing the similarities and differences.
        c) loglinear or VARBRUL analysis enables you to test combinations of different factors until you arrive at the most likely combination of factors.

CHAPTER 5

1.   The answers are given below.
        Sentence one
                The (Article) dog (Verb, Noun or Adjective) ate (Verb, Noun or Adjective) the (Article) bone (Verb, Noun or Adjective)
        The and *the* have been tagged from the lexicon.
        All other words have been given the default set of tags.

2.   Using your knowledge of grammar, you could deduce the parts of speech for each word. For example, you could work out that *bone* was a noun, acting as the head of a noun phrase pre-modified by an article. You could work out that *dog* was intended as a noun rather than a verb by a similar process. In the second sentence, *old* and *fat* are in a modifying position in a noun phrase, preceded by a modifying genitive phrase and followed by the head of the noun phrase. As *old* and *fat* are attributes of the cat, we would label them as adjectives. *getting* is a main verb premodified by a form of the primary verb *be* acting as an auxiliary. lazy is an adjective appearing in a complemetiser rôle.

3.   This is the answer to the question, working from left to right disambiguating pairs of words and then proceeding assuming that the correct answer has been found. The best answer is emboldened in each case.

        Using the transition tables, we arrive at the analysis 'The (A) dog (N) ate (V) the (A) bone (N)'.

The dog

Tag sequence	Diagram probabilities
A,N	**64**
A,V	0
A,J	29

dog ate

Tag sequence	Diagram probabilities
N,V	**17**
N,N	8
N,J	0

the bone

Tag sequence	Diagram probabilities
A,N	**64**
A,V	0
A,J	29

4. There is little doubt that with the resources provided you rapidly started to generate bad analyses for the sentences you chose. This is because the lexical resources given only cover the closed class parts-of-speech. Assuming that every unknown word can be noun, verb or adjective soon makes the potential number of part-of-speech combinations too large and the results too uncertain. If you generate a supplementary lexicon of nouns, adjectives and main verbs the results will improve accordingly.

CHAPTER 6

1. One important question you would have to ask is what corpus data you would need. Various corpora of speech data are available, but none seem to have the same categorisation as the written corpora. So unless you want to compare specific sections of a spoken corpus with specific parallel sections of a written corpus (if those could be found) you would be looking to create an overall comparison of the two. With that said, you may still subdivide one of the two corpora, and say compare female spoken data with written data, but the need for such a division would have to be apparent in the motivation for the study. In methodological terms, one may find difficulty getting access to as much spoken as written data (though that situation is slowly changing).

2. Two obvious strategies spring to mind. Firstly, collect a corpus of such writing yourself. Secondly. and preferably, access the scientific writing section of an existing corpus, such as LOB or the BNC, and edit the corpus texts to create the sub-view of the corpus appropriate to your study. Issues of representativeness and sampling would still remain – see chapter 3 for more details.

Bibliography

Aarts, J. (1991) 'Intuition-based and observation-based grammars' in Aijmer and Altenberg 1991, pp. 44–62.

Aarts, J. and Meijs, W. (eds) (1984) *Corpus Linguistics*, Amsterdam: Rodopi.

Aarts, J. and Meijs, W. (eds) (1986) *Corpus Linguistics II*, Amsterdam: Rodopi.

Aarts, J. and Meijs, W. (eds) (1990) *Theory and Practice in Corpus Linguistics*, Amsterdam: Rodopi.

Aarts, J., de Haan, P. and Oostdijk, N. (eds) (1993) *English Language Corpora: Design, Analysis and Exploitation*, Amsterdam: Rodopi.

Abercrombie, D. (1965) *Studies in Phonetics and Linguistics*, London: Oxford University Press.

Aijmer, K. (1988) 'Report from ongoing work on conversational phrases in English'', Paper Presented at ninth ICAME Conference, Birmingham. (Abstract in *ICAME Journal* 13 (1989): 42–3.)

Aijmer, K. and Altenberg, B. (eds) (1991) *English Corpus Linguistics: Studies in Honour of Jan Svartvik*, London: Longman.

Alt, M. (1990) *Exploring Hyperspace: A Non-Mathematical Explanation of Multivariate Analysis*. London: McGraw-Hill.

Altenberg, B. (1984) 'Causal linking in spoken and written English', *Studia Linguistica* 38: 20–69.

Altenberg, B. (1990) 'Automatic text segmentation into tone units', in Svartvik 1990, pp. 287–324.

Antaki, C. and Naji, S. (1987) 'Events explained in conversational "because" statements', *British Journal of Social Psychology* 26: 119–126.

Aone, C. and Bennett, S. W. (1994) 'Discourse tagging and discourse-tagged multilingual corpora', in *Proceedings of the International Workshop on Sharable Natural Language Resources*, Nara, Japan.

Atkins, B. T. S. and Levin, B. (1995) 'Building on a corpus: a linguistic and lexicographical look at some near-synonyms', *International Journal of Lexicography* 8:2, 85–114.

Baddeley, D. (1976) T*he Psychology of Memory*, New York: Basic Books.

Baker, J. (1995) *The Evaluation of Multiple Post-editors: Inter-rater Consistency in Correcting*

Automatically Tagged Data, Unit for Computer Research on the English Language Technical Papers 7, Lancaster University.

Bauer, L. (1993) 'Progress with a corpus of New Zealand English and some early results', In Souter and Atwell 1993, pp. 1–10.

Beale, A. (1987) 'Towards a distributional lexicon', in Garside, Leech and Sampson 1987, pp. 149–62.

Bellugi, U. and Brown, R. (eds) (1964). *The Acquisition of Language*. Monographs of the Society for Research in Child Development 29.

Bergenholtz, H. and Schaeder, B. (eds) (1979). *Empirische Textwissenschaft: Aufbau und Auswertung von Text-Corpora*, Königstein: Scripter Verlag.

Biber, D. (1988) *Variation across Speech and Writing*, Cambridge: Cambridge University Press.

Biber, D. (1993a) 'Co-occurrence patterns among collocations: a tool for corpus-based lexical knowledge acquisition', *Computational Linguistics* 19(3): 549–56.

Biber, D. (1993b) 'Representativeness in corpus design', *Literary and Linguistic Computing* 8(4): 243–57.

Biber, D. and Finegan, E. (1991) 'On the exploitation of corpora in variation studies', in Aijmer and Altenberg 1991, pp. 204–20.

Black, E., Garside, R. and Leech, G. (eds) (1993) *Statistically Driven Computer Grammars of English: The IBM/Lancaster Approach*, Amsterdam: Rodopi.

Bloom, L. (1970) *Language Development: Form and Function in Emerging Grammars*, Cambridge, MA: MIT Press.

Boas, F. (1940) *Race, Language and Culture*, New York: Macmillan.

Bod, R. (1993) 'Using an annotated corpus as a stochastic grammar', in *Proceedings of EACL '93*, Utrecht.

Bongers, H. (1947) *The History and Principles of Vocabulary Control*, Worden: Wocopi.

Brill, E. (1992) 'A simple rule-based part-of-speech tagger', in *Proceedings of the Third Conference on Applied Natural Language Processing* (ANLP-92), Trento, Italy.

Brill, E. (1993) 'A corpus-based approach to language learning', PhD thesis, Department of Computing, University of Pennsylvania.

Brill, E. and Marcus, M. (1992) 'Tagging an unfamiliar text with minimal human supervision', in *Proceedings of the Fall Symposium on Probabilistic Approaches to Natural Language*, American Association for Artificial Intelligence.

Brown, P., Cocke, J., Della Pietra, S., Della Pietra, V., Jelinek, F., Lafferty, J., Mercer, R. and Roosin, P. (1990) 'A statistical approach to machine translation', *Computational Linguistics* 16(2): 79–85.

Brown, P., Della Pietra, V., Della Pietra, S. and Mercer, R. (1993) 'The mathematics of statistical machine translation: parameter estimation', *Computational Linguistics* (19(2): 263–301.

Brown, R. (1973) *A First Language: The Early Stages*, Cambridge, MA: Harvard University Press.

Calzolari, N. and Bindi, R. (1990) 'Acquisition of lexical information from a large textual Italian corpus', in *Proceedings of the Thirteenth International Conference on Computational Linguistics*, Helsinki, Finland.

Carmichael, L. (ed.). (1954) *Manual of Child Psychology*, New York: Wiley.

Chafe, W. (1992) 'The importance of corpus linguistics to understanding the nature of language', in Svartvik 1992, pp. 79–97.

Charniak, E. (1993) *Statistical Language Learning*, Cambridge, MA: MIT Press.

Chomsky, N. (1957) *Syntactic Structures*, The Hague: Mouton.

Chomsky, N. (1962), paper given at the University of Texas 1958, 3rd Texas Conference on Problems of Linguistic Analysis in English, Austin: University of Texas.

Chomsky, N. (1964) 'Formal discussion', in Bellugi and Brown 1964, pp. 37–9.

Chomsky, N. (1965) *Aspects of the Theory of Syntax*, Cambridge, MA: MIT Press.

Chomsky, N. (1988) *Generative Grammar: Its Basis, Development and Prospects*, Kyoto: Kyoto University of Foreign Studies.

Church, K. (1988) 'A stochastic parts program and noun phrase parser for unrestricted text', in *Proceedings of the Second Conference on Applied Natural Language Processing*, Austin, TX, pp 136–43.

Church, K. and Hanks, P. (1989) 'Word association norms, mutual information and lexicography', in *Proceedings of the 27th Annual Meeting of the ACL*, Vancouver, Canada.

Church, K., Gale, W., Hanks, P. and Hindle, D. (1991) 'Using statistics in lexical analysis', in Zernik 1991, pp. 115–64.

Collier, A. (1994) 'A system for automating concordance line selection', in *Proceedings of the International Conference on New Methods in Language Processing*, CCL, UMIST, pp. 95–100.

Copeland, C., Durand, J., Krauwer, S. and Maegaard, B. (eds) (1991) *Studies in Machine Translation and Natural Language Processing*, Volume 1: *The Eurotra Linguistic Specifications*, Luxembourg: Office for Official Publications of the Commission of the European Communities.

Crowdy, S. (1993) 'Spoken corpus design', *Literary and Linguistic Computing* 8(4): 259–65.

Crystal, D. and Davy, D. (1969) *Investigating English Style*, London: Longman.

Cutting, D., Kupiec, J., Pedersen, J. and Sibun, P. (1992) 'A practical part-of-speech tagger', in *Proceedings of the Third Conference on Applied Natural Language Processing (ANLP-92)*, Trento, Italy, pp. 133–40.

Daille, B. (1995) *Combined Approach for Terminology Extraction: Lexical Statistics and Linguistic Filtering*, Unit for Computer Research on the English Language Technical Papers 5, Lancaster University.

de Haan, P. (1992) 'The optimum corpus sample size?' in Leitner 1992, pp. 3–19.

de Haan, P. (1984) 'Problem-oriented tagging of English corpus data', in Aarts, J. and Meijs, W. 1984, pp. 123–39.

de Haan, P. and van Hout, R. (1986) 'Statistics and corpus analysis', in Aarts, J. and Meijs, W. 1986, pp. 79–97.

DeRose, S. (1991) 'An analysis of probabilistic grammatical tagging methods', in Johansson and Stenström 1991, pp. 9–13.

Déroualt, A. M. and Merialdo, B. (1986) 'Natural language modeling for phoneme-to-text transcription', *IEEE Transactions on Pattern Analysis and Machine Intelligence* 8(6): 742–49.

Eaton, H. (1940) *Semantic Frequency List for English, French, German and Spanish*, Chicago: Chicago University Press.

Edwards, J. A. (1994) 'Survey of electronic corpora and related resources for language researchers', in Edwards and Lampert 1994, pp. 263–310.

Edwards, J. A. and Lampert, M. D. (eds) (1994) *Talking Data: Transcription and Coding in Discourse Research*, Hillside, NJ: Lawrence Erlbaum Associates.

El-Béze, M. (1993) 'Les modèles de langage probabilistes: quelques domaines d'applications', Habilitation à diriger des recherches, Université de Paris Nord.

Elithorn and Banerji (eds) (1984) *Artificial and Human Intelligence*, Brussels: NATO Publications.

Fillmore, C. (1992) '"Corpus linguistics" or "Computer-aided armchair linguistics"', in Svartvik 1992, pp. 35–60.

Fordham, A. and Croker, M. (1994) 'A stochastic government and binding parser', in *Proceedings of the International Conference on New Methods in Language Processing*, CCL, UMIST, pp. 190–7.

Francis, W. (1979) 'Problems of assembling, describing and computerizing large corpora', in Bergenholtz and Schaeder 1979, pp. 110–23.

Fries, C. (1952) *The Structure of English: An Introduction to the Construction of Sentences*, New York: Harcourt-Brace.

Fries, C. and Traver, A. (1940) *English Word Lists. A Study of their Adaptability and Instruction,* Washington, DC: American Council of Education.

Fries, U., Tottie, G. and Schneider, P. (eds) (1994) *Creating and Using English Language Corpora*, Amsterdam: Rodopi.

Garnham, A., Shillcock, R., Brown, G., Mill, A. and Cutler, A. (1981) 'Slips of the tongue in the London-Lund corpus of spontaneous conversation', *Linguistics* 19: 805–17.

Garside, R. (1987) 'The CLAWS word-tagging system',in Garside, Leech and Sampson 1987.

Garside, R. (1993a) 'The large-scale production of syntactically analysed corpora', *Literary and Linguistic Computing* 8(1): 39–46.

Garside, R. (1993b) 'The marking of cohesive relationships: tools for the construction of a large bank of anaphoric data', *ICAME Journal* 17: 5–27.

Garside, R. and McEnery, A. (1993) 'Treebanking: the compilation of a corpus of skeleton parsed sentences', in Black, Garside and Leech 1993, pp. 17-35.

Garside, R., Leech, G. and Sampson, G. (eds) (1987) *The Computational Analysis of English: A Corpus Based Approach*, London: Longman.

Gärtner, K., Sappler, P. and Trauth, M. (eds) (1991) *Maschinelle Verarbeitung altdeutscher Texte IV,* Tübingen: Niemeyer.

Gerbner, G., Holsti, O. R., Krippendorff, K. Paisley, W. J. and Stone, P. J. (eds) (1969). *The Analysis of Communication Content*, New York: John Wiley.

Gougenheim, G., Michéa, R., Rivenc, P. and Sauvegot, A. (1956) *L'Elaboration du français élémentaire*, Paris: Didier.

Greene, B. and Rubin, G. (1971) *Automatic Grammatical Tagging of English*, Technical Report, Department of Linguistics, Brown University, RI.

Halliday, M. (1991) 'Corpus studies and probabilistic grammar', in Aijmer and Altenberg 1991, pp. 30-43.

Halliday, M. and Hasan, R. (1976) *Cohesion in English*, London: Longman.

Harris, Z. (1951) *Methods in Structural Linguistics*, Chicago: University of Chicago Press.

Hockett, C. (1948) 'A note on structure', *International Journal of American Linguistics* 14: 269-71.

Hofland, K. and Johansson, S. (1982) *Word Frequencies in British and American English*, Bergen: Norwegian Computing Centre for the Humanities.

Holmes, J. (1988) 'Doubt and certainty in ESL textbooks', *Applied Linguistics* 9: 21–44.

Holmes, J. (1994) 'Inferring language change from computer corpora: some methodological problems', *ICAME Journal* 18: 27–40.

Horrocks, G. (1987) *Generative Grammar*, London: Longman.

Hughes, L. and Lee, S. (eds) (1994) *CTI Centre for Textual Studies Resources Guide 1994*, Oxford: CTI Centre for Textual Studies.

Hunt, K. (1965) *Gramatical structures written at three grade levels*, Champaign, Illinois: National Council of Teachers of English.

Ingram, D. (1978) 'Sensori-motor development and language acquisition', in Lock 1978, pp. 261–90.

Janssen, S. (1990) 'Automatic sense-disambiguation with LDOCE: enriching syntactically analyzed corpora with semantic data', in Aarts and Meijs 1990, 105–36.

Jelinek, F. (1985) 'The development of an experimental discrete dictation recognizer', *Proceedings of the IEEE* 73(11): 1616–24.

Johansson, S. (ed.). (1982) *Computer Corpora in English Language Research*, Bergen: Norwegian Computing Centre for the Humanities.

Johansson, S. (1991) 'Times change and so do corpora', in Aijmer and Altenberg 1991, pp. 305–14.

Johansson, S. and Norheim, E. (1988) 'The subjunctive in British and American English', *ICAME Journal* 12: 27–36.

Johansson, S. and Stenström, A.-B. (eds) (1991) *English Computer Corpora: Selected Papers and Research Guide*, Berlin: Mouton de Gruyter.

Johansson, S., Burnard, L., Edwards, J. and Rosta A. (1991) 'Text Encoding Initiative, Spoken Text Work Group'. Working paper on spoken texts.

Jones, D. (1992) 'Non-hybrid example-based machine translation architectures', in *Proceedings of TMI-92*, Montreal, pp. 163–71.

Käding, J. (1897) *Häufigkeitswörterbuch der deutschen Sprache*, Steglitz: privately published.

Karlsson, F., Voutilainen, A., Heikkilä, J. and Anttila, A. (eds) (1995) *Constraint Grammar: A Language-Independent System for Parsing Unrestricted Text*, Berlin: Mouton de Gruyter.

Kennedy, G. (1987a) 'Expressing temporal frequency in academic English', *TESOL Quarterly* 21: 69–86.

Kennedy, G. (1987b) 'Quantification and the use of English: a case study of one aspect of the learner's task', *Applied Linguistics* 8: 264–86.

Kennedy, G. (1992) 'Preferred ways of putting things', in Svartvik 1992, pp. 335–73.

Kenny, A. J. P. (1982) *The Computation of Style*, Oxford: Pergamon Press.

Kirk, J. (1993) 'Taking corpora to Lancaster: a new study of the modal verb "will"', talk given at Unit for Computer Research on the English Language, Lancaster University.

Kirk, J. (1994) 'Teaching and language corpora: the Queen's approach', in Wilson and McEnery 1994, pp. 29–51.

Kjellmer, G. (1986) '"The lesser man": observations on the role of women in modern English writings', in Aarts and Meijs 1986, pp. 163–76.

Kjellmer, G. (1991) 'A mint of phrases', in Aijmer and Altenberg 1991, pp. 111–127.

Knowles, G. (1991) 'Prosodic labelling: the problem of tone group boundaries', in Johansson and Stenström 1991, pp. 149–63.

Kytö, M., Ihalainen, O. and Rissanen, M. (eds) (1988) *Corpus Linguistics Hard and Soft*, Amsterdam: Rodopi.

Kytö, M., Rissanen, M. and Wright, S. (eds) (1994) *Corpora across the Centuries*, Amsterdam: Rodopi.

Labov, W. (1969) 'The logic of non-standard English', *Georgetown Monographs on Language and Linguistics* 22.

Lafon, P. (1984) *Dépouillements et statistiques en lexicométrie*, Geneva: Slatkine-Champion.

Lancashire, I. (ed.) (1991) *The Humanities Computing Yearbook 1989–90*, Oxford: Oxford University Press.

Leech, G. (1991) 'The state of the art in corpus linguistics', in Aijmer and Altenberg 1991, pp. 8–29.

Leech, G. (1992) 'Corpora and theories of linguistic performance', in Svartvik 1992, pp. 105–22.

Leech, G. (1993) 'Corpus annotation schemes', *Literary and Linguistic Computing* 8(4): 275–81.

Leech, G. and Fallon, R. (1992) 'Computer corpora – what do they tell us about culture?', *ICAME Journal* 16: 29–50.

Leech, G. and Short, M. (1981) *Style in Fiction*, London: Longman.

Leech, G., Garside, R. and Bryant, M. (1994) 'The large-scale grammatical tagging of text: experience with the British National Corpus', in Oostdijk and de Haan 1994b, pp. 47–63.

Leitner, G. (1991) 'The Kolhapur corpus of Indian English: intravarietal description and/or intervarietal comparison', in Johansson and Stenström 1991, pp. 215–32.

Leitner, G. (ed.) (1992) *New Dimensions in English Language Corpora*, Berlin: Mouton de Gruyter.

Lenat, D. and Guha, R. (1990) *Building Large Knowledge Based Systems*, New York: Addison Wesley.

Ljung, M. (1990) *A Study of TEFL Vocabulary*, Stockholm: Almqvist and Wiksell.

Lock, A. (ed.) (1978) *Action, Gesture and Symbol: The Emergence of Language*, London: Academic Press.

Lorge, I. (1949) *Semantic Content of the 570 Commonest English Words*, New York: Columbia University Press.

McCarthy, D. (1954) 'Language development in children', in Carmichael 1954, pp. 492–630.

McEnery, A. (1992) *Computational Linguistics*, Wilmslow: Sigma Press.

McEnery, A. and Oakes, M. (1995) 'Sentence and word alignment in the CRATER project: methods and assessment', in *Proceedings of the EACL–SIGDAT Workshop*, Dublin, pp. 77–86.

McEnery, A. and Oakes, M. (1996) 'Sentence and word alignment in the CRATER project', in Thomas and Short, 1996, 211–31.

McEnery, A. and Wilson, A. (1993) 'The role of corpora in computer-assisted language learning', *Computer Assisted Language Learning* 6(3): 233–48.

McEnery, A., Baker, P. and Wilson, A. (1995) 'A statistical analysis of corpus based computer vs traditional human teaching methods of part of speech analysis', *Computer Assisted Language Learning* 8(2/3): 259–74.

Magerman, D. (1994) 'Natural language as statistical pattern matching', Ph.D. thesis, Stanford University.

Markantonatou, S. and Sadler, L. (1994) *Studies in Machine Translation and Natural Language Processing, Vol 4: Grammatical Formalisms — Issues in Migration*, Luxembourg: The Office for the Official Publications of the European Communities.

Matthews, P. (1981) *Syntax*. Cambridge: Cambridge University Press.

Meijs, W. (ed.) (1987) *Corpus Linguistics and Beyond*, Amsterdam: Rodopi.

Merialdo, B. (1994) 'Tagging English text with a probabilistic model', *Computational Linguistics* 20(2): 155–71.

Meyer, C. and Tenney, R. (1993) 'Tagger: an interactive tagging program', in Souter and Atwell 1993, pp. 25–36.

Miller, G., Beckwith, R., Fellbaum, C., Gross, D., Miller, K. and Tengi, R. (1990/93) *Five Papers on WordNet*, CSL Report 43, Cognitive Science Laboratory, Princeton University.

Mindt, D. (ed.) (1988) *EDV in der angewandten Linguistik: Ziele — Methoden — Ergebnisse*, Frankfurt-am-Main: Diesterweg.

Mindt, D. (1991) 'Syntactic evidence for semantic distinctions in English', in Aijmer and Altenberg 1991, pp. 182–96.

Mindt, D. (1992) *Zeitbezug im Englischen: eine didaktische Grammatik des englischen Futurs*, Tübingen: Gunter Narr.

Minsky, M. and Riecken, D. (1994) 'A conversation with Marvin Minsky about agents', *Communications of the ACM* 37(7), pp. 22–29.

Myers, G. (1989) 'The pragmatics of politeness in scientific articles', *Applied Linguistics* 10: 1–35.

Myers, G. (1991) 'Pragmatics and corpora', talk given at Corpus Linguistics Research Group, Lancaster University.

Nagao, M. (1984) 'A framework of a mechanical translation between Japanese and English by analogy principle', in Elithorn and Banerji 1984.

Nakamura, J. (1993) 'Quantitative comparison of modals in the Brown and the LOB corpora', *ICAME Journal* 17: 29–48.

O'Connor, J. and Arnold, G. (1961) *Intonation of Colloquial English*, London: Longman.

Oostdijk, N. and de Haan, P. (1994a) 'Clause patterns in modern British English: a corpus-based (quantitative) study', *ICAME Journal* 18: 41–79.

Oostdijk, N. and de Haan, P. (eds) (1994b) *Corpus Based Research into Language*, Amsterdam: Rodopi.

Opdhal, L. (1991) '-*ly* as adverbial suffix: corpus and elicited material compared', *ICAME Journal* 15: 19–35.

Palmer, H. (1933) *Second Interim Report on English Collocations*, Tokyo: Institute for Research in English Teaching.

Pannek, G. (1988) 'Relativsätze im gesprochenen Englisch und in Lehrwerken für den Englischunterricht', in Mindt 1988, pp. 77–83.

Pearson, J. and Kenny, D. (1991) 'Terminology in Eurotra', in Copeland *et al.* 1991, pp. 161–3.

Peitsara, K. (1993) 'On the development of the *by*-agent in English', in Rissanen, Kytö and Palander-Collin 1993, pp. 217–33.

Pennington, M. and Stevens, V. (eds) (1991) *Computers in Applied Linguistics*, Clevedon: Multilingual Matters.

Preyer, W. (1889) *The Mind of a Child*, New York: Appleton.

Quirk, R. (1960) 'Towards a description of English usage', *Transactions of the Philological Society*, pp. 40–61.

Quirk, R., Greenbaum, S., Leech, G. and Svartvik, J. (1985) *A Comprehensive Grammar of the English Language*, London: Longman.

Rissanen, M. (1989) 'Three problems connected with the use of diachronic corpora', *ICAME Journal* 13: 16–19.

Rissanen, M., Kytö, M. and Palander-Collin, M. (eds) (1993) *Early English in the Computer Age*, Berlin: Mouton de Gruyter.

Sadler, V. (1989) *Working with Analogical Semantics*, Dordrecht: Foris.

Sampson, G. (1987) 'Evidence against the grammatical/ungrammatical distinction', in Meijs 1987, pp. 219–26.

Sampson, G. (1992) 'Probabilistic parsing', in Svartvik 1992, pp. 425–47.

Sánchez-León, F. and Nieto-Serrano, A. (1995) 'A public domain tagger for Spanish', CRATER working paper.

Schmidt, K. M. (1991) 'Ein Datenbanksystem für das Begriffwörterbuch mittelhochdeutscher Epik und Fortschritte bei der automatischen Disambiguierung', in Gärtner, Sappler and Trauth 1991, pp. 192–204.

Schmidt, K. M. (1993) *Begriffsglossar und Index zu Ulrichs von Zatzikhoven Lanzelet*, Tübingen: Niemeyer.

Schmied, J. (1993) 'Qualitative and quantitative research approaches to English relative constructions', in Souter and Atwell 1993, pp. 85–96.

Schreuder, R. and Kerkman, H. (1987) 'On the use of a lexical database in psycholinguistic research', in Meijs 1987, pp. 295–302.

Sebba, M. (1991) 'The adequacy of corpora on machine translation', *Applied Computer Translation*, vol 1, 1, pp. 15–27.

Sedelow, S. and Sedelow, W. (1969) 'Categories and procedures for content analysis in the humanities', in Gerbner *et al.* 1969, pp. 487–99.

Sekine, S. (1994) 'A new direction for sublanguage NLP', in *Proceedings of the International Conference on New Methods in Language Processing*, CCL, UMIST, pp 123–29.

Shannon, C. and Weaver, W. (1949) *The Mathematical Theory of Communication*. Urbana, IL: University of Illinois Press.

Short, M., Semino, E. and Culpeper, J. (1996) 'Using a corpus for stylistics research: speech presentation', in Thomas and Short 1996.

Smadja, F. (1991) 'From N-grams to collocations: an evaluation of Xtract', in *Proceedings of the 29th ACL Conference*, Berkeley.

Souter, C. (1990) 'Systemic-functional grammars and corpora', in Aarts and Meijs 1990, 179–212.

Souter, C. (1993) 'Towards a standard format for parsed corpora', in Aarts, de Haan and Oostdijk 1993, 197–212.

Souter, C. and Atwell, E. (eds) (1993) *Corpus Based Computational Linguistics*, Amsterdam: Rodopi.

Sperberg-McQueen, C. M. and Burnard, L. (1994) *Guidelines for Electronic Text Encoding and Interchange (P3)*, Chicago and Oxford: Text Encoding Initiative.

Stenström, A.-B. (1984a) 'Discourse items and pauses', Paper presented at Fifth ICAME Conference, Windermere. Abstract in *ICAME News* 9 (1985): 11.

Stenström, A.-B. (1984b) 'Discourse tags', in Aarts and Meijs 1984 , pp. 65–81.

Stenström, A.-B. (1987) 'Carry-on signals in English conversation', in Meijs 1987, pp. 87–119.

Stern, W. (1924) *Psychology of Early Childhood up to Six Years of Age*, New York: Holt.

Stone, P., Dunphy, D., Smith, M. and Ogilvie, D. (1966) *The General Inquirer: A Computer Approach to Content Analysis*, Cambridge MA: MIT Press.

Sutton, S. and McEnery, A. (1992) 'Information retrieval and corpora', in Leitner 1992, pp. 191–210.

Svartvik, J. (1966) *On Voice in the English Verb*, The Hague: Mouton.

Svartvik, J. (ed.) (1990) *The London-Lund Corpus of Spoken English*, Lund: Lund University Press.

Svartvik, J. (ed.) (1992) *Directions in Corpus Linguistics*, Berlin: Mouton de Gruyter.

Svartvik, J. and Quirk, R. (1980) *A Corpus of English Conversation*, Lund: C.W.K. Gleerup.

Swinscow, T. (1983) *Statistics at Square One*, London: British Medical Association.

Taylor, L., Grover, C. and Briscoe, T. (1989) 'The syntactic regularity of English noun phrases', in *Proceedings of ACL European Chapter Meeting*, Manchester, pp. 256–63.

Taylor, L., Leech, G. and Fligelstone, S. (1991) 'A survey of English machine-readable corpora', in Johansson, S. and Stenström, A.-B. 1991, pp. 319–54.

Thomas, J. and Short, M. (eds) *Using Corpora for Language Research*, London: Longman.

Thorndike, E. (1921) *A Teacher's Wordbook*, New York: Columbia Teachers College.

Thorndike, E. and Lorge, I. (1944) *The Teacher's Word Book of 30,000 Words*, New York: Columbia University Press.

Tottie, G. (1991) *Negation in English Speech and Writing: A Study in Variation*, San Diego: Academic Press.

Tsujii, J., Ananiadou, S., Carroll, J. and Sekine, S. (1991) *Methodologies for the Development of Sublanguage MT System II*, CCL UMIST Report No. 91/11.

Van Halteren, H. (1994) 'Syntactic databases in the classroom', in Wilson and McEnery (eds) pp. 17–28.

West, M. (1953) *A General Service List of English Words*, London: Longman.

Wichmann, A. (1989) *Tone of Voice: A Stylistic Approach to Intonation*, Lancaster Papers in Linguistics 70.

Wichmann, A. (1993) 'Gradients and categories in intonation: a study of the perception and production of falling tones', in Souter and Atwell 1993, pp. 71–84.

Wikberg, K. (1992) 'Discourse category and text type classification: procedural discourse in the Brown and the LOB corpora', in Leitner 1992, pp. 247–61.

Wilson, A. (1989) 'Prepositional phrase postmodifiers of nominals and their prosodic boundaries: some data from the Lancaster Spoken English Corpus', MA thesis, Lancaster University.

Wilson, A. (1992a) Review of 'The Oxford Psycholinguistic Database', *Computers and Texts* 4: 15–17.

Wilson, A. (1992b) *The Usage of Since: A Quantitative Comparison of Augustan, Modern British and Modern Indian English*, Lancaster Papers in Linguistics 80.

Wilson, A. and McEnery, A. (eds) (1994) *Corpora in Language Education and Research: A Selection of Papers from Talc94*, Unit for Computer Research on the English Language Technical Papers 4 (special issue), Lancaster University.

Wilson, A. (forthcoming), *Conceptual Glossary and Index to the Latin Vulgate Translation of the Gospel of John*, in preparation.

Woods, A., Fletcher, P. and Hughes, A. (1986) *Statistics in Language Studies*, Cambridge: Cambridge University Press.

Yates, S. (1993) 'The textuality of computer-mediated communication: speech, writing and genre in CMC discourse', Ph.D. thesis, Milton Keynes: The Open University.

Zanettin, F. (1994) 'Parallel words: designing a bilingual database for translation activities', in Wilson and McEnery 1994, pp. 99–111.

Zernik, U. (ed.) (1991) *Lexical Acquisition: Exploiting On-Line Resources to Build a Lexicon*, Hillsdale, New Jersey: Lawrence Erlbaum Associates.

Index